American Headway 4

THE WORLD'S MOST TRUSTED ENGLISH COURSE

SECOND EDITION

John and Liz Soars

OXFORD
UNIVERSITY PRESS

Scope and Sequence

SKILLS DEVELOPMENT

READING	LISTENING	SPEAKING	WRITING
A home away from home—two people describe their experiences of living abroad (jigsaw) p. 6	"Things I miss from home"—people describe what they miss when they travel abroad p. 10	Exchanging information about people who live abroad p. 6 Discussion—the pros and cons of living abroad p. 7	**Applying for a job** A resume and a cover letter p. 106
"Paradise Lost"—how tourism is destroying the object of its affection p. 15	An interview with Tashi Wheeler about her travels as a child with her parents, who founded the *Lonely Planet* guides p. 20	Information gap and role play—Tony and Maureen Wheeler p. 14 Dreams come true—things to do before you die p. 18	**Informal letters** Correcting mistakes p. 108
The Clinging Woman, a story by Ruth Rendell p. 26	The money jigsaw p. 28	**Retelling a news story** Responding to a news story p. 24 Talking about your favorite book or movie p. 25	**Narrative writing 1** Using adverbs in narratives *I used to go skiing frequently in the winter.* p. 109
"Diana and Elvis shot JFK!"—three of the world's most popular conspiracy theories (jigsaw) p. 34	"My most memorable lie"—people confess to untruths p. 33	Discussion—good and bad lies p. 33 Exchanging information about conspiracy theories p. 34	**Linking ideas** Conjunctions *whenever, so that, even though* p. 110
"Todays teenagers are just fine"—young people who have already achieved a great deal" p. 44	Arranging to meet—three friends decide a time and a place to get together (jigsaw) p. 48	Future possibilities in your life p. 43 Exchanging information about people arranging to meet p. 48	**Writing e-mails** E-mailing friends *Sorry, can't make next Sat.* p. 111
A profile of two famous brands—Starbucks and Apple Computers (jigsaw) p. 54	Radio advertisements—what's the product? What's the selling point? p. 53	A lifestyle survey p. 52 Writing an ad p. 53 Exchanging information about famous brands p. 54 Starting a restaurant p. 56	**Report writing** A consumer survey *TO: CEO* p. 112

SKILLS DEVELOPMENT

READING	LISTENING	SPEAKING	WRITING
"Meet the Kippers"—an article about grown-up children who won't leave home p. 62	Getting married—an Indian woman talks about her arranged marriage p. 61	The pros and cons of arranged marriages p. 61 Discussion—when should young people leave home? p. 62	**Arguing your case** For and against *first of all …, not only … but also* p. 114
"The wonder that's New York's Grand Central"—an article about a landmark train station p. 70	Extreme experiences—people describe their experiences in extreme weather conditions p. 69	Making descriptions longer p. 68 Talking about your experiences of extreme weather p. 69	**Describing places** My favorite part of town *I'm a New Yorker, and proud of it.* p. 115
"The man who planted trees"—how one man made the world a better place p. 78	A teacher I'll never forget—people describe a teacher who made a lasting impression on them p. 77	Discussion—a teacher I'll never forget p. 77 Discussion—your favorite TV programs p. 78	**Writing for talking** *What I want to talk about is …* p. 116
"The Tarzan of Central Park"—the story of a man who lived in trees p. 85	Hilaire Belloc's *Cautionary Tales for Children*—Jim, who ran away from his nurse and was eaten by a lion p. 88	It all went wrong! p. 85 Talking about children's stories p. 88	**Formal and informal letters and e-mails** Do's and don'ts *Hi Amber! How are things with you?* p. 117
"Have you ever wondered?"—the answers to some important questions in life p. 93	The interpretation of dreams—Paul's amazing dream p. 96	Practicing a conversation p. 93 Describing your dreams p. 96	**Narrative writing 2** Linking words and expressions *As soon as, eventually, by this time, finally* p. 118
"You're never too old"—a life in the day of Mary Hobson, who earned her PhD at age 74 p. 102	Happy days—people talk about what makes them happy and unhappy p. 101 A song—"That's Life" p. 104	Discussion—the different stages of life, and their pros and cons p. 101	**Adding emphasis in writing** People of influence *Michelangelo: sculptor, architect, painter, and poet* p. 119

1 No place like home

TEST YOUR GRAMMAR

1 Which time expressions from the box can be used with the sentences below?

1. My parents met in Paris.
2. They travel abroad.
3. They were working in Canada.
4. I was born in Montreal.
5. My grandparents have lived in Ireland.
6. I wrote to my grandmother.
7. I'm going to work in the U.S.
8. My brother's flying to Argentina on business.
9. He's been studying Spanish.
10. I'll see you.

when I was born   never   in the 1970s tonight   frequently   for years   years ago the other day   in two weeks   recently during a snowstorm   for a year since I was a child   later   sometimes

2 Talk to a partner about yourself and your family using some of the time expressions.

AWAY FROM HOME
Tense review and informal language

1 Read "Tyler's Tweets." What kind of text is this? Where is Tyler from? What does he find strange in London? What kind of person do you think Tyler is?

2 Complete the questions. Then ask and answer them with a partner.

1. "Where ___is___ Tyler _spending_ his junior year?"
   "In London."
2. "Is this his first trip abroad?"
   "No, it _____. He _____ _____ abroad once before. Last year he _____ to Mexico."
3. "Where _____ Dave _____?"
   "In north London."
4. "How long _____ Tyler _____ to stay with Dave?"
   "A few days."
5. "Why _____ the guy say 'cheers' to Tyler?"
   "Because he _____ the door open for him."
6. "_____ he like his host family?"
   "Yes, he _____. They _____ very nice."
7. "What _____ they _____ on Sunday?"
   "They _____ _____ Shakespeare's hometown."

3 **CD1** **2** Listen and check your answers.

2   Unit 1 · No place like home

Home Profile Find People Sign out

Tyler's Tw
4 followi
8 followe
3 listed

Search

RSS fee
Tyler's

Tyler's Tweets
I'm spending my junior year in London!

Tuesday, September 4, 1:42 p.m.
Still sitting in the airport in NYC. Been waiting three hours but seems like FOREVER!

Tuesday, September 4, 3:20 p.m.
Just boarded the plane for London. Finally! This is my first tr abroad except for a weekend in Tijuana, Mexico last year.

Tuesday, September 4, 3:25 p.m.
I'm going to stay with my buddy Dave for a few days in north London before I meet my host family. Dave lives in a place ca "Chalk Farm." I don't get it - a farm in London?

Thursday, September 6, 10:35 a.m.
London's fun but kind of weird. Why do people say "cheers" the time? I thought it was only for making toasts. A guy just said it to me when I held the door open for him.

Friday, September 7, 9.30 a.m.
Dave and I are in a hilarious English restaurant. There's this stuff called "black pudding" that looks like a sausage.

Saturday, September 8, 8:19 p.m.
First night with my host family, the Wilsons. They seem very nice, but their house is a million-mile walk to the subway! (They call it the 'Tube' here!) I miss my car! But they drive o the WRONG side of the road here. Crazy!

Saturday, September 8, 11:19 p.m.
Big day tomorrow. We're visiting Shakespeare's hometown. He's really famous, so I'm totally psyched!

4 Read Teresa's e-mail. Where is she? Is she working or on vacation? What are some of her likes and dislikes about the place?

5 Form the questions. Ask and answer them with a partner.

1. How long/Teresa/Africa?
2. What time/start work?
3. What/just buy?
4. Where/last Sunday?
5. What/bring home?
6. How many/collected already?
7. What/do at the beach?
8. What/sending?

CD1 3 Listen and check your answers.

A F R I C A

From: Teresa Sayers <teri.says@yoohoo.com>
Subject: RE: Re: Hello from Africa!
Date: Thurs. 17 March 8.56 pm
To: "dad n mom" <m.b.sayers@chatchat.net>
Attachments: piki-piki_003.jpg (501KB) ...

Hi, Mom! Hi, Dad!

Thanks for your messages - always love news from home. It's getting hotter and hotter here. Wish we had air conditioning and not just two junky fans. Since I arrived last September the heat's been getting worse and worse. Thank goodness I start work early, 7:00. It's the only cool (no - less hot) time of day in Tanzania. But hey, I have some cool news. I just bought a bike - well, not exactly a bike, a "piki-piki." It's a kind of little motorcycle. Everyone has one. Great for getting around. Don't freak, Mom! I'm really careful, especially on the bumpy road up to the school.

Last Sunday a group of us teachers (on our piki-pikis of course!) headed up the coast to a really awesome beach, Pangani Beach. Incredible white sand covered with fabulous shells. Did I tell you? Shelling is a real popular pastime here. I've already collected hundreds - some are huge and all shades of pink and orange. I'm going to bring them home. Anyway, we took a bunch of picnic stuff and barbecued fish and swam until the sun went down. The sunsets here are unbelievable - very quick but spectacular. I'm sending you a photo with this e-mail.

So that's it for now. Missing you tons. Can't wait to see you.

Love,
Teresa

PS Hey – I think I hear raindrops on the roof!

piki-piki_003.jpg

My_Class.jpg

PRACTICE

Identifying the tenses

1 Complete the tense charts. Use the verb *work* for the active and *make* for the passive.

ACTIVE	Simple	Continuous
Present	he works	we are working
Past	she	I
Future	they	you
Present Perfect	we	she
Past Perfect	I had worked	you
Future Perfect	they	he will have been working

PASSIVE	Simple	Continuous
Present	it is made	they are being made
Past	it	it
Future	they	
Present Perfect	they	
Past Perfect	it	
Future Perfect	they will have been made	

2 **CD1 4** Listen to the lines of conversation and discuss what the context might be. Listen again and identify the tenses. Which lines have contractions?

He's been working such long hours recently. He never sees the children.

- Could be a wife talking about her husband.
- Present Perfect Continuous, Present Simple.
- He's (He has) been working …

Discussing grammar

3 Compare the meaning in the pairs of sentences. Which tenses are used? Why?

1. Bianca **comes** from Rio.
   Bianca **is coming** from Rio.

2. You**'re** very kind. Thank you.
   You**'re being** very kind. What do you want?

3. What **were** you **doing** when the accident happened?
   What **did** you **do** when the accident happened?

4. I**'ve lived** in Singapore for five years.
   I **lived** in Singapore for five years.

5. When we arrived, he **made** lunch.
   When we arrived, he**'d made** lunch.

6. We**'ll have** dinner at 8:00, right?
   Don't call at 8:00. We**'ll be having** dinner.

7. How much **are** you **paying** to have the house painted?
   How much **are** you **being paid** to paint the house?

8. How **do you do**?
   How **are you doing**?

Talking about you

4 Complete these sentences with your ideas.

1. On weekends I often …
2. My parents have never …
3. I don't think I'll ever …
4. I was saying to a friend just the other day that …
5. I hate Mondays because …
6. I'd just returned home last night when …
7. I was just getting ready to go out today when …
8. I've been told that our teacher …
9. In my very first English class I was taught …
10. The reason I'm studying English is because …

CD1 5 Listen and compare. What are the responses?

5 Work with a partner. Listen to each other's sentences and respond.

SPOKEN ENGLISH Missing words

Which words are missing in these lines from conversations?

1. Heard about Jane and John splitting up?
   Have you heard about Jane and John splitting up?
2. Leaving already? What's wrong?
3. Failed again? How many times is that?
4. Sorry I'm late. Been waiting long?
5. Doing anything interesting this weekend?
6. Like the car! When did you get it?
7. Bye, Joe! See you tonight.
8. Just coming! Hang on!
9. Want a ride? Hop in.
10. Seen Jim lately?

Read the lines aloud to your partner and make suitable responses.

CD1 6 Listen and compare.

A long-distance phone call

6 Read through these lines of a phone conversation. Cara is calling her father. Where do you think she is? Why is she there? Where is he? Work with a partner to complete her father's lines in the conversation.

D ...
C Dad! It's me, Cara.
D ...
C I'm fine but still a bit jet-lagged.
D ...
C It's 16 hours ahead. I just can't get used to it. Last night I lay awake all night, and then today I nearly fell asleep at work in the middle of a meeting.
D ...
C It's early, but I think it's going to be really good. It's a big company, but everybody's being so kind and helpful. I've been trying to find out how everything works.
D ...
C I've seen a bit. It just seems like such a big, busy city. I don't see how I'll ever find my way around it.
D ...
C No, it's nothing like Denver. It's like nowhere else I've ever been—huge buildings, underground shopping centers, lots of buses, taxis, and people—so many people—but it's so clean. No litter on the streets or anything.
D ...
C Well, for the time being I've been given a tiny apartment, but it's in a great part of town.
D ...
C That's right. I won't be living here for long. I'll be offered a bigger place as soon as one becomes available, which is good 'cause this one really is tiny. But at least it's near where I'm working.
D ...
C Walk! You're kidding! It's not *that* close. It's a short bus ride away. And the buses and trains come so regularly—it's a really easy commute, which is good 'cause I start work very early in the morning.
D ...
C Again, it's too early to say. I think I really will be enjoying it all soon. I'm sure it's going to be a great experience. It's just that I miss everyone at home so much.
D ...
C I will. I promise. And you e-mail me back with all your news. I just love hearing from home. Give everyone my love. Bye.
D ...

CD1 7 Listen and compare. Identify some of the tenses used in the conversation.

▶▶ **WRITING** Applying for a job *p. 106*

READING AND SPEAKING
A home away from home

1 Why do people go to live abroad? Make a list of reasons and discuss with your class.

2 You are going to read about Ian Walker-Smith, who moved to Chile, and Daniel Allum, who moved to Kansas, in the U.S.

Which of these lines from the articles do you think are about Chile (**C**) and which are about Kansas (**K**)?

1. ☐ As we're 2,600 meters above sea level, I easily get out of breath when I'm exercising.
2. ☐ When we first arrived it was 106°F—so hot the road melted—and now it's freezing.
3. ☐ . . . we converse in what we call "Espanglish" . . .
4. ☐ We live in the middle of nowhere off Highway 54.
5. ☐ Its surrounding mines are said to make more money than any other city.
6. ☐ Our house has a basement for shelter from tornados.
7. ☐ I wish football (they call it "soccer") was more popular here.
8. ☐ We now have a pleasant walkway along the seafront.

3 Divide into two groups.

Group A Read about Ian on this page.
Group B Read about Daniel on page 8.

Check your answers to Exercise 2.

4 Answer the questions about Ian or Daniel.
1. Where did he go to live abroad? Why?
2. How long has he been there?
3. What does he do there?
4. What do you learn about his family?
5. What is the new hometown like?
6. Have there been any difficulties?
7. In what ways is he "in the middle of nowhere?"
8. Does he feel at home in his new home?
9. What does he like and dislike about his new life?
10. What does he miss?

5 Find a partner from the other group. Compare your answers. Who do you think is happier about the move? Which new home would you prefer?

Expat tales

IAN WALKER-SMITH IN CHILE

Ian Walker-Smith comes from Crewe, England but now lives and works in Chile. He's married to a Chilean woman, 05 Andrea, and works for a European astronomical agency in the town of Paranal.

Ian says: ❝I work shifts of eight days in Paranal and get six to rest at home—in my case, the mining town of Antofagasta, a 10 harrowing two-hour drive away on the coast. It takes a real toll on me being so far from Andrea. I miss her when I'm away.

Where he works

I work at Paranal Observatory, where every night the boundaries of our universe are probed by four of the world's largest telescopes. I'm part of a 12-strong I.T. team which looks after everything from 15 satellite ground stations to desktop support. My role is to make sure the computers run 24/7. As Paranal is in the middle of nowhere—up a mountain in the desert—the sky is truly amazing. As we're 2,600 meters above sea level, I easily get out of breath when I'm exercising, and each time I arrive for a week on shift, I can't think straight or 20 fast for the first day or so.

Why he moved

I decided to move to Chile four years ago when I was a 25-year-old with itchy feet (and wanted to get out of the way of an ex-girlfriend!). I was working for Littlewoods Home Shopping Group, and one day a colleague pointed out this job in Chile. We both thought it would be
25 a good idea, but I was the one who put a CV together.

Life in Chile

Landing at Santiago airport was my first experience of language being such a barrier. I couldn't speak more than a handful of words in Spanish, and would you believe that my baggage had gotten lost! So my first couple of hours in Chile were spent trying to locate my missing
30 possessions. Today I can order food in restaurants and argue with mechanics about my car, but I can't really make myself understood on any deeper level. I can't get my thoughts across as a native speaker could. Andrea speaks pretty good English, and we converse in what we call "Espanglish"—at least we can understand each other.

35 Antofagasta, the town where we have made our home, was once described in a Chilean advertising campaign as the "Pearl of the North." Let's just say that it's hardly a tourist destination (which is pretty much what you'd say about my hometown, Crewe!). Antofagasta and its surrounding mines are said to make more money
40 for Chile than any other city. During my time here, some money has been put back into the city. The municipal beach has been much improved. We now have a pleasant walkway along the seafront.

What he misses

Even after four years, I don't feel I belong. Over Christmas I went back to the UK for a month's holiday—on landing at Heathrow I felt at home
45 right away. What I miss most is greenery. My own culture still fits me like the winter gloves I left behind when I came to work in the desert sun. Shame I can't say the same of my old winter trousers ... "

Language work

Study the texts again and answer the questions about these expressions. Explain the meanings to a partner who read the other text.

Ian in Chile
1. *It takes a real toll . . .* L.10
   What takes a toll? On what or who?
2. *. . . the computers run 24/7.* L.16
   How long do the computers operate?
3. *I easily get out of breath . . .* L.18
   When and why does he get out of breath?
4. *. . . itchy feet . . .* L.22
   Why did he get itchy feet?
5. *. . . winter gloves . . .* L.46
   What still fits him like winter gloves?

Daniel in Kansas
1. *. . . we'll probably mess around inside.* L.13
   What will Daniel probably do inside?
2. *Dad got sick of leaving for work so early.* L.26
   I don't get car sick anymore. L.62
   Who was actually sick, Daniel or his father?
3. *. . . who's six and whinges.* L.37
   Does Daniel like it when she whinges?
4. *. . . Everyone laughs when I say "lorry" instead of "truck."* L.44
   Why do they think this is funny?
5. *American football stinks.* L.61
   Does he like American football?

Express all the lines marked with an asterisk (*) in more formal English.

What do you think?

Work in groups.

- Close your eyes and think about your country. What would you miss most if you went to live abroad? Compare ideas.
- Make a list of the disadvantages of moving abroad. Then for every disadvantage (–) try to find an advantage (+).

  ⊖ The language barrier—maybe you don't speak the language.

  ⊕ But this is an opportunity to learn a new language.

- Have any of your friends or family gone to live in a foreign country? Why?
- Do you know anyone who has come to live in your country from another country? Why? Do they have any problems?
- Which other countries would you like to live in for a while? Why?

Expat tales

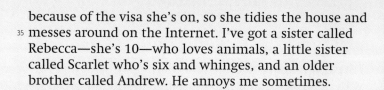

"Christmas is exciting when you're 12 - and even more so when it's your first abroad and your first with a guaranteed blanket of snow," says Daniel Allum from Oakley, England.

Daniel says: "I am excited about having a white Christmas—it'll be fun. When we first arrived in the U.S. it was 106° F—so hot the road melted—and now it's freezing with the grass covered in snow and ice. We've built a snowman outside, and there's a big hill for sledding. On Christmas Day we'll probably mess around inside as there's meant to be eight inches of snow. In some ways the snow makes it feel more like Christmas, but I'm used to having relatives around, and they won't take the 12-hour flight here just for one day.

Why they moved

My family and I—four kids and two adults—lived in a little town called Oakley in Bedfordshire, and now we live in a smaller one in Kansas called Hugoton. Hugoton is flat with no trees and just tumbleweed everywhere. We live in the middle of nowhere off Highway 54. It's one of those towns that you can just drive through in two minutes. We moved here because Dad, who worked for a farming company, got sick of leaving for work so early and getting home so late. Last November he called us all down from our rooms and said he'd started job interviews to move to another country, and in June we packed up and left. We spend more time together now. Dad gets home from work much earlier, and Mum can't work because of the visa she's on, so she tidies the house and messes around on the Internet. I've got a sister called Rebecca—she's 10—who loves animals, a little sister called Scarlet who's six and whinges, and an older brother called Andrew. He annoys me sometimes.

Life in Kansas

Life's different here. Our house has a basement for shelter from tornados—we don't have basements in England or tornados. Tornados are not uncommon in Kansas. And I think there's a language barrier because everyone laughs when I say "lorry" instead of "truck" or "petrol" instead of "gas." My friends try to talk like me, but they just sound like the Queen. School is better than in England, but I hate saying the pledge of allegiance. Every day before school we have to say it. In England we don't sing "God Save the Queen" every morning. And everyone here likes country music. I like Eminem and Jay-Z, but if I went to school singing them, I'd probably get suspended.

What he misses

What I miss most is fish and chips. Mum really misses being close to a main town—when she sees three shops in a row she gets all excited. Also I wish football (they call it "soccer") was more popular here. No one knows what I'm talking about. Last week there was meant to be an Arsenal game on TV, but instead it got changed to Oklahoma football. American football stinks. But I really like living here. The people are really nice, and I don't get car sick anymore as the roads are so long and straight."

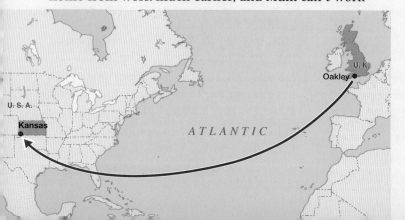

VOCABULARY AND PRONUNCIATION
House and home

1 How many new words can you make by combining a word on the left with a word on the right? Which are nouns and which are adjectives?

home
house

work	made	maker	sick	page
plant	town	coming	sit	less
grown	bound	warming		

2 **CD1 8** Listen to the conversations. After each one, discuss these questions. Who is talking to whom? What about? Which compounds from Exercise 1 are used?

3 Complete these lines from the conversations.

1. I'm going away for two weeks. Do you think you could possibly water my _____ for me?

2. I'll make sure everything stays clean and tidy. I don't mind doing _____.

3. Let's give her a spectacular _____ party when she gets back from Hong Kong.

4. Me? I'm just a _____. Four kids, _____ pies, and _____ vegetables!

5. We're having a _____ party on the 12th. Can you come? I'll give you our new address.

6. The problem is, with the place being much bigger, there's much more _____ to do!

7. Her grandmother's sick and _____, so they have to go and help.

"Please turn it down—Daddy's trying to do your homework."

4 **CD1 9** Practice saying the lines in Exercise 3 with the correct stress and intonation. Listen and check. Try to remember more of each conversation. Act some of them out with a partner.

5 Work in groups. Make compounds by combining words from one of the boxes in **A** with as many words as possible from **B**. Use your dictionary to help.

A

book	tea
computer	sleeping
air	door
junk	open
food	fire
word	head

B

pill	line	mail	way	case
bell	light	air	house	bag
software	escape	office		
food	poisoning	pot	step	
rest	alarm	shelf	program	

Share your words with a different group and explain the meanings.

LISTENING AND SPEAKING
Things I miss from home

1 When have you spent time away from home? Where did you go? Why? Did you have a good time? What did you miss from home?

2 Write down one thing that you missed on a piece of paper and give it to your teacher. You will use this later.

3 **CD1 10** Listen to people talking about things they miss when they are away. What do they miss? What do they do about it? Complete the chart.

	What do they miss?	What do they do?
Andrew		
Gabriele		
Paul		
Anna		
Sylvia		
Chris		

4 **CD1 10** Read the lines below. Then listen again. Who is speaking? What do the words in *italics* refer to?

1. That sounds very silly, but I like to see *them* every once in a while.
2. I don't eat much of *it* at home.
3. *It* doesn't happen with newspapers.
4. As soon as I'm checked in, I go straight *there*.
5. I know it sounds crazy, but *this one* I take is just the way I like it.
6. When I'm away on business *it's* not like that.

5 Read aloud the things the class wrote down in Exercise 2. Guess who wrote them. Whose is the funniest? The most interesting? What do the most people miss?

EVERYDAY ENGLISH
Social expressions and the music of English

1 Work with a partner. Match a line in **A** with a line in **B**.

A	B
1. Great to see you. Come on in.	a. Let me see. No, actually, I think I'll pass on dessert.
2. Excuse me, don't I know you from somewhere?	b. Thanks. I was just passing through and thought I'd drop by.
3. What do you mean you're not coming to my party?	c. Really? That's too bad. I was hoping to meet her.
4. I think I'll have the chocolate cake. What about you?	d. No, I don't think so.
5. My roommate can't make it to your party.	e. Well, I'm just not up for going out tonight.
6. How come you're not going on vacation this year?	f. Fantastic! I knew you'd come through for us.
7. You'll get yourself sick if you keep working at that pace.	g. Because we just can't afford it.
8. I got you the last two tickets for the show.	h. That may be, but I have to get this finished by Friday.

CD1 11 Listen and check. Pay particular attention to the stress and intonation. Practice the lines with your partner.

> ### Music *of* English ♫
>
> **CD1 12** The "music" of a language is made up of three things.
>
> 1 **Intonation**—the up and down of the voice:
>
> *Excuse me!* *Really?*
>
> 2 **Stress**—the accented syllables in individual words:
>
> *chocolate* *fantastic* *dessert*
>
> 3 **Rhythm**—the stressed syllables over a group of words:
>
> *What do you mean you're not coming?*

2 **CD1 13** Listen to the conversation and concentrate on the "music." Who are the people? Do they know each other? Where are they?

3 Work with a partner. Look at the conversation on page 149. Take the roles of **A** and **B** and read the conversation aloud. Use the stress shading to help you.

CD1 13 Listen again and repeat the lines one by one. Practice the conversation again with your partner.

4 Complete these conversations. The stressed words are already given. Practice saying the lines as you go.

1.

A Excuse ... , ... know you ... somewhere?
B Actually, ... think so.
A ... Gavin's party last week?
B Not me. ... don't know anyone ... Gavin.
A Well, someone ... looked just like
... there.
B Well, that may be, ... certainly
wasn't me.
A ... am sorry!

2.

A Tony! Hi! Great ... see ... !
B Well, ... just passing through,
... drop by ... "hello."
A ... in! Tell ... new!
B ... sure? ... too busy?
A Never ... busy ... talk ... you.
B Thanks. ... really nice ...
chat.
A Fantastic! Let ... coat.

5 **CD1 14** Listen and compare your ideas and pronunciation.

2 # Been there, done that!

- **Grammar:** Present Perfect Simple and Continuous
- **Vocabulary:** Hot verbs—*make, do*
- **Everyday English:** Exclamations

TEST YOUR GRAMMAR

1 What is strange about these sentences? What should they be?

1. Columbus has discovered America.
2. Man first walked on the moon.
3. I traveled all my life. I went everywhere.
4. I've learned English.
5. I've been losing my passport.

2 Which of these verb forms can change from simple to continuous or vice versa? What is the change in meaning?

1. What do you do in New York?
2. I know you don't like my boyfriend.
3. I had a cup of tea at 8:00.
4. Someone's eaten my sandwich.
5. I'm hot because I've been running.

EXPLORERS AND TRAVELERS
Present Perfect

1 Look at the pictures. Why did people go exploring hundreds of years ago? Why do young people go traveling these days?

2 Read the first and last paragraphs of two articles about Marco Polo and Tommy Willis. Then match the sentences with the correct person. Put **MP** or **TW** in the boxes.

1. **MP** He was born in Venice, the son of a merchant. When he was 17, he set off for China. The journey took four years.

2. **TW** He's visited royal palaces and national parks in South Korea and climbed to the summit of Mount Fuji in Japan.

3. ☐ He's been staying in cheap hostels along with a lot of other young people.

4. ☐ His route led him through Persia and Afghanistan.

5. ☐ He was met by the emperor Kublai Khan. He was one of the first Europeans to visit the territory, and he traveled extensively.

6. ☐ "I've had diarrhea a few times." Apart from that, his only worry is the insects. He's been stung all over his body.

7. ☐ He stayed in China for 17 years. When he left, he took back a fortune in gold and jewelry.

8. ☐ He's been traveling mainly by public transportation.

3 **CD1 15** Listen and check. What other information do you learn about the two travelers?

MARCO POLO 1254–1324

MARCO POLO was the first European to travel the entire 5,000-mile length of the Silk Route, the main trade link between Cathay (China) and the West for over two thousand years.

He wrote a book called *The Travels of Marco Polo*, which gave Europeans their first information about China and the Far East.

4 Match a line in A with a line in B. Practice saying them. Pay attention to contracted forms and weak forms.

A	B
He's been stung	in cheap hostels.
He's visited	all over his body.
He's been staying	a lot of really great people."
"I've been	to Vietnam and Japan.
"I've met	pickpocketed and mugged."
He's been	royal palaces.

CD1 16 Listen and check.

TOMMY WILLIS backpacker in Asia

Tommy Willis is in Fiji. He's on a nine-month backpacking trip around Asia. He flew into Bangkok five months ago. Since then, he's been to Vietnam, Hong Kong, South Korea, and Japan.

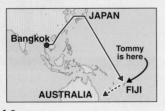

He's looking forward to taking things easy for another week then setting off again for Australia. "Once you've got the travel bug, it becomes very hard to stay in the same place for too long," he said.

GRAMMAR SPOT

1 What is the main tense used in the sentences about Marco Polo? Why?

What are the main tenses used in the sentences about Tommy Willis? Why?

2 Compare the use of tenses in these sentences.

1. I've read that book. It's good.
   I've been reading a great book. I'll lend it to you when I've finished.
   I've been reading a lot about Orwell recently. I've just finished his biography.
2. She's been writing since she was 16.
   She's written three novels.
3. He's played tennis since he was a kid.
   He's been playing tennis since he was a kid.

▶▶ **Grammar Reference 2.1 pp. 137–138**

PRACTICE

Questions and answers

1 Read the pairs of questions. First decide who each question is about, Marco Polo or Tommy Willis. Then ask and answer the questions.

1. Where did he go?
   Where has he been?
2. How long has he been traveling?
   How long did he travel?
3. How did he travel?
   How has he been traveling?
4. Who has he met?
   Who did he meet?
5. Did he have any problems?
   Has he had any problems?

2 Here are the answers to some questions. Write the questions.

About Marco Polo
1. In 1254 in Venice.
2. Four years.
3. For 17 years.
4. Gold and jewelry.
5. *The Travels of Marco Polo.*

About Tommy Willis
6. For five months. **How long ... away from home?**
7. Thailand, Vietnam, Hong Kong, South Korea, and Japan. **What ...?**
8. In cheap hostels.
9. A few times. **How many ...?**
10. Yes, once. **Has ...?**

CD1 17 Listen and check your answers.

Discussing grammar

3 Put the verb in the correct tense.

1. Charles Dickens _____(write) *Oliver Twist* in 1837.
   I _____(write) two best-selling crime stories.
   She _____(write) her autobiography for the past 18 months.
2. _____ you ever _____(try) Mexican food?
   _____ you _____(try) *chiles rellenos* when you were in Mexico?
3. How many times _____ you _____(marry)?
   How many times _____ Henry VIII _____(marry)?
4. I _____(live) in the same house since I was born.
   He _____(live) with his brother for the past week.
5. Cindy _____ finally _____(get) her driver's license. She _____(try) to pass the test for years.

Simple and continuous

> **GRAMMAR SPOT**
>
> **1** Simple verb forms see actions as a complete whole.
> *He **works** for IBM.   It **rained** all day yesterday.   I**'ve lost** my passport.*
>
> **2** Continuous verb forms see actions in progress, with a beginning and an end.
> *I**'m working** with Jim for a couple of days.*
> *It **was raining** when I woke up.*
> *The company **has been losing** money for years.*
>
> **3** Stative verbs don't tend to be used in the continuous.
> *I **know** Peter well.   I've always **liked** him.*
> *I **don't understand** what you're saying.*
>
> Do you know more verbs like these?
>
> ▶▶ **Grammar Reference 2.1 pp. 137–138**

4 Match a line in **A** with a line in **B**. Write a or b in the box.

A	B
1. ☐ Peter comes	a. from Switzerland.
2. ☐ Peter is coming by	b. at 8:00 tonight.
3. ☐ I wrote a report this morning.	a. I'll finish it this afternoon.
4. ☐ I was writing a report this morning.	b. I sent it off this afternoon.
5. ☐ I heard her scream	a. when she saw a mouse.
6. ☐ I heard the baby screaming	b. all night long.
7. ☐ What have you done	a. since I last saw you?
8. ☐ What have you been doing	b. with my dictionary? I can't find it.
9. ☐ I've had	a. a headache all day.
10. ☐ I've been having	b. second thoughts about the new job.
11. ☐ I've known	a. my new neighbors.
12. ☐ I've been getting to know	b. Anna for over ten years.
13. ☐ I just cut	a. my finger. It hurts!
14. ☐ I've been cutting	b. wood all morning.

▶▶ **WRITING** Informal letters—Correcting mistakes *p. 108*

Exchanging information

5 Tony and Maureen Wheeler are the founders of the *Lonely Planet* travel guides. There are now over 650 books in the series.

Work with a partner. You each have different information. Ask and answer questions.
Student A Look at page 149.
Student B Look at page 151.

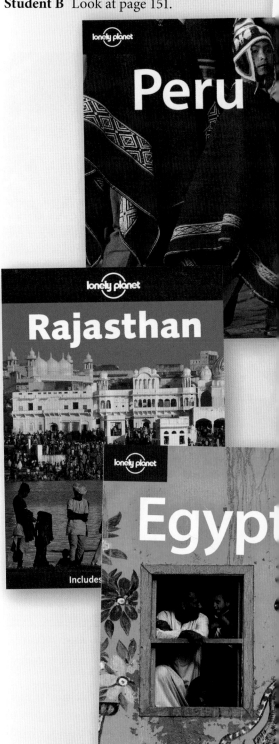

READING AND SPEAKING
Paradise Lost

1 Look at the pictures of tourist destinations in the world. Where are they? Have you been to any of them?

6 Work in groups to prepare an interview with Tony Wheeler. One half of the class will be the interviewers (look at the ideas below) and the other half Tony Wheeler (look at the ideas on page 151).

Interviewers

BACKGROUND
Where ... grow up?
What ... father do?

EDUCATION
Where ... school?
Which college ...?

WORK
What work ... after college?

FAMILY
How many children ...?

VACATIONS
What ... like doing ...?

LONELY PLANET GUIDES
When ... the first guidebook come out?
Where ... idea come from?
What ... the best and worst moment?
What ... secret of your success?
What advice ... people who want to get into travel writing?

FUTURE
Where would you like ...?

2 Think about the most important tourist spots in your country. Does tourism cause any problems there?

3 What are the main problems associated with the tourist industry in the world?

Turn to page 17.

Paradise lost

What can be done to stop tourism from destroying the object of its affection? Maurice Chandler reports on the boom in world travel.

On the sun-soaked Mediterranean island of Majorca, the locals are angry. Too late. In the last quarter of the 20th century, they cashed in on foreign nationals, mainly Germans, wanting to buy up property on their idyllic island. Suddenly, it occurred to Majorcans that the island no longer belonged to them. They don't deny tourism's vital contribution to the local economy. The industry has transformed Majorca from one of Spain's poorest parts to the richest in per capita income. But the island's 800,000 inhabitants are increasingly convinced that the 24 million foreign visitors a year are far too much of a good thing. Water is rationed, pollution is worsening, and there is no affordable housing left for them to buy.

On the other side of the world, 250 Filipinos were recently evicted from their homes. Their lakeshore village of Ambulong was cleared by hundreds of police officers, who demolished 24 houses. The intention of the authorities was to make way for a major business venture—not oil, logging, or mining but an environmentally-friendly vacation resort.

A growth industry

Tourism is the world's largest and fastest-growing industry. In 1950, 25 million people traveled abroad; last year it was 922 million. The World Tourism Organization estimates that by 2020 1.6 billion people will travel each year, spending over two trillion U.S. dollars.

The effects of tourism

To millions of tourists foreign destinations are exotic paradises, unspoiled, idyllic, and full of local charm. But many of the world's resorts are struggling to cope with relentless waves of tourists, whose demands for more and more swimming pools and golf courses are sucking them dry.

"The issue is massive and global," says Tricia Barnett, director of Tourism Concern, a charity which campaigns for more responsible approaches to travel. "Tourists in Africa will be taking a shower and then will see a local woman carrying a pot of water on her head, and they are not making the connection. Sometimes you'll see a village with a single tap when each hotel has taps and showers in every room."

The problem is that tourists demand so much water. It has been calculated that a tourist in Spain uses 880 liters of water a day, compared with 250 liters by a local. An 18-hole golf course in a dry country can consume as much water as a town of 10,000 people. In the Caribbean, hundreds of thousands of people go without piped water during the high tourist season as springs are piped to hotels.

In 1950, 25 million people traveled abroad; last year it was 922 million.

Winners and losers

The host country may not see many benefits. In Thailand, 60% of the $4 billion in annual tourism revenue leaves the country. Low-end package tourists tend to stay at big foreign-owned hotels, cooped up in the hotel compound, buying few local products. They have no contact with the local community beyond the waiters and chambermaids employed by the hotel. "Mass tourism usually leaves little money inside the country," says Tricia Barnett. "Most of the money ends up with the airlines, the tour operators, and the foreign hotel owners."

These days the industry's most urgent question may be how to keep the crowds at bay. A prime example of this is Italy, where great cultural centers like Florence and Venice can't handle all the tourists they get every summer. In Florence, where the city's half-million or so inhabitants have to live with the pollution, gridlock, and crime generated by 11 million visitors a year, there's talk not only of boosting hotel taxes, but even of charging admission to some public squares. The idea is to discourage at least some visitors, as well as to pay for cleaning up the mess.

The future

However, for many poorer countries, tourism may still offer the best hope for development. "The Vietnamese are doing their best to open up their country," says Patrick Duffey of the World Tourism Organization. "Iran is working on a master plan for their tourism. Libya has paid $1 million for a study. They all want tourists. And people always want to discover new parts of the world. They are tired of mass tourism. Even if a country doesn't have beaches, it can offer mountains and deserts and unique cultures."

Yet if something isn't done, tourism seems destined to become the victim of its own success. Its impact on the environment is a major concern. In hindsight, tourist organizations might have second thoughts about what exactly they were trying to sell.

As Steve McGuire, a tourist consultant, says, "Tourism more often than not ruins the very assets it seeks to exploit, and having done the damage, simply moves on elsewhere."

For poorer countries, tourism may still offer the best hope for development.

Reading

4 Read the title and the quotes in the article. What do you think the article will be about?

5 Read the article. Answer the questions.
   1. Which of the places in the pictures on page 15 are mentioned?
   2. What is said about them?
   3. What other places are mentioned?
   4. Does the article talk about any of the problems you discussed in Exercises 2 and 3?
   5. The author asks, "What can be done to stop tourism from destroying the object of its affection?" What would Steve McGuire's answer be?

6 In groups, discuss these questions.
   1. How is tourism destroying the object of its affection in Majorca and the Philippines?
   2. What are the statistics of the global tourist industry?
   3. What are the effects of tourism?
   4. Who are the winners and losers?
   5. What are possible future developments?

What do you think?

1 Give your personal reactions to the text, using these phrases.

I didn't know/I already knew that ...	What surprised me was ...
It must be really difficult for ...	It's hard to believe that ...
I wonder what can be done to ...	It's a shame that ...

2 In groups, think of questions to ask the other groups about the text. Use the prompts below for help.

Who ...?	Why ...?	In what way ...?
What is meant by ...?	How many ...?	
What exactly ...?	What are some of the problems ...?	

Who has bought nearly all the property on the island of Majorca?

Vocabulary work

1 Work with a partner. Discuss the meaning of the words highlighted in the article.

2 Match a line in **A** with a line in **B**. Can you remember where these phrases appeared in the text?

A	B
the boom	destinations
tourism's vital	venture
per capita	for development
a major business	income
foreign	example
consume	in world travel
a prime	as much water
the best hope	contribution to the economy

SPEAKING AND LISTENING
Dreams come true

1 20,000 Americans were asked what they most wanted to do before they die. Here are the top 15 activities.

What are your top five? Number them 1–5. Which ones don't interest you at all? Put an **X**.

- [ ] go whale-watching
- [ ] see the Northern Lights
- [ ] visit Machu Picchu
- [ ] get away to a paradise island
- [ ] go white-water rafting
- [ ] fly in a fighter plane
- [ ] fly in a hot-air balloon
- [ ] climb Sydney Harbor Bridge
- [ ] swim with dolphins
- [ ] walk the Great Wall of China
- [ ] go on safari
- [ ] go skydiving
- [ ] dive with sharks
- [ ] drive a Formula 1 car
- [ ] go scuba diving on the Great Barrier Reef

Compare your lists in groups.

2 You can read the actual results of the poll on page 150. Does anything surprise you? What do you think is missing from the list?

3 Do you know anyone who has done any of these things? What was it like?

4 **CD1 18** Listen to three people describing their experience of one of these activities. Which one are they talking about? What do they say about it?

VOCABULARY
Hot verbs—*make, do*

1 There are many expressions with *make* and *do*. Look at these examples from the text on pp. 16–17.

- They wanted . . . to *make way* for a vacation resort.
- They aren't *making the connection*.
- The Vietnamese are *doing their best* to open up their country.
- Tourism, having *done the damage*, moves on elsewhere.

2 Put the words in the right box.

a good impression	business	arrangements	a decision
a difference	research	a profit	your best	progress
a good job	an effort	sb a favor	a suggestion	sth clear

MAKE	DO

3 Complete the sentences with some of the expressions in Exercise 2.

1. When you go on a job interview, it's important to _____.
2. I think we're all getting tired. Can I _____? Let's take a break.
3. A lot of _____ has been _____ into the causes of cancer.
4. I think the CEO is basically _____. He's reliable, he's honest, and he gets results.
5. I'd like to _____ right now that I am totally opposed to this idea.
6. We can't _____ in this business unless we raise prices.
7. I don't mind if we go now or later. It _____ no _____ to me.
8. Could you _____ me _____ and lend me some money till tomorrow?

CD1 19 Listen and check.

4 Match an expression in **A** with a line in **B**. Underline the expression with *make* or *do*.

A	B
1. She's made it big as an actress.	"She's an accountant."
2. We'll never make it there in time.	"I can make myself understood."
3. "What does she do for a living?"	"Yeah. It really made my day."
4. "You'll all have to work weekends from now on."	The traffic's too bad.
5. "How much do you want to borrow? $20?"	She can command $20 million a movie.
6. "How much Spanish do you speak?"	"Yes, that'll do."
7. "I heard the boss said you'd done really well."	"That does it! I'm going to look for another job!"

Phrasal verbs

5 Complete the sentences with a phrasal verb with *do*.

do away with sth	do without sth
could do with sth	do sth over

"I'm tired of wondering what I'd do without you. I want to find out for sure."

1. I'm so thirsty. I _____ a glass of tea.
2. Your homework was full of mistakes. You'll have to _____ it _____.
3. I think we should _____ pennies. You can't buy anything with them anymore.
4. I could never _____ my assistant. She organizes everything for me.

CD1 20 Listen and check.

6 Do the same with these phrasal verbs with *make*.

make sth up	make up for sth
make (sth) of sth	make off with sth

1. Thieves broke into the mansion and _____ jewelry and antique paintings.
2. Jake's parents buy him lots of toys. They're trying to _____ always being at work.
3. What did you _____ the lecture? I didn't understand a word.
4. You didn't believe his story, did you? He _____ the whole thing _____.

CD1 21 Listen and check.

LISTENING AND SPEAKING
Tashi Wheeler—girl on the move

1 What are some of your earliest memories of vacations as a child? Tell the class.

2 Look at the photos of Tashi Wheeler, the daughter of Tony and Maureen (p. 14). In each photo …
- How old is she?
- Where do you think she is—Mexico, Singapore, Kenya (x2), the U.S. (Arizona), or Peru?
- What is she doing?

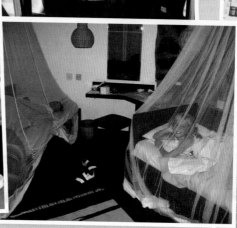

3 Tashi began traveling when she was eight months old. What questions would you like to ask her?

What was the first foreign country you went to?
What are your earliest memories?
Which countries have you been to?

4 **CD1 22** Listen to part one of an interview with Tashi. Does she answer any of your questions?

What memories does she have of …?
- the transportation
- being on safari
- her mother
- trekking in Nepal

5 **CD1 23** Listen to part two. Correct the wrong information.

> On vacation, the Wheeler family is very relaxed. They get up late and go to bed early. They spend a lot of time on the beach. Tony Wheeler reads the paper. They go to the same restaurant every day. Tashi and her brother spend a lot of time watching movies. She doesn't feel that travel broadens the mind.

6 **CD1 24** Listen to part three and answer the questions.
1. How did her attitude to travel change as she got older?
2. What did she find difficult socially?
3. Why was "adjusting back and forth" difficult?
4. What did the kids at school have that she didn't? What did she have that they didn't?
5. Where does she feel comfortable? Where does she feel uncomfortable?
6. What are Tashi's final words of advice for future travelers?
7. "I get very itchy-footed." Which phrase with a similar meaning did Tommy Willis use on page 13?

SPOKEN ENGLISH Fillers

When we speak (in any language!), we can be vague and imprecise. We also use fillers, which don't mean very much, but fill the gaps!

| Tashi | And the Galapagos Islands, Philippines, *and stuff like that*. . . . monkeys swinging off the, *um*, rearview mirrors, *and things*. The getting up at *like* four in the morning . . . |
| Interviewer | And when you were on these travels, *I mean*, did your dad *sort of* have a notebook, and he'd be *sort of* stopping everywhere . . . ? |

Look at the audio script on page 122. Find more examples of imprecise language and fillers.

EVERYDAY ENGLISH
Exclamations

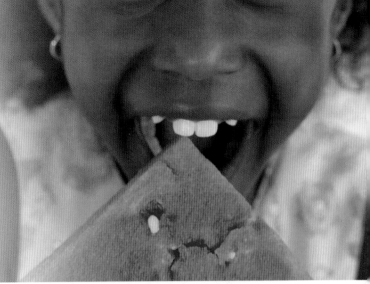

1 Look at these examples of exclamations. When do we use
What a(n) ... !, *What ... !*, and *How... !*?

What an exciting experience!   What nonsense!   How horrible!

2 Match an exclamation in **B** with a line in **C**.

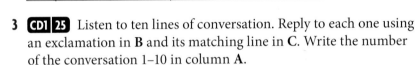

A	B	C
1	**Mmm!**	How interesting!
	Wow!	That's disgusting!
	Hey, Peter!	That's unbelievable! How amazing!
	Oh, really?	Sorry about that! I dropped it!
	Ah!	It's absolutely delicious!
	Ouch!	That's nonsense! What a weird thing to say!
	Yuck!	What a shame!
	Huh?	That really hurt!
	Phew!	Come over here and sit with us.
	Whoops!	What a relief! Thank goodness for that!

3 **CD1 25** Listen to ten lines of conversation. Reply to each one using
an exclamation in **B** and its matching line in **C**. Write the number
of the conversation 1–10 in column **A**.

4 What is the next line in each conversation? Put a number 1–10 next
to the correct line.

> **A** How's your steak? Is it OK?
> **B** Mmm! It's absolutely delicious! *Just the way I like it.*

- [ ] Don't worry. I'll get you a new one.
- [ ] Triplets! That'll keep them busy!
- [ ] You must be so disappointed!
- [1] Just the way I like it.
- [ ] I hadn't done any studying for it at all.
- [ ] You wouldn't catch me eating that!
- [ ] I've got to watch where I'm going!
- [ ] Tell us what's new!
- [ ] You know it's not true.
- [ ] I haven't seen her for weeks. How is she?

CD1 26 Listen and check. Practice the conversations, paying special
attention to intonation. You could act some of them out and make
them longer!

Music *of* English ♪♫

With exclamations using *What . . . !* and *How . . . !*, your intonation should
rise and fall on both the adjective and noun:

What awful shoes!   *What a fantastic view!*   *How amazing!*

CD1 27 Listen and repeat.

---

5 Put *What ...*, *What a ...*, or *How ...*
to complete the exclamations.

1. _____ silly mistake!
2. _____ brilliant idea!
3. _____ ridiculous!
4. _____ terrible weather!
5. _____ nonsense!
6. _____ mess!
7. _____ awful!
8. _____ wonderful!
9. _____ relief!
10. _____ terrible thing to happen!

Which are positive reactions? Which
are negative?

6 **CD1 28** Listen to these statements.
Respond to them using one of the
exclamations in Exercise 5.

7 Write a dialogue with a partner. Use
some of the exclamations on this page.
You could ask about a party, a meal, a
vacation, or a sports event.

Begin with a question.

> **What was the ... like?**
> **Well, it was ...**

Act out your conversations for the class.

3 What a story!

> **Grammar:** Narrative tenses
> **Vocabulary:** Books and movies
> **Everyday English:** Showing interest and surprise

TEST YOUR GRAMMAR

Read the story. Put the events into chronological order. What happened first? What happened last?

Burglar arrested

▶ LAST SATURDAY night a couple came home at midnight to find their house had been robbed. Dave and Janet Jones had left home at 6:00 pm to go to have dinner with friends. When they got home, the back door had been smashed, and money and jewelry had been stolen. Mrs. Jones told police she had seen a man who had been acting suspiciously in the area days before the robbery. A man answering her description was later arrested.

WHAT'S IN THE NEWS?
Narrative tenses

1 Look at the newspaper headlines. What do you think is the whole story?

2 What would you like to know? Write some more questions.

> *Did he mean to fall over?*
> *Where was she climbing?*
> *How did he manage to hack into their computers?*

3 **CD1 29** Listen to three conversations about the stories. Which of your questions were answered?

4 Here are the answers to some questions. What are the questions?

1. Just ordinary clothes.
2. For a dare.
3. Three hours.
4. In a shelter.
5. His own software program.
6. To download from the Internet.

5 Match lines in **A** and **B**. Practice saying them with contracted and weak forms.

A	B
He was wearing	with a partner.
He'd been talking	he wouldn't do it.
His friends had bet him	the next night.
She was climbing	about doing it for years.
They were rescued	ordinary clothes.

CD1 30 Listen and check.

Man survives plunge over Niagara Falls

180ft drop

Climber saved by

Need heli rescue off north ridge of Piz Badile, Switzerland!

Send   Cancel

The nerd who hacked into U.S. military computers

text plea to friend

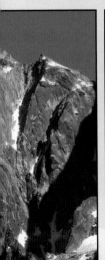

GRAMMAR SPOT

1 Complete the chart using the verb in parentheses.

Past Simple	Past Continuous
(fall)	(read)

Past Perfect	Past Perfect Continuous
(hear)	(act)

Past Simple passive	Past Perfect passive
(arrest)	(rob)

Look at audio script **CD1 29** on page 123. Find an example of each tense. When do we use the Past Perfect? When do we use continuous tenses?

2 Why are different tenses used in these paragraphs?

John cooked a delicious meal. His guests had a good time. They left at midnight.

Just after midnight John was looking at the mess. His guests had just left. He'd cooked a delicious meal, and everyone had had a good time.

▶▶ **Grammar Reference 3.1–3.5 pp. 138–139**

PRACTICE

Discussing grammar

1 Compare the use of tenses in these sentences. How do the tenses change the meanings?

1.
I read	
I was reading	a book on the plane.

2. When Alice arrived,
I made a cake.
I was making a cake.
I had made a cake.

3.
The movie started	
The movie had started	when we got to the theater.

4. He was fired because
he had stolen some money.
he had been stealing money for years.

5. When I got to the garage, my car
was being repaired.
had been repaired.

Writing narratives

2 Rewrite the sentences as one sentence, beginning with the part in **bold**.

She won $2,000 in a contest. **Last night Sally was celebrating.**
Last night Sally was celebrating because she'd won $2,000 in a contest.

1. He got up at dawn. He was driving for ten hours. **Peter was tired when he arrived home.**
2. I parked my car in a no-parking zone. It was towed away. **I went to get my car, but it wasn't there.** (*When ...*)
3. He wasn't always poor. He had a successful business. Unfortunately, it went bust. **Mick was a homeless beggar.**
4. They were shopping all day. They spent all their money on clothes. **Jane and Peter arrived home.** They were broke. (*When ...*)
5. He saw a house in Maine. He first saw it while he was driving on vacation. **Last week John moved to the house.**

The news

3 **CD1 31** Listen to the first story. Correct the mistakes in the sentences.

1. Ten workers have died.
2. They'd been trapped up a mountain.
3. They'd been building a new road.
4. There was an avalanche.
5. Sixteen men managed to escape.
6. Ten were fatally injured.
7. The men were recovering at home.
8. The cause of the accident is known.

4 **CD1 32** Listen to the second news story. Here are the answers to some questions. Write the questions.

1. For two days.
2. After school on Wednesday.
3. Their photographs.
4. Nearby houses.
5. A neighbor.
6. In a garden shed.
7. No, they hadn't. (*... realized ...?*)

▶▶ **WRITING** Narrative writing 1—Using adverbs in narratives *p. 109*

VOCABULARY AND SPEAKING
Books and movies

1 We usually want to know some things about a book before we start reading it. Here are some answers. Write in the questions.

1. <u>Who wrote it</u>_____?
   Charles Dickens/Agatha Christie.

2. _____?
   It's a romantic novel/a crime thriller/a biography.

3. _____?
   It's about a relationship that goes wrong/war and peace.

4. <u>Where and</u>_____?
   In India in the 1800s/In New York in the '80s.

5. _____?
   A lawyer named Potts and his client, Lady Jane /A detective named Blunket.

6. _____?
   Yes, it has. It came out a few years ago and starred Johnny Depp.

7. _____?
   It ends really tragically/It's frustrating because we don't really know/They all live happily ever after.

8. _____?
   I thought it was great/I couldn't put it down/I didn't want it to end/It was OK, but I skipped the boring parts.

9. _____?
   Yes, I would. It's great if you like a good love story/ It's great beach reading.

2 Which questions could also be asked about a movie? Some might have to change. What extra questions can be asked about a movie?

3 **CD1** **33** Listen to two people, one talking about a movie and the other a book. Take notes under these headings.

Title	Setting	Characters	Plot	Personal opinion

4 Work with a partner. Ask and answer the questions in Exercise 1 about your favorite book or movie.

5 Look at the front and back covers of *The Fallen Curtain*, a collection of short stories. Which of the questions in Exercise 1 can you answer?

The FALLEN CURTAIN

S T O R I E S

BY
RUTH RENDELL

CRIME/FICTION

"Suspense at its best."
—*The Times*

Awarded an Edgar by the Mystery Writers of America

These are short stories from a crime writer at the height of her powers. Ruth Rendell employs all her spine-chilling crafts to produce a page-turner that makes the heart pound.

The Clinging Woman, the first story in the collection, opens with the attempted suicide of a young woman, hanging by her hands from a balcony on the twelfth floor of a London apartment building. The prompt action of a neighbor saves her life. But what made Lydia Simpson want to end her life? Was it an unhappy childhood? Or perhaps a failed relationship?

The man who saved her life thinks he has done nothing to deserve being called a hero. He simply called the police. He wants to forget all about the episode. But he is drawn into a relationship with the mysterious woman who he rescued from certain death.

As they become closer, he glimpses character traits in Lydia that at first worry him, then disturb him. Why doesn't she have any friends? Does she want to possess him? Why can't he ever do anything without her?

In *The Clinging Woman,* Ruth Rendell – the queen of literary mystery – exposes the twisted inner workings of an unbalanced mind. It is a haunting psychological thriller with unexpected twists and a shocking conclusion.

"One of the best inventors of plots since Agatha Christie." –*Daily Telegraph*

"Ruth Rendell is at the top of her class."
– *The Observer*

ISBN 0-385-72095-5

51495

9 780385 720953

READING AND SPEAKING
The Clinging Woman

1 Look at the picture. What can you see? What is the woman doing? What is the man doing? What is she thinking? What is he thinking? What do you think happens next?

2 Here is the opening of the story "The Clinging Woman." Read Part 1 and answer the questions. Then do the same for Parts 2–4.

Part 1

1. A lot of facts are established in the first paragraph. What are they?
   It's 6:30 in the morning.
   There are two characters.
   He lives ...

Part 2

1. What is the man's initial interpretation of what he sees?
2. What is his second interpretation?
3. If this was a "stunt," what would there be on the ground?
4. How does he know this second interpretation is wrong?
5. What is his third interpretation?
6. What does he do?

Part 3

1. How do the neighbors react?
2. How does the man react to this attention?
3. What happened two weeks (a fortnight) later?
4. Why doesn't he recognize the person at the door?

Part 4

1. How does the man feel as she talks? What does he say?
2. What does he want her to do?
3. What doesn't he want to happen?
4. How does he feel as she goes? How does she appear?

Language work

Match a word from lines 1–49 of the text with a synonym or near synonym.

Word in the text	Synonym
clinging	look
awakened	holding tightly
gaze	courage
vanishing	woken up
deserted	disappearing
obviously	final
nerve	center
ultimate	empty
focus	warned
alerted	clearly

What do you think?

1. Why doesn't the writer give the characters' names at first? (In fact, we never actually learn the man's name.)

2. What do you think happens at the bus stop?

3. Do they get to know each other? Go out together? Get married? Have children?

4. What worrying character traits are mentioned on the back cover?

> "My life has been yours ever since you saved it."

> "We don't need children to bring us together. You're my husband and my child and my friend all in one."

> The first thing he noticed when he let himself in at his front door at six was the stench of gas.

> "How long," she asked dully, "will you be gone?"
> "Three months."
> She paled. She fell back as if physically ill.

> ... she had been lying there, the empty bottle of pills still clutched feebly in her hand.

5. Here are some lines from the rest of the story.

What do you think happens?

Look at page 153 and read a synopsis of the story.

Discussing a book or movie

- Work in groups. Talk about a movie you have seen recently, or a book you're reading at the moment.
- Use the expressions on page 25. Here are some more lines that might help.

   It is set in ...
   It's a thriller/a romance/a true story ...
   It describes how ...
   It's about a man who ...
   We watch the characters as they ...
   There's a moment in the film/book when ...
   In the end ...

The CLINGING WOMAN

Part 1

The girl was hanging by her hands from the railings of a balcony. The balcony was on the twelfth floor of the high-rise building next to his. His apartment was on the ninth floor, and he had to look up to see her. It was half-past six in the morning. He had been awakened by the sound of an aircraft flying dangerously low overhead and had gotten out of bed to look. His sleepy gaze, descending from the blue sky which was empty of clouds, empty of anything but the bright vanishing arrow of the aircraft, alighted—at first with disbelief—on the hanging figure.

Part 2

He really thought he must be dreaming, for this sunrise time was the hour for dreams. Then, when he knew he wasn't, he decided it must be a stunt. This was to be a scene in a film. There were cameramen down there, a whole film unit, and all the correct safety precautions had been taken. Probably the girl wasn't even a real girl but a dummy. He opened the window and looked down. The parking lot, paved courts, grass spaces between the blocks, all were deserted. On the balcony railing one of the dummy's hands moved, clutching its anchorage more tightly, more desperately. He had to believe then what was obviously happening— unbelievable only because melodrama, though a frequent constituent of real life, always is. The girl was trying to kill herself. She had lost her nerve and now was trying to stay alive. All these thoughts and conclusions of his occupied about thirty seconds. Then he acted. He picked up the phone and dialed the emergency number for the police.

Part 3

The arrival of the police cars and the ultimate rescue of the girl became the focus of gossip and speculation for the tenants of the two buildings. Someone found out that it was he who had alerted the police, and he became an unwilling hero. He was a modest, quiet young man and, disliking

this limelight, was relieved when the talk began to die away, when the novelty of it wore off, and he was able to enter and leave his apartment without being pointed at as a kind of St. George* and sometimes even congratulated.

About a fortnight after that morning of melodrama, he was getting ready to go to the theater, just putting on his overcoat, when the doorbell rang. He didn't recognize the girl who stood outside. He had never seen her face. She said, "I'm Lydia Simpson. You saved my life. I've come to thank you."

Part 4

His embarrassment was acute. "You shouldn't have," he said with a nervous smile. "You really shouldn't. That's not necessary. I only did what anyone would have done."

She was calm and tranquil, not at all his idea of a failed suicide. "But no one else did," she said.

"Won't you come in? Have a drink or something?"

"Oh, no, I couldn't think of it. I can see you're just going out. I only wanted to say thank you very, very much."

"It was nothing."

"Nothing to save someone's life? I'll always be grateful to you."

He wished she would either come in or go away. If this went on much longer the people in the other two apartments on his floor would hear, would come out, and another of those bravest-deeds-of-the-year committee meetings would be convened. "Nothing at all," he said desperately. "Really, I've almost forgotten it."

"I shall never forget, never."

Her manner, calm yet intense, made him feel uncomfortable, and he watched her retreat into the elevator—smiling pensively with profound relief. Luckily, they weren't likely to meet again. The curious thing was that they did, the next morning at the bus stop.

*St. George: A hero who, according to legend, killed a dragon that was terrorizing a town.

LISTENING AND SPEAKING
The money jigsaw

Our $2,000 jigsaw

1 Look at the headlines and photographs. What story are they telling? Use the prompts to invent the story.

going to school / ripped-up cash / flying all over / a trash can / a plastic bag / jammed full / torn-up bills / had to go to school

after school playing / police / told them where / police took away / U.S. Treasury / long time / gave back / stick together

Stick-up job on torn money
leaves schoolgirls $1,200 richer

What do you think?

Why do you think someone tore up the money? Rachel and her friend have two theories.

• Maybe an old lady decided she wasn't going to leave it to anyone.
• It could have been a divorce—one person didn't want the other to have it.

Do you agree? Do you have any better explanations?

2 **CD1 34** Listen to one of the girls, Rachel Aumann, being interviewed. Compare your story with hers.

3 Answer the questions.

1. Where did the girls find the money?
2. How big are the pieces?
3. Are they being allowed to keep it?
4. Is it easy to stick the notes together?
5. How do they do it?
6. How long have they been doing it?
7. How much money is there?

> **SPOKEN ENGLISH** *like*
>
> Rachel uses the word *like* a lot.
>
> > Yeah, it was, um, *like* really bizarre.
> > . . . we followed it to, *like*, a garbage can.
>
> This use of *like* suggests that the speaker (often a younger person) is not making an effort to be precise when describing or reporting a situation.
>
> Look at the audio script on p. 123. Find more examples of *like*. Which example shows the correct use of *like* as a preposition?

EVERYDAY ENGLISH
Showing interest and surprise

1 **CD1 35** Listen to the conversation. Write in **B**'s answers. How does she show interest and surprise?

A Jade's got a new boyfriend.
B _____? Good for her!
A Apparently, he lives in a castle.
B _____? How amazing!
A I know. She met him in Slovenia.
B _____? That's interesting.
A Unfortunately, he can't speak much English.
B _____? I thought everyone could these days!

2 **B** uses *echo questions* and *reply questions*. Which are which? Practice the conversation with your partner. Pay particular attention to the stress and intonation.

> ### Music of English 🎵
> To show interest, the intonation on echo and reply questions should start high, go down, and then go up high at the end.
>
> She has?   He does?   She did?   You are?
>
> **CD1 36** Listen and repeat.
>
> If you use these short questions without any intonation, you will sound bored and uninterested!

3 Complete the conversations with either an echo or a reply question.

1. **A** Sam wants to apologize.
   B _____?
   A Yes. He's broken your mother's Chinese vase.
   B _____? Oh, no!

2. **A** We had a terrible vacation.
   B _____?
   A Yes. It rained all the time.
   B _____?
   A Yes. And the food was disgusting!
   B _____? What a drag!

3. **A** I'm broke.
   B _____? How come?
   A Because I just got a phone bill for $500.
   B _____? Why so much?
   A Because I have a girlfriend in Korea.
   B _____? How interesting!

4. **A** It took me three hours to get here.
   B _____?
   A Yes. There was a traffic jam ten miles long.
   B _____? That's awful!
   A Now I've got a headache!
   B _____? Poor thing. I'll get you something for it.

5. **A** I'm watching the sun set over the ocean.
   B _____?
   A Yes. And I've got something very important to ask you.
   B _____? What is it? I can't wait!
   A You'd better sit down. I'd like to marry you.
   B _____? Wow!

CD1 37 Listen and compare. Practice them with a partner.

4 Work with a partner. Take turns saying surprising things (they don't have to be true!) and responding with a reply question or an echo.

> I was born in a taxi cab!

> You were? That's incredible!

Grammar: Questions and negatives
Vocabulary: Prefixes and antonyms
Everyday English: Being polite

TEST YOUR GRAMMAR

1 Make the sentences negative. Sometimes there is more than one possibility.

> *I disagree/don't agree with you.*

1. I agree with you.
2. I think you're right.
3. I told her to go home.
4. "Is John coming?" "I hope so."
5. I knew everybody at the party.
6. I've already done my homework.
7. You must get a visa.
8. My sister likes hip-hop, too.

2 Write in the missing word in each question.

1. "What ____ of music do you like?" "Jazz."
2. "How ____ do you wash your hair?" "Every other day."
3. "Who do you look ____?" "My mother."
4. "How ____ does it take you to get to school?" "Nearly an hour."
5. "What were you talking ____ to the teacher?" "Oh, this and that."
6. "Do you know what ____ the time?" "Just after three."

Ask and answer the questions with a partner.

TELLING LIES
Questions and negatives

1 Think of some lies that these people might tell.

a teenage girl to her parents	a car salesman
a student to the teacher	a politician
a husband to his wife	

2 All the people in the cartoons are lying. Who to? Why?

3 [CD1 38] Listen to what the people are really thinking. What is the truth? Why did they lie? Do you think any of the people have good reasons to lie?

4 Which question was each person asked before they lied? Put a–f in the boxes.

1. ☐ What did you make that face for? Doesn't it look good?
2. ☐ Can I speak to Sue Jones, please? It's urgent.
3. ☐ How come you're sick today? You looked just fine yesterday!
4. ☐ Who gave you that black eye? Haven't I told you not to get into fights?
5. ☐ Where are you going? How long will you be? I hope you won't be late.
6. ☐ I want to know if you'll marry me. I don't think you will.

GRAMMAR SPOT

1 In Exercise 4, find and read aloud . . .

Questions
. . . questions with auxiliary verbs.
. . . questions without auxiliary verbs.
. . . two ways of asking *Why?*
. . . a question with a preposition at the end.
. . . a question word + an adverb.
. . . an indirect question.

Negatives
. . . negative questions.
. . . a future negative.
. . . negatives with *think* and *hope*.

2 Indirect questions
Make these direct questions indirect using the expressions.

Where does he work? I don't know . . .
What's her name? Do you have any idea . . . ?
Did she buy the blue one? I wonder . . .

▶▶ **Grammar Reference 4.1–4.2
pp. 139–140**

PRACTICE

Quiz time!

1 Work in two groups. You are going to write some questions for a general knowledge quiz.

Group A Look at the information on p. 150.
Group B Look at the information on p. 152.

Write the questions for your quiz in your group. Ask and answer questions between groups.

2 Look at the other group's information. How did your group do? Discuss with your group, using indirect questions.

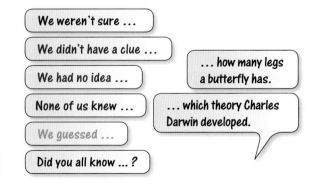

We weren't sure ...

We didn't have a clue ...

We had no idea ...

None of us knew ...

We guessed ...

Did you all know ... ?

... how many legs a butterfly has.

... which theory Charles Darwin developed.

Asking for more information

3 We can respond to a statement with a short question to ask for more information.

I went out for dinner last night. — Who with?

My aunt sent me a postcard. — Where from?

Write short questions with a preposition to ask for more information about these statements.

1. She gave away all her money.
2. We need to have a talk.
3. I danced all night.
4. I need $5,000 urgently.
5. I got a great present today.
6. I bought a birthday card today.
7. Shh! I'm thinking!
8. Do you think you could give me a ride?

4 Make the short questions into longer ones.

Who did you go out for dinner with?   Where did she send it from?

CD1 39 Listen and check your answers. Notice that all the questions end with a preposition.

Negative questions and pronunciation

5 **CD1 40** Listen and compare the negative questions in 1 and 2. Which expresses surprise? Which is just checking the information?

> 1. **A** **Don't you like** pizza?
>   **B** I know most people do, but I don't.

> 2. **A** **Haven't we met** somewhere before?
>   **B** Yes, we have. **Wasn't it** at Maria's party?

Listen again and repeat. Practice the stress and intonation.

6 Ask and answer about these things with a partner using negative questions.

> **I'm surprised!**
> like/ice cream   have/a computer   can/swim

> **I'm just checking.**
> is/hot today   is/this your pen   live/in New York

CD1 41 Listen and compare.

How come you don't eat meat?

7 Make a negative sentence about these people. Use your dictionary.

Vegetarians don't eat meat.

> vegetarians   insomniacs   atheists
> dyslexics   pacifists

8 **CD1 42** Listen to the first part of a description of a man named Norman. Which words in Exercise 7 describe him?

> **SPOKEN ENGLISH** *How come?*
>
> *How come?* can be used in informal spoken English instead of *Why?* They do not have exactly the same meaning. Read the questions. Which express surprise?
>
> > *Why are you studying English?*
> > *How come you speak English so well?*
> > *Why did you go to Japan?*
> > *How come you've never been abroad?*

9 **CD1 43** Listen to the second part. There are lots of contradictions. Complete the sentences about Norman below with a question using *How come?*

My friend Norman

He lives in a tiny studio apartment, so *how come he came downstairs to the living room?*
He's an insomniac, so *how come he slept so long?*
He's single, so ...
He doesn't have any pets, so ...
He's an atheist, so ...
He's dyslexic, so ...
He's unemployed, so ...
He's a vegetarian, so ...

Who is it?

10 Write three sentences about yourself using *only* negative sentences. Distribute them among the students in the class. Read them aloud and guess who it is.

I can't cook.   I'm not wearing jeans.
I don't sit next to Maria.

LISTENING AND SPEAKING
My most memorable lie

Work in small groups.

1 Did you ever tell lies as a child? Can you remember any? Talk about them in your groups. Decide which is the most interesting lie in your group and tell the class.

2 **CD1 44** Listen to six people talking about their most memorable lie. Correct the statements.

1. **Andrew**'s boss fired him for lying about where he was.
2. **Paul** only lied once as a child because he swore and stole cookies.
3. **Carolyn** went to London for her sister's wedding.
4. **Kiki** finally told her grandmother the truth.
5. **Sean** took karate lessons at school.
6. **Kate**'s mother never discovered the truth.

3 Listen again and answer the questions.

1. Andrew says, *like an idiot, I put pictures of it online.* Pictures of what? Why was it stupid of Andrew to do this?
2. Paul says, *strangely what you end up doing is lying ... so that you've got something to say.* Lying to who? When? Why is it strange?
3. Carolyn says, *I had to tell a white lie.* What was it? Why was it a white lie? What *did nothing* for whose figure?
4. Kiki says, *I know where I lost it.* What did she lose? Where did she lose it? What was her lie?
5. Sean says, *somebody's mom called my mom to get all the details.* To get details of what? Why did he lie in the first place?
6. Kate says, *I put him in the box and forgot about him.* Who did she put in the box? Which box? How does she excuse her behavior?

4 Which words go with which lie? What do they refer to?

confession	frumpy	toy box	bugging	a robbery
cookies	page	necklace	the playground	pictures
vacation	hungry and scared	sins		

What do you think?

- Which of the six lies do you think are "good" reasons to lie? Which are "bad?" Which are "white lies?"
- Work alone. List other occasions when you think it might be good to lie and occasions when it is definitely not.
- Discuss your ideas with your group. Do you all agree about what are "good" and "bad" lies?

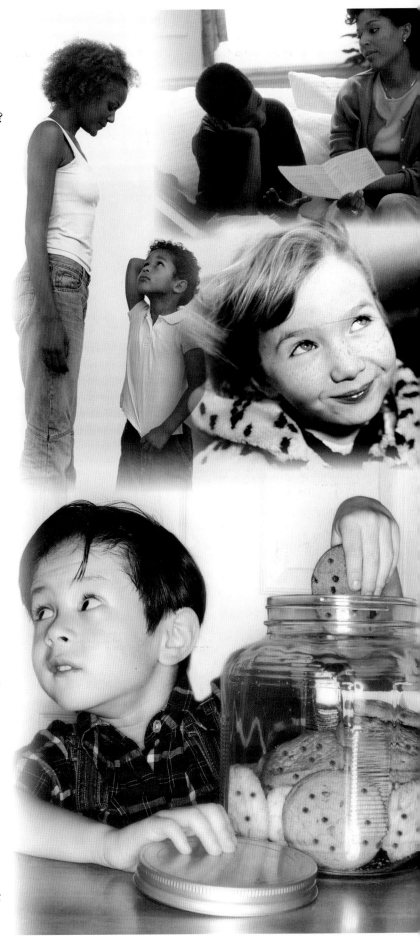

READING AND SPEAKING
Diana and Elvis shot JFK!

1 What do you know about the following events? Discuss in groups and share information.
- The deaths of President John F. Kennedy, John Lennon, Elvis Presley, Princess Diana.
- The Apollo moon landings.

2 There are many conspiracy theories about these events. What are conspiracy theories? How are they usually circulated nowadays? Do you know any theories about the events in Exercise 1?

3 Read the introduction to three of the world's most popular conspiracy theories. Which events are mentioned? Why do people like these theories? What is a "juicy" theory?

CLASSIFIED

EVERYBODY loves a good conspiracy theory. Whether it is the CIA shooting President Kennedy or Elvis being alive and well and living on the Moon, there are few things that appeal to the imagination more than a mixture of mystery and a hint of evildoing in high places. When horrifying, historic events shake our world, we seek to make sense of them by creating bizarre theories. These theories, however unlikely, are preferable to the cold fact that sometimes accidents happen. Many of the juiciest theories circulate on the Internet.

4 Work in groups of three.

Student A Read the article on page 35.
Student B Read the article on page 36.
Student C Read the article on page 37.

Answer the questions.
1. When and what was the event?
2. How many theories are mentioned? Write a list of the different ones in note form.
3. What proof is given to support them?
4. What reasons are suggested for hiding the true facts?
5. Which people, individual or groups, are mentioned in relation to the event?

Compare your answers with the others in your group.

Vocabulary work

Find words in your text to replace those in *italics*. Explain them to the others in your group.

Diana
1. The huge number of websites is *absolutely amazing*.
2. The florists *devised* a *clever but wicked* plot to murder Diana.
3. The car crash was a *carefully planned trick*.
4. I don't *believe* any of these theories.
5. Someone in the royal family *devised* a plot to *interfere* with the brakes.

Moon landing
1. Rumors have been *going around* for many years.
2. The U.S. flag is seen *blowing*, but there is no *wind* on the moon.
3. A *fantastic exhibition* of stars.
4. Scientists have *all* agreed that the theorists don't have *any argument at all*.
5. NASA has been desperately *trying to hide* evidence of life.

JFK, Jr.
1. There are many *strange* theories—one of the *craziest* claims that he was murdered by Clinton supporters.
2. Explosives were *stuck* to the tail of the plane.
3. The plane *hit violent air movements*.
4. The crash happened *strangely and coincidentally* on the 30th anniversary.
5. Some explanations are *clearly stupid*. Others are *quite believable*.

What do you think?
- Which theories are the most believable/unbelievable?
- What is it about the Internet that breeds such theories?
- Think of a recent major news event and work in your groups to devise conspiracy theories about it. Describe the event and your theories to the class.

 WRITING Linking ideas—Conjunctions *p. 110*

CONSPIRACY THEORY 1

THE DEATH OF DIANA

The first Diana conspiracy site appeared on the Internet in Australia only hours after her death on August 31, 1997. Since then an estimated 36,000 Diana conspiracy websites have been set up—breathtaking by anyone's standards. Hypotheses range from pure James Bond ("it was all a government plot to protect the monarchy") to farce ("it was a fiendish murder plot thought up by the world's florists to sell lots of flowers"). And the most popular theory of all is that Diana, Princess of Wales, isn't dead after all—that car crash in Paris was an elaborate hoax to enable the Princess and her boyfriend, Dodi Fayed, to fake their own deaths so that they could live in blissful isolation for the rest of their lives. Subscribers to this theory say that Diana was fed up with the intrusions into her private life and used the wealth and resources of the Fayed family to fake her death. Now she and Dodi are living on a small tropical island, communicating with her sons by satellite video conferencing. Think about it, they say. We never actually saw her body, did we?

> "We never actually saw her body, did we?"

You don't buy into any of these theories? Don't worry. There are plenty more to choose from. For example, Paul Burrell, Diana's former butler, claims that the princess predicted her own death in a car crash. Apparently, she was so frightened that ten months before her death she wrote to Burrell saying that a plot was being hatched by a member of the royal family. She said her car's brakes would be tampered with and she would suffer serious head injuries. And all of this so that her ex-husband, the Prince of Wales, could marry again.

These theories multiply because it is so hard for us to believe that a princess, with all her wealth and bodyguards, could be killed by something as arbitrary and mundane as a traffic accident. Psychologically, we need conspiracy theories to make the tragedies of life more bearable. And the Internet helps feed the global paranoia.

CONSPIRACY THEORY 2

THE APOLLO MOON LANDING

For over 30 years rumors have been circulating that the Apollo Moon landings were faked. They say astronaut Neil Armstrong made no "giant leap for mankind." They assert that the 1969 Moon mission was a hoax to prove America won the space race, that the astronauts were "astro-nots!" The high point in the great Moon landing conspiracy came when the Fox television network broadcast a program entitled *Did We Land on the Moon?* This program alleged that the whole Moon landing had been staged inside a movie studio on a U.S. military base somewhere in the Mojave desert.

The program claimed:
1. The U.S. flag planted on the Moon's surface is seen fluttering, but there is no breeze of any kind on the Moon.
2. The photographs taken by the astronauts do not include any of the Moon's night sky, where there would have been a stunning array of stars on view.

"Was the whole Moon landing staged inside a movie studio?"

3. The shadows in the pictures are clearly coming from more than one angle—an impossibility on the Moon, where the only light source is the Sun, but more than plausible inside a movie studio.
4. One of the famed Moon rocks brought back by the Apollo astronauts is marked with a telltale letter "C," suggesting the markings not of some alien life force but of a movie prop.

After the program, the Internet went crazy with theories and countertheories. However, scientists have unanimously agreed that the conspiracy theorists don't have even the beginnings of a case. Too many things about the Apollo missions were impossible to fake, from the radio signals picked up at listening stations around the world to the Moon rocks, which have been subjected to repeated geological analysis and clearly date back several millennia.

Finally there are the UFO "nuts." They actually do believe that astronauts went to the Moon and found not only a lot of rocks but also widespread evidence of an ancient alien civilization—a discovery so terrifying that NASA has been desperately seeking to conceal it from the public ever since.

Moon rock

CONSPIRACY THEORY 3

THE DEATH OF JOHN F. KENNEDY, JR.

John F. Kennedy, Jr., son of the assassinated U.S. president, was killed on July 17, 1999 when his tiny Piper Saratoga aircraft crashed over Martha's Vineyard near Boston. He was piloting the plane on the way to a family wedding with his wife, Carolyn. To millions of Americans JFK, Jr. was the closest thing to royalty the United States has ever had, and, as with his father, with every anniversary of his death they come up with more and more bizarre conspiracy theories to explain the tragedy.

One of the wildest theories claims that Kennedy, Jr., known as "John John," was murdered by Clinton supporters because he planned to run against Hillary Clinton in the New York Senate race.

Another theory asserts that an explosion, heard over Martha's Vineyard at the time of the crash, suggests that terrorists placed a bomb on the tiny plane. It is claimed that leaked FBI documents record the discovery of explosives glued within its tail.

> "Some of the explanations for the plane crash are patently ridiculous."

A third theory blames Kennedy's beautiful blonde wife, Carolyn. It is suggested that she caused the crash by chatting on her cell phone just as the plane ran into turbulence over Martha's Vineyard, thus interfering with the controls while her husband was desperately trying to make an emergency landing. However, the most popular theory of all blames the crash on the legendary Irish curse said to have taken the lives of so many of the Kennedy clan. This curse, reputed to have followed the Kennedy dynasty over from Ireland, is said to strike when Kennedy members are around water. John John's uncle Joseph Kennedy, Jr. died in a flight over water during World War II, while another uncle, Ted Kennedy, drove off a bridge into water at Chappaquiddick—eerily, the plane crash happened on the 30th anniversary of the Chappaquiddick incident.

"Some of the explanations for the plane crash are patently ridiculous," says a Kennedy watcher. "Others, like the cell phone theory, are based on recorded information and are pretty plausible."

VOCABULARY
Saying the opposite

Antonyms

1 Compare these sentences.
Which antonyms are used?
Which one sounds better in context?

Some theories are plausible but others are implausible.

Some theories are plausible but others are ridiculous.

2 Antonyms can sometimes be formed with a negative prefix. What is the negative prefix for these words?

believable   honest   responsible
legal   complete   probable

1 What part of speech are these words? Write antonyms for them, using prefixes if possible.

Word	Antonym(s)
fake **adj**	genuine, real, authentic
like **vb**	dislike, hate, can't stand
tiny	
happiness	
guilty	
safe	
admit	
sincere	
success	
mature	
encourage	
kind	
appear	

2 Complete the conversations with antonyms from the box. Put the words in the correct form.

improve	safety	~~success~~	criticize	generosity
fail	stingy	encourage	get worse	danger

1. **A** Gary's a really <u>successful</u> businessman.
   B Yeah, but he's a complete _____ as a family man. He never sees his children.
2. **A** My grandpa's so _____ he gives me $20 every time I see him.
   B Lucky you. My grandpa's famous for his _____. A quarter every birthday, if he remembers.
3. **A** Well, Henry, I'm pleased there's been some _____ in your behavior this semester, but sadly your work has _____.
   B So I didn't do OK on the test?
4. **A** You're not going bungee jumping! It sounds really _____.
   B No, honestly, it's perfectly _____ as long as you're careful.
5. **A** Our teacher is always _____ us. I feel useless.
   B I know. It's not fair—he should give us more _____ if he wants us to work hard.

3 What is the effect of using antonyms in these conversations?

A What **lousy** weather!
B Yes, it's not exactly **tropical**, is it?

A Jenny's **dense**, isn't she?
B Well, she isn't the **brightest of people**, it's true.

Write similar conversations with a partner about these topics. How could you describe the following both honestly and tactfully?
• a boring party   • an awful vacation   • a stingy friend   • a hard test

4 What's the opposite of ... ?

1. a tough question
   tough meat
2. a clear sky
   a clear conscience
3. fair hair
   a fair decision
4. a hard mattress
   a hard test
5. a live animal
   live music
6. a light color
   a light sleeper

5 Match the words and their meanings.

1. **ab**used	not ever used
2. **dis**used	not used any more
3. **un**used	used cruelly or badly
4. **mis**used	used too much
5. **over**used	not used enough
6. **under**used	used in the wrong way

EVERYDAY ENGLISH
Being polite

1 What "white lies" might you tell in these situations? Role-play them with a partner.

> 1. You're having a meal with your host family. You've just forced yourself to eat something you don't like, when your host says, "You must have some more!" What do you say?
>
> 2. A friend has just had a baby, who you think looks like any other newborn baby. "Isn't he gorgeous?" she coos. What do you say?
>
> 3. Your aunt invites you to go on vacation with her for two weeks. You love her but know it would be a disaster, and it would be no vacation for you. What do you say?

CD1 45 Now listen and compare your answers.

2 **CD1 46** Listen to the pairs of lines and conversations. Which one is more polite?

3 Make these requests and offers more polite. Use the expressions below.

1. Give me a ride.
2. Help me find my glasses!
3. Come over for dinner tomorrow!
4. Lend me your dictionary.
5. Can I help you with this exercise?
6. Stop whistling!

Could you possibly ... ?

Would you mind (not) ...?

I wonder if you could ... ?

Do you happen to know ... ?

4 Work with a partner. Take turns making the requests and offers in Exercise 3 and refusing them politely, using one of these expressions.

I'd love to, but . . .   That's really nice of you, but . . .
I'm really sorry . . .   I would if I could, but . . .
I'm afraid I . . .   Sorry! I've got to . . .

CD1 48 Listen and compare your answers.

Role play

5 Anna and Ben have invited friends for dinner. Look at the conversation on page 152. Work in groups of four to complete the conversation.

B   Kim! Hello! Great to see you. Come on in. Let me take your coat.
Kim   Thanks so much. Oh, these are for you.

CD1 49 Listen and compare. Act your role play out for the class.

5 An eye to the future

Grammar: Future forms
Vocabulary: Hot verbs—*take, put*
Everyday English: Phone calls

TEST YOUR GRAMMAR

1 Which future form expresses . . . ?

| an intention   a prediction   a future fact based on a timetable   an arrangement between people   a spontaneous decision |

1. Tomorrow's weather will be warm and sunny.
2. The train to Denver leaves at ten past ten.
3. I'm going to be a race-car driver when I grow up.
4. We're seeing Sue for lunch on Thursday.
5. I'll make some coffee.

2 Name the different future forms.

HOW DO YOU SEE YOUR FUTURE?
Future forms

1 **CD2 2** Look at the pictures and listen to these people talking about the future. Who says what? Put a number 1–6 next to the names.

a. Tony

b. Mickey

c. Elsie

d. Katie

e. Janine

f. Marco

2 Answer the questions.

1. What is Katie going to study?
   When do the classes start?
2. What is Mickey doing tomorrow?
   What time does the game start?
3. Why are Tony and Marie excited?
   When is the baby due?
4. What's happening tomorrow?
   What will they do together?
5. Why is Janine packing?
   How's she getting to the airport?
6. What are Marco's ambitions?
   What will he have done before he's 25?

CD2 3 Listen and check.

3 Here are the answers to some questions.
Write the questions.

1. New York University. (*Which ...?*)
2. His son.
   Chicago and St. Louis.
3. Jamie or Heather.
4. Some cookies.
5. It leaves at 10:30.
6. In much bigger places.

CD2 4 Listen and check.

GRAMMAR SPOT

1 Do these sentences refer to the present
or the future?

Marie's having a baby soon . . .
Right now I'm packing . . .

I play guitar.
The plane leaves at 10:30.

2 What's the difference between
these sentences?

*What **do** you **do** in the evenings?*
*What **are** you **doing** this evening?*

*Get in the car. I**'ll give** you a ride.*
*I**'m going to give** Dave a ride to the
airport tomorrow.*

*We**'ll have** dinner at 8:00.*
*We**'ll be having** dinner at 8:00.*

*I**'ll write** the report tonight.*
*I**'ll have written** the report by tonight.*

▶▶ **Grammar Reference 5.1–5.8
pp. 140–142**

PRACTICE

Discussing grammar

1 Complete the sentences with the correct verb form.

1. **'ll see / 'm going to see**

   I'm very excited. I <u>'m going to see</u> my whole family this weekend.

   I don't know if I have time to come this evening. I <u>'ll see</u>.

2. **are you going to do / will you do**

   So you're off to Canada for a year! What _____ there?

   I'm sure you will pass your exams, but what _____ if you don't?

3. **'ll come / 'm coming**

   I _____ with you if you like.

   I _____ with you whether you like it or not.

4. **are you doing / are you going to do**

   Your latest grades are terrible. What _____ about it?

   What _____ this evening?

5. **'m giving / 'm going to give**

   I've had enough of her lazy attitude. I _____ her a good talking-to.

   I _____ a presentation at 3:00 this afternoon. I'm scared stiff.

6. **leaves / is leaving**

   John! Peter _____ now. Come and say good-bye.

   The bus _____ at 8:00, so don't be late.

7. **'ll see / 'll be seeing**

   I _____ you outside the theater at 8:00.

   I _____ Peter this afternoon, so I'll tell him the news.

8. **'ll see / 'll have seen**

   You _____ enough of me by the end of this visit.

   I'm going to be a star one day. You _____.

   CD2 5 Listen and check.

2 Put the verbs in the correct tense. Use Present Simple, Present Perfect, *will*, or the Future Continuous.

"**This is your captain speaking...**"

Good morning, ladies and gentlemen. Welcome on board this United Airlines flight to Tokyo. In a very short time we (1)_____ (take) off. When we (2)_____ (reach) our cruising speed of 550 miles per hour, we (3)_____ (fly) at 35,000 feet. Our flight time today is about 12 hours, so we (4)_____ (be) in Tokyo in time for breakfast tomorrow!

The cabin crew (5)_____ (serve) refreshments during the flight. If you (6)_____ (need) any assistance, just press the button, and a flight attendant (7)_____ (come) to help you.

[*Near the end of the flight*]
In just a few minutes, the crew (8)_____ (come) around with duty-free goods. We (9)_____ also _____ (give out) landing cards. When you (10)_____ (fill) them in, place them in your passport. They (11)_____ (collect) as you (12)_____ (go) through passport control.

In 20 minutes we (13)_____ (land) at Narita Airport. Please put your seats in the upright position. You are requested to remain seated until the plane (14)_____ (come) to a complete stop.

We hope you (15)_____ (fly) again soon with United Airlines.

CD2 6 Listen and check.

3 Complete the sentences with the correct form of the verb. Use *will*, the Future Continuous, or the Future Perfect.

> **go**

1. I can get the tickets. I _____ past the theater on my way home.
2. I'll say good-bye now. You _____ by the time I get back.
3. He _____ crazy when I tell him I crashed his car.

> **make**

4. "Should we have some tea? "Good idea. I _____ it."
5. Dave is so ambitious. I bet he _____ a fortune by the time he's 30.
6. You'll know where the party is. We _____ so much noise!

> **read**

7. I'll lend you this book next time I see you. I _____ it by then.
8. We're studying Shakespeare next year, so I _____ his plays over the summer.
9. I just got an e-mail from Megan. I _____ it to you.

Talking about you

4 Complete the questions with the most natural future form. Sometimes there are several possibilities.

1. Where _____ (you go) on vacation this year?
2. How _____ (you get) there?
3. How long _____ (you be) away for?
4. Which hotel _____ (you stay) in?
5. What time _____ (your flight arrive)?
6. What _____ (you do) while you're on vacation?

In pairs, ask and answer the questions about your next vacation. If you don't have a vacation planned, make one up!

I hope so/I don't think so

5 **CD2** **7** Listen to the conversations and complete them.

1. "Do you think you'll ever be rich?"
   "I _____ so."
   "I _____ one day."
   "It's possible, but I _____ it."
   "I'm sure I _____."
   "I'm sure I _____."

2. "Are you going out tonight?"
   "Yes, I am."
   "I think _____, but I'm not sure."
   "I _____ be."

3. "Do you think the world's climate will change dramatically in the next 50 years?"
   "I _____ so."
   "I hope _____."
   "Who _____? Maybe."

6 Ask and answer similar yes/no questions about future possibilities in your life.

1. be famous
   go to Florida
   marry a millionaire
   speak perfect English
   have grandchildren

2. go to the movies soon
   meet friends this weekend
   eat out in the next few days

3. we discover life on another planet
   people live for 150 years
   find a cure for cancer

TO THE FAR EAST
Independent Tours Around the World

NORDDEUTSCHER LLOYD
BREMEN

CANADIAN NATIONAL
RAILWAYS

6004

THE CONTINENTAL LIMITED
IN THE CANADIAN ROCKIES

ACROSS CANADA
SERCOMBE & HAYES 9, South Street,

INDIA

BY IMPERIAL
AIRWAYS

READING AND SPEAKING
Today's teenagers are just fine!

1 In your country, what do
- old people think of young people?
- young people think of old people?
- parents think of teenagers?
- teenagers think of their parents?

2 Look at the photos. Read the headings and the introduction. Why do you think young people "get a bad rap?" What does this mean?

3 Work with a partner and answer these questions about each person.
1. What is their particular talent?
2. What do you learn about their family or childhood?
3. Who has influenced their life and career?
4. What have they achieved in life so far?
5. What is their ambition?
6. Do they spend time with friends?

4 Compare Sarah's life with the three boys.

5 Which person might have said …?
1. "She won't be able to walk at all soon."
2. "By the time I'm 20 I'll be giving concerts all over the world."
3. "I'm going to take my grandmother on a world cruise."
4. "I'm playing in a major tournament in China next month."

What do you think?
- Who do you think is the most successful now?
- Who will be most successful in the future?
- Which *two* teenagers do you most admire? Why?

Language work

Complete the chart of adjectives and nouns. Mark the stress. The missing words are all in the articles.

Adjective	Noun
am'bitious	am'bition
poor	
competitive	
memorable	
	success
influential	
responsible	
	pride
	health
	necessity

Judith Woods and Fiona Holloway report

Today's teenagers

Today's teenagers get a bad rap, but they are not all sulking in their bedrooms. The ones featured here—like millions of teens all over the world—are ambitious, talented, and making the most of their lives, often against the odds.

Darius Knight, 18
The future Olympian

Darius grew up in poverty, but discovering table tennis turned his life around. He is now a youth champion and has set his sights on the Olympics.

"My childhood was tough. It was an everyday thing for me to get into fights. Then, when I was ten I took up table tennis and joined an after-school group. The teacher, Gideon Ashison, made me see that it was up to me if I wanted to be successful. I started to enter competitions and trained from the age of 12. When I was 17 I was accepted to the Institute of Sport, where I now live and train full-time. My goal is to become the world's number one table tennis player. I still see my friends, but table tennis isn't their kind of thing."

Fraser Doherty, 19
The entrepreneur

are just fine!

Harry Byart, 15
The recording artist

Harry Byart (AKA Fugative) released his first album, *Prince of the Playground*, last September, and his single *Summertime* is available to download from MySpace and has been played on British radio.

"My family has always encouraged me and my music. I play the keyboard and I sing. I've co-written all the songs with my producer Darren Martyn, who has worked with many well-known musicians. He's been a big influence on me. I write about things that matter to me, such as my friends, school, and real life. I plan to make music my career, but at this stage my ambition is just to make my mom proud of me."

Fraser set up the healthy jam brand SuperJam when he was just 16. Today it is sold in 1,000 stores, and he's about to launch it in Europe.

"When I was 14 my grandma told me her secret recipe for jam. I made a batch and sold it locally for $3.00 a jar. It was really popular, and within 18 months I was making 1,000 jars a week.

My story made the local newspaper, and I was spotted by a businessman. Thanks to his advice I began researching jam companies and I developed the line to include blueberries and cranberries, and, because I was using these so-called "superfoods," I called it SuperJam.

Today I make more money than both my parents combined. People ask if I feel I've missed out on being a "normal teenager," but I still do all the things with my friends that the average teenager does—I just get to do unusual stuff as well, like having dinner with famous politicians. My ambition is to sell my jam worldwide."

Sarah Thomas, 14
The caregiver

Sarah cares for her mother Carol, 51, who has multiple sclerosis (MS).

"I'll never forget my first day at school. I saw the other children being dropped off by their parents, and I suddenly realized that not all mothers were in a wheelchair. The thing is, my mom has had MS for 26 years, so I have no memory of her being anything other than sick.

As an only child, I've had to grow up quickly to cope with the responsibilities of Mom's condition. Although she's relatively mobile, she falls over daily, suffers from fatigue, and can't do much. In the mornings I make sure Mom has taken her pills, and I give her an injection. After school I cook dinner. I don't have much time for friends. Then someone told me about a project that gives young caregivers the chance to meet each other. That helps a lot. Caring for my mom isn't a burden. I'm going to keep doing it as long as it's necessary."

SPOKEN ENGLISH *thing*

The word *thing* is used a lot in English!

1 Look at the examples of *thing* from Darius's story on page 44.

> It was an everyday **thing** for me to get into fights.
> Table tennis isn't their kind of **thing**.

Find an example of *thing(s)* in each of the other texts.

2 Ask and answer the questions with a partner about you.
- How are things with you at the moment?
- What's the thing you like most about studying English?
- Generally speaking, do you try to do the right thing?
- Do you like doing your own thing?
- Is horse racing your kind of thing?
- Do you ever say the wrong thing in company?
- Do you have a thing about people wearing fur?
- If your friend keeps you waiting, do you make a big thing of it?

SPEAKING
A career quiz

1 Who do you know that is rich and successful? Think of people you know personally and famous people. What have they done? Share ideas with the class.

2 Are you ambitious? Do you want to be rich and successful, or do you think there's more to life than work?

3 Do the quiz. Circle an answer a, b, or c. Compare your answers with a partner.

4 Turn to page 150 and find out how ambitious you are. Do you agree? Discuss as a class. Who are the most ambitious? What do they want to do? Who are the least ambitious? Why?

How ambitious are you?

1 It's 8.30am on Monday morning. Are you …?
a. already working at your desk
b. just walking through the door
c. just walking out of the shower

2 You've been asked to present your team's findings at a meeting with your boss. Do you …?
a. take credit yourself for most of the findings
b. present a balanced report, taking care to give credit to colleagues where it's due
c. forget your notes for the meeting

3 Your boss is really pleased with your team's work and takes you all out to a restaurant to celebrate. Do you …?
a. make sure that you are sitting next to your boss to explain why the project was so successful
b. chat to your boss for a while and then talk to your colleagues
c. enjoy the meal and chat to anyone and everyone

4 You are at a conference, and your name badge has your name but your boss's job title. Do you …?
a. just leave it because you hope to have the title yourself one day
b. ask politely for it to be changed
c. fail to notice? You never bother to put name badges on anyway.

5 If your colleagues chose an adjective to describe you, which would it be?
a. Highly-motivated.
b. Supportive.
c. Lazy.

6 You and a colleague are both put up for a promotion, but you don't get it. Do you …?
a. find it very difficult to congratulate him or her
b. congratulate him or her warmly but feel very disappointed
c. feel relieved that you won't have any extra work

7 The head office sends an e-mail asking staff for suggestions to cut costs in the workplace. Do you …?
a. already have a list of suggestions
b. refuse to take part because you believe they are trying to cut jobs
c. delete the e-mail

8 Your boss is going away on a training course, and you are going to take over his or her job for that period. Are you going to …?
a. work hard and make sure your colleagues work hard
b. discuss your plans with your colleagues to get their support
c. enjoy the freedom of your boss being away

9 What is your motto at work?
a. Work hard and make sure the boss notices what you do.
b. Make sure you work well with your team.
c. Work to live, don't live to work.

VOCABULARY
Hot verbs—take, put

1 There are many expressions with *take* and *put*. Look at these examples from the text on pages 44–45 and the quizzes on pages 46 and 150.

> I make sure Mom has **taken her pills**.
> Do you **take credit** yourself **for** most of the findings?
> You and a colleague are both **put up** for a promotion.
> You will have to **put yourself first** sometimes.

2 Put the words in the right box.

| offense   a stop to sth   place   words in sb's mouth   (no) notice   part |
| sb in charge of sth   sb/sth for granted   my advice   your best foot forward |
| a risk   your work first   responsibility for sth   pressure on sb   forever |

TAKE	PUT

3 Complete the sentences with expressions from Exercise 2 in the correct form.

1. The wedding _____ in an old country church. It was lovely, but it was miles away. It _____ to get there.
2. My son's always hanging out at the mall, but I'll _____ _____ to that. I won't give him any more pocket money.
3. Please don't _____, but I don't think your work has been up to your usual standard recently.
4. I told you that boy was no good for you. You should have _____ _____ and had nothing to do with him.
5. The older you get, the more you have to learn to _____ for your own life.
6. My boss is _____ on me to resign, but I won't go.
7. I tried to get the teacher's attention, but she _____ _____ of me at all.
8. Children never say "Thank you" or "How are you?" to their parents. They just _____ them _____.

CD2 8 Listen and check.

4 Match a line in **A** with a line in **B**. Underline the expressions with *take* or *put*.

A	B
1. Take your time.	Put it on your calendar.
2. The party's on the 21st.	What would you do?
3. Their relationship will never last.	Calm down. There's no need to panic.
4. "I told her a joke about the French, and it turned out she *was* French."	There's no need to hurry.
5. Take it easy.	No one's out to get you.
6. Put yourself in my shoes.	Take my word for it. I know these things.
7. You always take things too personally.	"Whoops! You really put your foot in in your mouth, didn't you?"

Phrasal verbs

5 Use a dictionary. Complete the sentences with a phrasal verb with *take*.

> take sth back   take sth in
> take off   take on sb

1. The store _____ extra workers every Christmas.
2. The lecture was too complicated, and the students couldn't _____ it all _____.
3. My business really _____ after I picked up six new clients.
4. You called me a liar, but I'm not. _____ it _____ and apologize!

CD2 9 Listen and check.

6 Complete the sentences with these phrasal verbs with *put*.

> put sth out   put sb off
> put away sth   put sth on

1. _____ some music _____! Whatever you want.
2. That article about factory farming has really _____ me _____ eating chicken.
3. Could you _____ your toys, please? Your room's a mess.
4. The kitchen fire was scary, but luckily I _____ it _____.

CD2 10 Listen and check.

"Well, I wouldn't eat it. But don't let that put you off."

LISTENING AND SPEAKING
The reunion

1 Three friends, Jack, Amy, and Gabe, were all in college together in Boston. Now, ten years later, they are planning a reunion. Divide into two groups.

Group A
CD2 **11** Listen to Jack calling Amy.

Group B
CD2 **12** Listen to Amy calling Gabe.

Listen and complete as much as possible of the chart. The following names are mentioned.

> Washington Street   Bombay House   New York
> Park Plaza   Back Bay Hotel   San Francisco
> Curry Cafe   Newbury Street   Newton

2 Check your answers with people in your group.

	Jack	Amy	Gabe
1. Traveling from?			
2. How?			
3. Leaving at what time?			
4. Arrival time in Boston?			
5. Staying where?			
6. Going to which restaurant?			
7. Where is it?			
8. Where are they going to meet?			
9. What time?			

3 Find a partner from the other group. Exchange information to complete the chart.

4 What might go wrong with their plans? Will everything work out all right? Who's meeting who where?

▶▶ **WRITING** E-mailing friends *p. 111*

EVERYDAY ENGLISH

Beginning a telephone conversation

1 **CD2 13** Listen to the beginning of three phone calls. What's the difference between them?

- When and why do we make small talk? Who with? What about?
- Why do some places have recorded menus?
- Why do people find them frustrating?

2 Here is the beginning of a telephone conversation between two people who *don't* know each other. Put it in the right order.

- [1] **A** Hello. TVS Computer Services. Samantha speaking. How can I help you?
- [ ] **A** Thank you. One moment, please.
- [ ] **C** Hello. Customer service.
- [ ] **B** Yes, could I speak to your customer service manager, please?
- [ ] **A** Certainly. May I ask who's calling?
- [ ] **B** This is Keith Jones.
- [7] **B** Hello, I was wondering if you could help me . . .

CD2 14 Listen and check your answers.

Ending a telephone conversation

3 Here is the end of a telephone conversation between Irene and her daughter Lily, a student. Put it in the right order.

- [1] **A** So that's about all that's new here, Mom. It was good to talk to you.
- [ ] **B** I know, we should do it more often. By the way, are you still seeing that nice guy from Boston? Brian, wasn't it?
- [ ] **B** OK, don't want to keep you. Oh, one more thing, you're coming home for Thanksgiving, right?
- [ ] **A** Mom. I told you, Brian's just a friend, not a boyfriend. I really don't have time to date right now. Anyway, Mom...
- [ ] **A** I know, Mom, I know. Look, I'll book a flight right after dinner, I promise. All right. Love you, Mom. Love to Dad!
- [ ] **A** Of course.
- [ ] **A** Don't worry, I get out pretty often, just not with Brian. Listen, Mom, I've got to run. I've got dinner on the stove.
- [ ] **B** But have you booked your flight yet? You know it's a very busy time of year.
- [ ] **B** What a shame! You know you should get out more, Lily. It's not good to...
- [10] **B** Love you, too, honey! Thanks for calling! Bye now.

CD2 15 Listen and check your answers.

4 Discuss the questions.

- Who's trying to end the conversation? Who wants to chat?
- How does Lily try to signal that she wants to end the conversation?
- How do they confirm their arrangements?

6 Making it big

Grammar: Expressions of quantity
Vocabulary: 'export and ex'port
Everyday English: Business expressions and numbers

TEST YOUR GRAMMAR

1 Circle the words that can complete the expressions of quantity.

a few . . . cars/traffic/delays/pollution
not many . . . crimes/criminals/violence/accidents

very little . . . time/room/hope/spaces
a bit of . . . luck/opportunity/fun/help

a lot of . . . enthusiasm/energy/people/ingredients
plenty of . . . fresh air/fluids/sleep/walks
hardly any . . . money/experience/clothes/friends

2 What do you notice about the three groups of quantifiers?

THE NAKED CHEF
Expressions of quantity

1 Jamie Oliver is a famous British chef. Read the article. Why is he famous? Why is he known as "The Naked Chef?"

2 Answer the questions.
1. How many restaurants does he have?
2. How many books has he written?
3. How many TV series has he made?
4. How much money did he earn cooking at his parents' pub?
5. How much time did he spend in France?
6. How many chefs did he work with in London?
7. How much experience did he have when he was first on TV?
8. What is his recipe for success?

Jamie Oliver

Jamie Oliver became an extremely successful and well-known chef at a very young age. He has several restaurants in different parts of the world. He has written eleven books and made over 20 TV series. He doesn't have much free time anymore. How did he make it big?

His rise to fame came early and swiftly. By the age of eight he had already started cooking at his parents' pub, earning a little money. After two years in cooking school and a few months in France, he started working in restaurants. He worked with three famous chefs in London before he was spotted by a TV producer at 21, and his life changed.

Even though he had very little experience, he had a great deal of enthusiasm for cooking and was very natural in front of the camera. His first TV program featured him zipping around London on his scooter buying ingredients and cooking for his friends. His recipes were simple—they didn't involve complicated cooking techniques and used plenty of fresh ingredients. That's why he is known as "The Naked Chef."

He opened a restaurant called Fifteen, where he trained a group of unemployed young people to work in the business. There are now similar restaurants in Holland and Australia. He also started a campaign to improve the meals children eat at school, trying to replace junk food with fresh, nutritious dishes.

So what is his recipe for success? "A little bit of luck and a lot of passion!" he says.

3 **CD2 16** Listen to a similar text about Jamie Oliver. Write down the differences you hear.

GRAMMAR SPOT

1 Why do we say . . .?

a *few* restaurants	but	a *little* money
not much free time	but	*not many* free days

2 **CD2 16** Read and listen to the texts again. Complete the chart with the expressions of quantity.

Reading text	Listening text
several restaurants	<u>quite a few</u> restaurants
_____ books	a lot of books
over 20 TV series	_____ TV series
_____ in France	a little time in France
three famous chefs	_____ famous chefs
_____ experience	hardly any experience
a great deal of enthusiasm	_____ of enthusiasm
_____ of fresh ingredients	lots of fresh ingredients

▶▶ **Grammar Reference 6.1 pp. 142–143**

4 Close your books. What can you remember about Jamie Oliver?

PRACTICE

Countable or uncountable?

1 With a partner, ask and answer questions.

How much . . .?   How many . . .?

1. money/in your pocket
2. cups of coffee/day
3. times/been on a plane
4. time/spend watching TV
5. sugar/in your coffee
6. pairs of jeans/have
7. books/read in one year
8. homework/a night
9. English teachers/had
10. movies/a month

CD2 17 Listen and compare your answers.

2 Some nouns can be both countable (**C**) and uncountable (**U**).

Fish is good for you. **U**
I caught a fish today. **C**

I do a lot of business in Russia. **U**
We opened a business together. **C**

Complete the sentences with *a* or nothing.

1. I'd like ___ single room for the night.
   Is there ___ room for me to sit down?

2. You shouldn't let children play with ___ fire.
   Can we light ___ fire? It's getting cold.

3. Canada is a land of ___ great beauty.
   You should see my new car. It's ___ beauty.

4. There was ___ youth standing in front of me.
   ___ youth is wasted on the young.

3 Find pairs of words with similar meanings. Write them in the correct column.

~~dollar~~ truck suitcase job furniture advice apple fact ~~money~~ suggestion fruit trip chair work traffic information luggage travel

Countable nouns	Uncountable nouns
dollar	money

With a partner, choose a pair of words. Write two sentences to illustrate their use. Use the countable nouns in the plural.

We need some new furniture.   We need four more chairs.

Expressing quantity

4 Rephrase the sentences. Use the prompts.

She earns a dollar a day.

  much / very little / hardly any

She doesn't earn much money.
She earns very little money.
She earns hardly any money.

1. She has two friends.
   many / very few / hardly any

2. There are six eggs in the fridge.
   some / a few / enough

3. There are two eggs in the fridge.
   many / only a couple of

4. There aren't any tomatoes.
   no / not a single

5. Did you spend many weeks in France?
   much / a lot of

6. I have five days of vacation a year.
   much / hardly any

7. I must lose weight. I've put on 20 pounds!
   a huge amount of / far too much / lots of

8. Ninety percent of my friends have a car.
   almost all / most / the majority

9. Ten percent of them still live at home.
   very few / hardly any / not many

10. There isn't one of my friends who's married.
    none / not one

11. Ken was at work 100 percent of the time.
    all / the whole

12. Yesterday I ate hardly anything at all.
    not much / very little / almost nothing

5 Choose the correct alternative.

1. I have *a few / few* cousins but not many.
2. We have *very little / a little money*, I'm afraid.
3. I earn *less / fewer* money than I did in my old job!
4. *Less / fewer* people buy CDs these days.
5. *All people / Everyone* came to my party.
6. My house was robbed last month. *All / Everything* was stolen.
7. *Everyone / All the people* was watching the World Cup final.
8. Last week the *all / whole* school had the flu.

SPOKEN ENGLISH Expressing quantity

There are many ways of expressing quantity in spoken English.

  *She's got **lots of** clothes.*

CD2 18 Listen and write the expression of quantity you hear.

_____ of time   _____ of food   _____ of things
_____ of money   _____ of laundry   _____ of people

What do your friends have a lot of?

  Tania's got millions of shoes.

A lifestyle survey

Conduct a survey of the habits of your class using the activities listed. When you are ready, tell the class what you heard, using expressions from the box.

Most of us like shopping.

- like shopping
- spend a lot of money on sneakers
- go out with friends
- buy designer clothes
- like *The Simpsons*
- go to coffee shops
- go clubbing regularly
- do a lot of exercise

all of us

most of us

a few of us

hardly anybody

quite a lot of us

nobody

(almost) everybody

none of us

 WRITING Report writing—A consumer survey *p. 112*

---

52   Unit 6 · Making it big

LISTENING AND SPEAKING
Advertisements

1 What's your favorite advertisement at the moment? What's it for? Does it have a story?

2 **CD2 19** Listen to six radio advertisements and answer the questions. Write a number 1–6.

Which ad ...

... is advertising a football game? ☐
... is selling a chocolate bar? ☐
... is selling laundry detergent? ☐
... is for a new car with free gasoline? ☐
... is for car insurance for women? ☐
... is advertising a store's opening hours? ☐

3 Complete the chart.

	Name of the product	Characters involved	Setting/ place
1.			
2.			
3.			
4.			
5.			
6.			

4 What is the selling point for each ad?

5 Answer the questions about each ad.
   1. Describe Sarah's T-shirt.
      What's special about this laundry detergent?
   2. What do the men think of the woman driver?
      Why and how do they change their minds?
   3. What has the daughter done that she's so proud of?
      Why is her father so horrible to her?
   4. How can the daughter afford a new car?
      In what ways does she make fun of her father?
   5. What does the man want to invite Sue to do?
      In what ways does he say the wrong thing?
   6. How does the priest try to hurry up the wedding?
      Why is he in a hurry?

Writing an ad

Write a radio or television ad. Choose a product or service of your own, or one of the following.

a BMW sports car   Bonzo dog food
Dazzle dishwashing liquid
Green Mountain coffee   a bank for students
a restaurant in town
a computer

READING AND SPEAKING
Two famous brands

1 What do you know about these brands? What is their reputation? Are they popular among your friends and family? Who are their rivals?

2 Work in two groups.

Group A Read about Starbucks on this page.
Group B Read about Apple Computers on p. 55.

Read your article and answer the questions.

1. When and where did the company begin?
2. Who founded it?
3. Where did the name of the company come from?
4. Why did the product become a success?
5. Has business always been easy for the company?
6. What makes the brand special?
7. What features of the product or company do people see as negative?
8. What are some examples of the company's products?

3 Find a partner from the other group. Exchange information.

4 Here are eight answers. Decide which four are about your article. Then write the questions.

- In Silicon Valley.
- About 600.
- $5 billion.
- In 1997. (*When . . . launched?*)
- Ten years. (*How long . . . take . . . ?*)
- Because he argued with his partner. (*Why . . . resign?*)
- Because they can't compete. (*Why . . . out of business?*)
- By selling some of their possessions. (*How . . . ?*)

STARBUCKS COFFEE

ANYONE FOR COFFEE? What about a Skinny Latte, or perhaps an Almond Truffle Mocha, or even a Raspberry Mocha Chip Frappuccino? These are just a few of the many specialty coffees on offer at Starbucks, the world's leading coffee roaster and retailer.

Starbucks serves over 25 million customers a week in 15,000 stores in 44 countries around the world. And this figure is increasing rapidly. So how did a company currently worth $5 billion get started?

Starbucks Coffee, Tea, and Spice, as it was originally known, roasted its first coffee beans in 1971. This tiny coffee house in Seattle, named after a character in the novel *Moby Dick*, was the vision of three men—Baldwin, Siegel, and Bowker—who cared passionately about fine coffee and tea. Their determination to provide the best quality coffee helped their business to succeed, and a decade later, their fourth store in Seattle opened.

Meanwhile, in New York, Howard Schultz, a businessman specializing in kitchen equipment, noticed that a small company in Seattle was ordering a large number of a special type of coffeemaker. Out of curiosity, he made the cross-country trip to Seattle to find out more. As soon as he saw the Starbucks store, he knew that he wanted to be a part of it. The three founding members weren't initially very eager, but a persistent Schultz was eventually hired to be the head of Starbucks marketing in 1982. He modeled the Starbucks stores on Italian espresso bars and made them comfortable places to relax. Within the next ten years, Schultz had already opened 150 new stores and had bought the company! There are now stores all over Europe, Asia, and the Middle East. Today Starbucks is one of the world's most recognized brands.

❚❚ 15,000 stores in 44 countries. ❚❚

But global success comes at a price. Facing competition from lower-priced coffee offered by McDonald's, Starbucks recently closed about 600 stores in the U.S. And although Starbucks has a company policy of fair trade and employee welfare, it has been the recent target of antiglobalization protests. Many people feel that big corporations, even responsible ones, are never a good thing, as small, independent companies can't compete and go out of business. However, Starbucks's continued success in the face of opposition shows that its blend of commercialism and comfy sofas is still proving an irresistible recipe for world domination.

Apple Computers

ARE YOU A MAC USER? For many, home computers have become synonymous with Windows and Bill Gates, but there has always been a loyal band of Apple and Macintosh users whose devotion to the Apple brand and its co-founder Steven Jobs is almost religious.

Steven Jobs and Steven Wozniak dropped out of college and got jobs in Silicon Valley, where they founded the Apple Computer company in 1976, the name based on Jobs's favorite fruit. They designed the Apple I computer in Jobs's bedroom, having raised the capital by selling their most valued possessions—an old Volkswagen bus and a scientific calculator. The later model, the Apple Macintosh, introduced the public to point and click graphics. It was the first home computer to be truly user friendly, or as their advertisements put it, "the computer for the rest of us." When IBM released its first PC in 1981, Jobs realized that Apple would have to become a more grown-up company to compete effectively. He brought in John Sculley, the president of Pepsi-Cola, to do the job, asking him, "Do you want to just sell sugared water, or do you want to change the world?" Sculley and Jobs began to argue bitterly, however, and after a power struggle, Jobs was reluctantly forced to resign.

❝ The computer for the rest of us. ❞

By 1996 Apple was in trouble due to the dominance of Windows software and the increasing number of PC clones that used it. Jobs, having had great success with his animation studio Pixar, was brought back to the ailing firm for an annual salary of $1, and the company gradually returned to profitability.

Apple's computers cost more than most PCs and have a more limited range of software available for them, but their great appeal has been the attention to design, making Apple the cool computer company. The launch of the stunning multicolored iMac in 1997, followed by the sleek new iMac in 2002, marked the end of the computer as an ugly, utilitarian machine and brought the home computer out of the study and into the lounge. As Steve Jobs put it, "Other companies don't care about design. We think it's vitally important."

Apple's fortunes were transformed again with the development of the iPod in 2003 and the iPhone in 2007, which soon became must-have gadgets that brought about a boom in Internet music sales and transformed the cell phone industry. And, of course, they were beautifully stylish.

Vocabulary work

Find adverbs ending in *-ly* in the texts that have these meanings.

Starbucks

a. at great speed
b. at the present time
c. in the beginning, before a change
d. with strong feeling and enthusiasm
e. at the beginning
f. after a long time, especially after a delay

Apple Macintosh

a. really/genuinely
b. in a way that produces a successful result
c. in a way that shows feelings of sadness or anger
d. in a way that shows hesitation because you don't want to do sth
e. slowly over a long period of time
f. in a very important way

What do you think?

- What arguments do the antiglobalization protesters make against Starbucks and other multinational corporations? Do you agree?
- Do you have a computer? What kind? What are your favorite websites?

VOCABULARY AND PRONUNCIATION
export: /ˈɛkspɔrt/ or /ɪkˈspɔrt/?

1 **CD2 20** Listen and repeat these words, first as nouns and then as verbs. How does the word stress change?

| a. export | c. decrease | e. progress | g. produce | i. insult |
| b. import | d. increase | f. record | h. permit | j. protest |

2 Practice the words with a partner. Give instructions like this.

> c as a noun! 'decrease

> g as a verb! pro'duce

3 Complete the sentences with one of the words in its correct form. Read the sentences aloud.

1. Japan _____ a lot of its oil from other countries. Its _____ include cars and electronics.
2. I'm very pleased with my French. I'm making a lot of _____.
3. Government officials are worried. There has been an _____ in the unemployment rate.
4. But the number of crimes has _____, so that's good news.
5. How dare you call me a liar and a cheat! What an _____!
6. There was a demonstration yesterday. People were _____ about the price of gasoline.
7. He ran 100 meters in 9.45 seconds and broke the world _____.
8. Don't touch the DVD player! I'm _____ a movie.
9. Britain _____ about 50% of its own oil.

CD2 21 Listen and check.

refuse: /ˈrɛfyus/ or /rɪˈfyuz/?

1 **CD2 22** These words have different meanings according to the stress. Check the meaning, part of speech, and the pronunciation in your dictionary. Listen and repeat.

| a. refuse | c. minute | e. content | g. invalid |
| b. present | d. desert | f. object | h. contract |

2 Practice saying the words in Exercise 1 with a partner.

> g as an adjective! in'valid

3 Answer the questions using the words in Exercise 1.

1. What's another name for garbage?
2. What's a UFO?
3. What's the Sahara?
4. What do you get lots of on your birthday?
5. What are pages ii–v of this book?
6. What's another way of saying ...?
   - happy
   - a written agreement
   - incorrect (PIN number)
   - very small
   - you won't do something

CD2 23 Listen and check.

SPEAKING
Starting a restaurant

1 Think of some restaurants that are popular where you live. What makes them successful?

2 Work in small groups. You are going to start your own restaurant. You have to make many important decisions. Discuss these questions.

1. What kind of restaurant will you open?
2. How will you raise money to start the restaurant?
3. Where will the restaurant be located?
4. What kind of customers do you want to attract?
5. How will you advertise your restaurant to attract these cusomers?
6. How many workers will you hire, and how much will you pay them?

3 Your restaurant is now successful! Discuss these questions.

1. Should you raise prices?
2. Should you expand?
3. The economy enters a recession and business slows. What do you do to stay profitable?

What do you think?

- Appoint a spokesperson from each group. Tell the rest of the class what decisions you made and why you think those decisions would make your restaurant successful.

- As a class, vote on the group whose restaurant is most likely to continue to succeed.

EVERYDAY ENGLISH
Business expressions and numbers

1 This exercise practices fixed expressions in a work context. Match a line in **A** with a reply in **B**.

> We need to get together sometime. When would suit you best?

> Monday and Tuesday are out for me, but Wednesday would be fine. Let's say 9:30.

A	B
1. Mike! Good to see you again! How's business?	a. Sorry, you're breaking up. Can you repeat that last part?
2. I'm afraid something's come up, and I can't make our meeting on the 6th.	b. Sure. I'll e-mail them to you as an attachment.
3. What are your travel arrangements?	c. You win some, you lose some.
4. Could you confirm the details in writing?	d. No. There's no point. I'm not qualified for it. I wouldn't stand a chance.
5. They want a deposit of 2 ½ percent, which is $7,500, and we ha. . . ge. . . t. . .	e. I'm on flight UA 2762 at 6:45.
6. I'll give you $5,250 for your car. That's my final offer.	f. Good, thanks, Jeff. Sales are up again. How about yourself?
7. I don't know their number offhand. Bear with me while I look it up.	g. Great! It's a deal. It's yours.
8. OK. Here's their number. Are you ready? It's 708-555-2200.	h. That's OK. Let's try for the following week. Is Wednesday the 13th good for you?
9. I got a pay raise, but I didn't get a better office.	i. No problem. I'll hold.
10. Did you apply for that job?	j. I'll read that back to you. Seven oh eight, five five five, twenty-two hundred.

CD2 24 Listen and check.

2 Work with a partner. Cover the lines in **B**. Try to remember the conversations. Then cover the lines in **A** and do the same.

Music of English 🎵🎵

Use the stress shading to help you get the rhythm of each sentence right.

MANKOFF

"No. Thursday's out. How about never— is never good for you?"

3 Practice the numbers in the conversations. How is the phone number said in two different ways?

4 Practice saying these numbers.

375	1,250	13,962	23,806	150,000	5,378,212

½   ¾   ⅓   ¼   ⅔

4.3   7.08   10.5   3.142   0.05

Sept. 17   Feb. 3   Nov. 22   Aug. 14

19th century   21st century   1960s

2007   1980   1786   1902

12:00 P.M.   12:00 A.M.   2:05 P.M.   10:30 P.M.

1-773-360-7220   800-667-7433   917-220-4500

(baseball) 2–0   (tennis) 30–0

CD2 25 Listen and check.

5 Write down some numbers. Dictate them to your partner. Ask your partner to read them back to you.

7 Getting along

Grammar: Modals and related verbs (1)
Vocabulary: Hot verb *get*
Everyday English: Exaggeration and understatement

TEST YOUR GRAMMAR

1 Read the sentences 1–10 and <u>underline</u> the modal verbs. Rewrite them with a correct expression a–j.

1. You <u>shouldn't</u> wear red. It doesn't suit you.
2. May I make a suggestion?
3. You can smoke in the designated area only.
4. I can take you to the airport, after all.
5. You must obtain a visa to work in Australia.
6. You should always make an appointment.
7. You'll pass. Don't worry.
8. You can't walk on the grass.
9. I couldn't get through. The line was busy.
10. I won't discuss the matter any further.

a. I'll be able to . . .
b. I didn't manage to . . .
c. You're sure to . . .
d. You are required to . . .
e. Is it OK if . . . ?
f. You're allowed to . . .
g. If I were you . . .
h. I refuse to . . .
i. It's always a good idea to . . .
j. You aren't permitted to . . .

2 **CD2 26** Listen and check.

3 Complete the lines a–j with your own ideas and compare with a partner.

I'll be able to come on Saturday, after all.

WE CAN WORK IT OUT
Modals and related verbs

1 **CD2 27** Read and listen to the two conversations. Who are the speakers? What are they talking about? Find all the examples of modal verbs.

1. **A** What the ... where do you think you're going?
B What do you mean?
A Well, you can't turn right here.
B Who says I can't?
A That sign does. "Do Not Enter." Can't you read?
B Hey, I couldn't see it, all right?
A You should get your eyes tested. You're not fit to be on the roads.

2 **CD2 28** Listen to two similar conversations. What expressions are used instead of modal verbs?

3 Choose one of the conversations. Learn it by heart and act it out for the class with your partner.

1 Modal verbs have many meanings. Match a sentence in **A** with a meaning in **B**.

A	B
1. He can ski.	
2. Can I go to the party?	
3. You must stop at the intersection.	ability
4. You must see the movie.	advice
5. He must be rich.	obligation
6. I'll help you.	permission
7. I won't help you.	probability
8. You should exercise more.	(un)willingness
9. It will be a good party.	
10. It might rain.	

2 Which meanings in **B** do these related verbs express?

> be able to   manage to   be allowed to   be sure to
> be supposed to   promise to   refuse to   have to
> be required to   be likely to   had better   Why don't you . . .?

3 What are the **question**, **negative**, and **third person singular** forms of these sentences?

I can speak Japanese.   I'm able to speak three languages.
I must go.   I have to go.   I've got to go.

Put the sentences into the past and future.

▶▶ **Grammar Reference 7.1–7.3 pp. 143–145**

2. A You won't tell anyone, will you?
  B Of course I won't.
  A You really can't tell a soul.
  B Trust me. I won't say a word.
  A But I know you. You'll tell someone.
  B Look. I really can keep a secret, you know. Oh, but can I tell David?
  A That's fine. He's invited too, of course. It's just that Ben and I want a really quiet affair, this being the second time around for both of us.

PRACTICE

Negotiating

1 Read the conversation. What is it about?

A *If I were you*, *I'd* swallow *my* pride and forgive and forget.
B Never! I *refuse to*.
A You'll *have no choice* in the end. You *won't be able to* ignore each other forever.
B *Maybe I'll* forgive him, but *I'll never be able to* forget.
A *It has to be* possible to talk it over and work something out. You *have to* for the sake of the children.
B Oh, I just don't know what to do!

2 **CD2 29** Replace the words *in italics* with suitable modal verbs. Listen and compare.

3 **CD2 30** Do the same with this conversation. Listen and compare.

A I don't know if I'll *be able to* come tonight.
B But you *have to*. You *promised to*.
A Yeah, but *I'm not supposed to* go out on weeknights. My parents won't let me.
B *Why don't you* tell your parents that you're going over to the library to study?
A *Not possible*. Somebody's *sure to* see me and tell them.
B We *have no choice but to* cancel the party then. Lots of kids *aren't able to* go out during final exams.

4 Practice the conversations with a partner.

Discussing grammar

5 Work with a partner. Which verbs or phrases can fill in the blank correctly? Cross out those which cannot.

1. I _____ be able to help you.

   a. won't   b. can't   c. might   d. may

2. Did you _____ keep it secret?

   a. could   b. manage to   c. able to   d. have to

3. You _____ be exhausted after such a long trip.

   a. must   b. can   c. had better   d. are sure to

4. The book is optional. Our teacher said that we _____ read it if we don't want to.

   a. can't   b. don't have to   c. don't need to
   d. aren't supposed to

5. I absolutely _____ work late again tonight.

   a. will not   b. should not   c. might not   d. refuse to

6. _____ hold your breath for more than a minute?

   a. Are you able to   b. Can you   c. May you   d. Could you

7. _____ tell me where the station is?

   a. May you   b. Could you   c. Are you able to   d. Can you

8. _____ I have some more dessert?

   a. Could   b. May   c. Will   d. Would

9. Will you _____ go on the trip with us?

   a. can   b. be able to   c. be allowed to   d. may

10. You _____ go to England to learn English.

    a. should   b. don't have to   c. shouldn't   d. could

11. You _____ worry so much. Everything will be OK.

    a. couldn't   b. shouldn't   c. don't have to   d. can't

12. I _____ call home.

    a. 'd better   b. ought to   c. am likely to   d. had to

6 Rewrite the sentences using the words in parentheses.

1. I just know it'll rain this weekend. (*sure*)
2. He passed his driver's test after three tries. (*manage*), (*succeed*)
3. Can you tell which twin is which? (*able*)
4. My parents say I can't have a cat. (*allow*), (*let*)
5. You should take it back and complain. (*If*), (*better*)
6. I should wear a suit for work, but I often don't. (*supposed*)
7. You can't tell anyone about it. (*better*), (*promise*)
8. He said he wouldn't turn down the volume. (*refuse*)

Exciting news

7 Read one side of a telephone conversation between Maria and Rebecca.

R Hello?
M . . .
R Maria, hi! Why all the excitement?
M . . .
R Yes, I can. I remember you doing it in the coffee shop. It was the one in the *Post*, wasn't it? Didn't you have to name a bunch of capital cities?
M . . .
R No way! I don't believe it. What's the prize?
M . . .
R You must be kidding! That's great! For how long?
M . . .
R Well, you should be able to do a lot in three days. And the Ritz Carlton! I'm impressed! Doesn't that overlook Central Park?
M . . .
R I thought so. Can't say I've been there, of course.
M . . .
R What do you mean? How would I ever be able to?
M . . .
R You can't be serious! You know I'd love to! But why me? Surely you should be taking David.
M . . .
R Oh, I'm sorry! I didn't know. When did this happen?
M . . .
R Well, what can I say? How could I possibly refuse an offer like that?
M . . .
R I definitely will!

Can you work out the answers to these questions?

• Why is Maria so excited?
• Where is she going?
• What is the relationship between Maria and David?

8 What do you think Maria's exact words were in the conversation? Practice it with a partner.

9 **CD2 31** Listen to the actual conversation between Maria and Rebecca. Compare your ideas.

LISTENING AND SPEAKING
Getting married

1 Look at the photos of three weddings and describe them.

2 What do you think are good reasons to get married? What do you think are bad reasons? Discuss ideas with the class.

3 This is Pratima Kejriwal, an Indian woman who had an arranged marriage. What would you like to know about her marriage? Write questions with a partner.

Who arranged the marriage?

How old was she when she got married?

4 **CD2 32** Listen to Pratima. Answer the questions.

1. Which of the questions you wrote were answered? What are the answers?
2. How did Pratima's father find the two men?
3. What did he want to know about them?
4. What were the similarities and differences between the two men?
5. Why did her father choose Shyam and not the first man?
6. Why did Shyam dress badly?
7. What happened between the time of the interview and the wedding?
8. How do you know that Pratima believes in arranged marriages?

SPOKEN ENGLISH Other question forms

1 What is unusual about these questions from the interview?

> And your father arranged your marriage?
> And this one your father chose?
> He had to?

These are *declarative questions* and are used when the speaker thinks he/she has understood something but wants to make sure or express surprise. Find more examples in the audio script on page 128.

2 Look at this question from the interview.

> For my sister, my elder sister, he saw over one hundred men before …
> **He saw how many?**

What emotion does this question form express? Make similar questions in reply to these statements.

1. My friends went to Alaska on vacation. **They went …?**
2. I got home at 5:00 this morning.
3. I paid $300 for a pair of jeans.
4. I met the president while I was out shopping.
5. He invited me to the White House for lunch.

CD2 33 Listen and check.

What do you think?

- Do you think arranged marriages are a good or bad thing? Work in groups and make a list of all the advantages and disadvantages that you can think of.
- What other ways do people meet marriage partners? Do you believe some ways are better than others? If so, which?

Discuss your ideas with the class.

 WRITING Arguing your case—For and against *p. 114*

READING AND SPEAKING
Meet the kippers

1 When do young people usually leave home in your country? Why do they leave? Work in two groups. List reasons for and against leaving home when you grow up.

Group A Make a list from the children's point of view.
Group B Make a list from the parents' point of view.

Share ideas with the class.

2 Read the introduction to the article and answer the questions.
1. Who are the kippers? What do they refuse to do?
2. What do the letters stand for?
3. What exactly does "eroding retirement savings" mean?
4. What does "leave the nest" mean?

3 Read about two kipper children and answer the questions in your groups.

Group A Read about **Vicki**.   **Group B** Read about **Martin**.

1. Who does she/he live with? Do they get along?
2. Why does she/he still live at home?
3. Has she/he ever lived away from home?
4. What advantages and disadvantages are mentioned?
5. What do her/his friends say?

Work with someone from the other group and compare the two children. Who do you think is more spoiled?

4 Read about two parents of kippers, Bill and Sandra. Compare their views.
1. Who is happy with the arrangement? Why? Who is not? Why not?
2. Who is at their "wits' end?"
3. What do they say about foreign travel?
4. What do they say about money?

Vocabulary work

Complete the sentences with words from the text. Who does each sentence refer to?

1. She isn't able to **r**_____ an apartment.
2. He couldn't **a**_____ to pay **o**_____ his **d**_____.
3. Her friends are always **s**_____ for **c**_____ because they have to pay **h**_____ rents.
4. She **c**_____ to the phone **b**_____.
5. She doesn't **c**_____ him **r**_____ because he wouldn't pay it.
6. He **r**_____ **u**_____ $8,000 in debt.
7. They're tired of their kids sponging **o**_____ them.
8. He can **s**_____ all his **s**_____ on enjoying himself.
9. He believes that **m**_____ isn't **e**_____.

What do you think?

- Check your list of reasons from Exercise 1. Which were mentioned?
- What's your opinion of Vicki and Martin?
- Do you sympathize more with Bill's views or Sandra's? Why?
- Is it possible to "grow up" while still living at home?
- Do you know any kippers?

MEET

Who are they?
They're the children who just WON'T leave home.

Kippers is an acronym for "Kids In Parents' Pockets Eroding Retirement Savings." Or, to put it another way, it refers to all those grown-up children who stay at home into their 20s and 30s, unwilling or unable to leave the nest.

THE CHILDREN

VICKI SARGENT, 30, lives with her father, Norbert, 65.

IF I WASN'T living at home, I wouldn't be able to afford to live in such a beautiful house. I would only be able to rent a room in an apartment. This way I have my father for company and money for a social life. It's just too comfortable to move out.

My dad and I get along well. We usually have dinner together, and if I'm not out, I'll spend the evening with him watching TV. He spoils me a lot and treats me at least once a week to dinner at a nearby restaurant.

My friends don't get it. They say I'm living in a bubble away from the real world, and I guess they're right. But they also admit they're jealous—they are always so strapped for cash because of their high rents. I don't pay my father any rent, but I buy the food and contribute to the phone bill.

Apart from three months when I went traveling in my early 20s, I have never lived away from home.

THE K.I.P.P.E.R.S.

MARTIN GIBBS, 28, lives with his parents Kathy, 52, and Robert, 54.

I HAVE TO admit that I'm spoiled at home, so it's hard to imagine moving out. My mom always has my breakfast on the table when I get up in the morning. We all get along really well together, although my parents can get on my nerves when they tell me what to do. But I'm sure I get on their nerves too sometimes.

At 23 I moved out for two years. I lived with a friend for a short time then went traveling in Asia. It was an amazing experience, but I got into debt, about $5,000, and I had to come back and live at home again so that I could afford to pay it off. My parents don't charge me rent, so I can spend all of my salary on enjoying myself. Sometimes girls call me a "mama's boy," but I think they like it. It's a nice, cozy place to bring girls back to because there is always an open fire and something cooking in the oven.

THE PARENTS

BILL KENNEDY tells why his children, Anna, Simon, and Andrew, can stay as long as they like!

NO ONE TOLD ME, but it seems I was the father of kippers for years without knowing it. My three children all lived at home well into their late 20s. I know there'll be some parents at their wits' end with their "lazy kids sponging off them." Actually, we don't want an empty nest. What puzzles me is why parents would ever want their children to leave home at 18. My wife, Judy, and I made it very easy for them to stay with us. It allowed them to postpone growing up. And it helped us postpone getting old. Honestly, I would happily forfeit any number of retirement perks—golfing, snorkeling, trips to Paris, Peru, or wherever—for just a few more years with our children at home. And why? Because money isn't everything. Family is.

SANDRA LANE, 49, says it's domestic hell with her son, Alan, 27.

THE FRIDGE IS the main issue. He's always helping himself to some tidbit that I've been saving for dinner. And he puts the empty milk cartons back! The phone is another cause for complaint—he's always getting calls from his buddies, but when I get angry he just says I should get a cell phone. And he borrows the car without asking, so I suddenly find myself unable to go out. He's been living at home since he graduated from college five years ago. By the time he finished school he had racked up $8,000 in debt. I can't charge him rent. There's no point. He couldn't and wouldn't pay it. But he's always got money for clothes and nights out. I'm at my wits' end with it all. I had been planning to go on a dream cruise as soon as Alan left home. Now that's all it can be—a dream.

VOCABULARY AND SPEAKING
Hot verb *get*

1 The verb *get* is very common in English. It has many different uses. Here are some examples from the texts on pp. 62–63.

1. My dad and I **get along well**.
2. My friends don't **get it**.
3. ... my parents can **get on my nerves** ...
4. ... it helped us postpone **getting** old.
5. ... he's always **getting** calls from his buddies ...
6. ... when I **get** angry ...
7. ... he just says I should **get** a cell phone.
8. ... he's always **got** money for clothes ...

Replace the words in **bold** with one of the expressions from the box.

> annoy/irritate   me   buy   become
> receiving   growing   understand
> have a good relationship   has

Talking about you

2 Ask and answer these questions with a partner.

1. Do you get along with your parents?
2. What have you got to do when you get home tonight?
3. How do you get to school?
4. What time do you usually get to school?
5. When did you last get angry? Why?
6. Name three things you've got in your bag.
7. If you have a problem with your computer, who do you get to help you?
8. How often do you get your hair cut?
9. In what ways is your English getting better?
10. What are two things that always get on your nerves?

Work together to rewrite the questions without using *get*. Is *get* generally more formal or informal?

Phrasal verbs with *get*

3 *Get* can combine with many particles to make phrasal verbs. Complete each group of sentences with the same particle from the box below. (Careful, only six of the particles are used.)

to	away	into	off	on	out	over	around	through	up

1. You always get How did our secret get I got a great book	_____	of doing the dishes. It's not fair. ? Everyone knows now! of the library. You can borrow it after me.
2. The police finally got Just to get All his teasing got	_____	the truth about the robbery. work I have to take three buses. me. It really hurt my feelings.
3. It took forever to get He still can't get I can't get	_____	the flu. the death of his pet cat. how much your children have grown!
4. He got We got I had to get	_____	to 300 pounds before he went on a diet. to page 56 in the last class. at 5 A.M. to catch the plane.
5. I couldn't get I tried to get Sue got	_____	to Joe. His phone was busy. to her, but she ignored my advice. the test quickly, but I took forever.
6. You can always get I'm sorry. I haven't gotten I can't see how we can get	_____	the rules if you hire a good lawyer. to replying to your invitation yet. this problem. It's a difficult one.

DID YOU MAKE ANY SALES?

I GOT TWO ORDERS: 'GET OUT AND STAY OUT !!'

EDGAR ARGO

Do you know anyone you would describe as being passionate, spontaneous, or temperamental? Why? Do you know anyone very controlled and reserved?

Which of these remarks about a wealthy man are exaggerated? Which are understated?

He's absolutely rolling in it.

He's not short a few pennies.

He hasn't done too badly for himself.

He's got a dollar or two.

He's stinking rich.

Match a line in **A** with a line in **B**. Use your dictionary to look up new words.

A	B
1. ☐ I'm dying for a cup of coffee.	a. Yes, it was a nice little break, but all good things must come to an end.
2. ☐ His parents are pretty well off, aren't they?	b. That's for sure. He's as dumb as dirt.
3. ☐ You must have hit the roof when she told you she'd crashed your car.	c. I wouldn't mind one myself.
4. ☐ I think Tony was a little rude last night.	d. No kidding! He was completely out of line!
5. ☐ I can't stand the sight of him!	e. I guess it is a little chilly.
6. ☐ He isn't very smart, is he?	f. Yeah, they do seem to get along well.
7. ☐ I'm fed up with this weather! It's freezing.	g. Yeah. I'm a little tired, too.
8. ☐ Well, that was a fantastic trip!	h. Well, yeah, I was a little upset.
9. ☐ I'm wiped out. I've got to go to bed.	i. You can say that again! They're totally loaded!
10. ☐ They're obviously madly in love.	j. I have to say I'm not too big on him, either.

4 **CD2 34** Listen and check your answers. Which words are examples of exaggeration? Which are understatements? Practice the conversations with a partner.

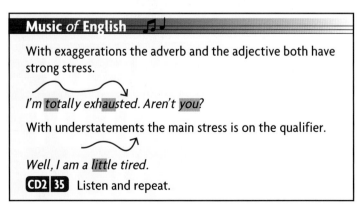

Music of English ♪♩

With exaggerations the adverb and the adjective both have strong stress.

I'm totally exhausted. Aren't you?

With understatements the main stress is on the qualifier.

Well, I am a little tired.

CD2 35 Listen and repeat.

5 Work with a partner. Read aloud these understated remarks and give exaggerated replies.

> I'm pretty tired. Can we finish this tomorrow?
>> Yeah, let's stop now. I'm completely exhausted.

1. Is that a new watch? I bet that cost something.
2. It's a little chilly in here, don't you think?
3. These shoes aren't bad, are they?
4. Can we pull over at the next rest stop? I could use something to eat.

CD2 36 Listen and compare.

8 People and places

Grammar: Relative clauses
• Participles
Vocabulary: Adverb collocations
Everyday English: The world around you

TEST YOUR GRAMMAR

1 Complete the sentences with one of the words below.

who	which	where	what	when	whose

1. The man _____ you met was my brother.
2. My other brother, _____ lives in London, is a teacher.
3. He suddenly quit his job, _____ came as a shock.
4. He says that _____ he wants to do is move to Australia.
5. His girlfriend, _____ parents live in Melbourne, is delighted.
6. They're not sure exactly _____ or _____ they're going.
7. Their house, _____ they bought last year, is up for sale.
8. The house _____ I want to buy is on Acacia Avenue.

2 In which sentences can the relative pronoun be replaced by *that*?

3 Underline the present and past participles in these sentences. Rewrite them with relative pronouns.

1. The woman standing next to him is his wife.
2. Most TVs sold in the U.S. are imported models.

PILOT SUPERSTAR
Relative clauses and participles

1 What do you know about John Travolta? Look at the photos and read the text quickly. What do you learn about his lifestyle? What is his passion?

2 Read the text again and complete it with the clauses a–j.

a. which is built
b. who lives
c. who isn't full of himself
d. where the super-rich can commute
e. including a Gulfstream executive jet
f. whose $3.5 million mansion
g. Walking out of his door
h. which means
i. previously owned by Frank Sinatra
j. most of whom share

CD2 37 Listen and check your answers.

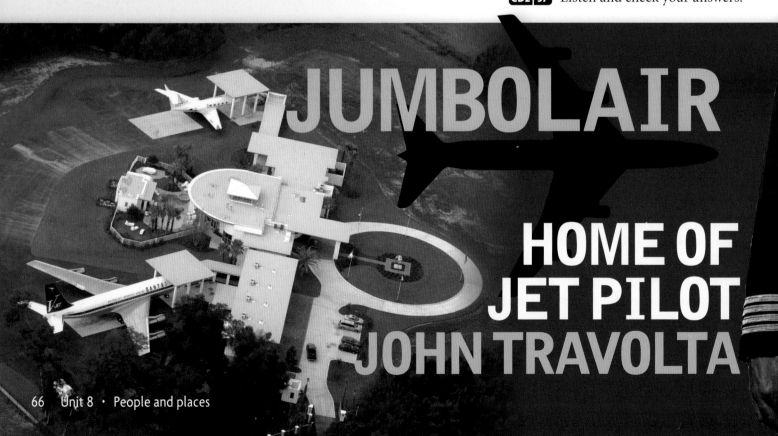

JUMBOLAIR

HOME OF JET PILOT JOHN TRAVOLTA

3 Answer the questions.

1. What kind of people live in Jumbolair?
2. Does John Travolta own three planes or more than three?
3. Who owned the Boeing 707 before Travolta?
4. What is Travolta's home like?
5. Why is it called "the ultimate boys' fantasy house?"
6. Why don't the neighbors complain about the noise?
7. Does Travolta behave like a typical movie star?

Welcome to JUMBOLAIR, Florida–the world's only housing development (1)_____ to work by jet plane from their own front doors.

Jumbolair's most famous resident is Hollywood movie star John Travolta, (2)_____ is big enough to park a row of airplanes, (3)_____ , a two-seater jet fighter, and a four-engine Boeing 707, (4)_____ .

Travolta holds a commercial pilot's license, (5)_____ he's qualified to fly passenger jets. He can land his planes and taxi them up to his front gates. His sumptuous Florida home, (6)_____ in the style of an airport terminal building, is the ultimate boys' fantasy house made real. As well as the parking lots for the jets, there is a heliport, swimming pool and gym, stables for 75 horses, and of course a 1.4-mile runway. Family man Travolta, (7)_____ with wife Kelly and daughter Ella Bleu, flies daily from his home when filming. (8)_____ and into the cockpit, he is airborne in minutes. His neighbors, (9)_____ his love of aviation, don't seem to mind the roar of his jets. They say it's nice to meet a superstar (10)_____ . "He's just a regular guy, very friendly," says one neighbor.

GRAMMAR SPOT

Relative clauses
Relative clauses are like adjectives. They give more information about nouns.
*We have a Korean neighbor **who comes from Seoul**.*

1 Read these sentences aloud, paying attention to the punctuation. Underline the relative clauses.
I met a man who's a pilot.
My friend Adam, who lives in Chicago, is a pilot.
The house which you walked past is my aunt's.
My aunt's house, which I don't like, is very modern.

2 In each pair of sentences, which relative clause . . .
. . . tells us exactly *who* or *what* is being talked about? (A **defining** relative clause)
. . . gives us an extra piece of information? (A **nondefining** relative clause)
Explain the use of commas. How do they affect the pronunciation?

3 In which sentence in Exercise 1 can the relative pronoun be omitted? Why?

Present and past participles
Underline the participles in these sentences. Which are adjectives? Which are present and which are past?
Who is that boring man standing at the bar?
The curtains and carpets included in the sale were old and worn.
They own four houses, including a ruined castle in Scotland.
Having lost all his money, he was a broken man.

▶▶ **Grammar Reference 8.1–8.2 pp. 145–146**

PRACTICE

Pronunciation and punctuation

1 Work with a partner. Read the sentences aloud, then write in the correct punctuation where necessary.

1. The area of New York I like best is Soho.
2. My father who's a doctor plays the drums.
3. The book that I'm reading now is fascinating.
4. Paul passed his driver's test on the first try which surprised everybody.
5. People who smoke risk getting all sorts of illnesses.
6. I met a man whose main aim in life was to visit every capital city in the world.
7. The Channel Tunnel which opened in 1995 is a great way to get from England to France.
8. What I like best about work are the vacation days.
9. A short bald man seen running away from the scene of the crime is being sought by the police.

CD2 38 Listen and compare your pronunciation. Repeat the sentences.

Discussing grammar

2 Read these sentences and decide which need *more* information to make sense.

1. People _____ live longer.
2. The apple tree in our garden _____ needs to be cut down.
3. She married a man _____ .
4. The Great Barrier Reef _____ is the largest coral reef in the world.
5. Did I show you the photos _____ ?
6. Let me introduce you to Kim Lee _____ .
7. I'm looking for a book _____ .
8. I was speaking to someone _____ .

3 Add these sentences to the ones in Exercise 2, using relative clauses. Leave out the pronoun if possible.

People who do regular exercise live longer.

a. She works in our Paris office.
b. You know this person.
c. We took them in Barbados.
d. She met him on vacation in Turkey.
e. It teaches German grammar.
f. They do regular exercise.
g. My grandfather planted it 60 years ago.
h. It is situated off the coast of Australia.

Depress -ed or *depress -ing*?

4 Which words in **B** go with the topics in **A**?

A	B
1. test results	challenging/challenged
2. a vacation	shocking/shocked
3. gossip	disappointing/disappointed
4. a trip	boring/bored
5. a job	relaxing/relaxed
6. a hard luck story	exhausting/exhausted
7. a TV documentary	amusing/amused
8. a social situation	embarrassing/embarrassed

CD2 39 Listen to conversations about the topics. For each, say how the people feel and why. Use the adjectives in **B**.

"It's raining again!"
"Oh, no! Another miserable day when we're stuck indoors."

She's depressed.   The weather is depressing.

5 Complete each pair of sentences with the correct form of the same verb, once as a present participle (*-ing*) and once as a past participle.

1. I hurt my leg _____ football.
   Bridge is a card game _____ by four people.
2. It says _____ *in Korea* on my camera.
   I have a job in a cafe _____ sandwiches.
3. I've spent the whole morning _____ an essay.
   On the wall was some graffiti _____ in big letters.
4. Items _____ on sale cannot be returned.
   I've spent all my money _____ Christmas presents.
5. The police caught the burglar _____ into a house.
   Careful! There's a lot of _____ glass on the floor.

Making descriptions longer

6 Add *all* the words and phrases from the box to this short sentence to make one long sentence.

A man walked along a street.

on a cold and rainy night   carrying a briefcase   wearing a rumpled suit
mysterious   deserted   nervously   full of $100 bills   young

CD2 40 Listen and check.

7 Work with a partner. Choose two sentences and make them longer. Read them aloud to the class. Who has the longest sentence?

1. *A woman was sitting in her garden.*
2. *Peter has a farmhouse in the country.*
3. *Ann Croft, the actress, was seen having lunch in a restaurant.*
4. *The trip to Hawaii was a disaster.*
5. *A boy found a wallet on Main Street.*

CD2 41 Listen and compare your ideas.

1 What's the coldest, hottest, or wettest you've ever been? Where were you? What were you doing? Work in groups and then tell the class.

2 You are going to listen to Simone and Anna recalling their extreme experiences of heat and cold. Look at the words and discuss what you think happened.

Simone	Anna
a night club	a tram
the pyramids	scarves
sunrise	frozen nostrils
a taxi	an anonymous landscape
a motorcycle	huge apartment blocks
heat exhaustion	an old lady
salt tablets	bonfires

3 **CD2 42** Listen to Simone and answer the questions.

1. Where was she?
2. What was the temperature?
3. What did she do that was stupid or silly?
4. What kind(s) of transportation did she use?
5. Where was she going to? Why?
6. What did she see when she arrived?
7. Who did she meet? Was this person helpful?
8. How did the temperature affect her?
9. What happened in the end?

4 Guess the answers to the same questions about Anna's story. Use the words in Exercise 2 to help.

5 **CD2 43** Listen and answer the questions in Exercise 3 about Anna. Compare your ideas.

Language work

6 Complete the sentences with the adverbs used by Simone and Anna.

| completely | dramatically | exactly | extremely |
| profusely | properly | really | seriously | stupidly |

1. It was _____ hot, and _____ we decided to go dancing.
2. We were sweating _____.
3. The temperature rises _____.
4. My brain wasn't working _____.
5. It was _____ anonymous, this landscape.
6. They all looked _____ the same.
7. I was beginning to _____, _____ panic.

SPOKEN ENGLISH adding a comment

In conversation we can add a comment with *which* as an afterthought. This often expresses our reaction to what we have said.

He gave me a ride home, which was nice.

1 Add a suitable comment from **B** to Simone's and Anna's comments in **A**. Sometimes more than one is correct.

A	B
1. We went dancing in temperatures of over 104°F,	which is hard to believe.
2. My friends were worried I'd get lost,	which was just amazing.
3. We visited the pyramids at sunrise,	which was a pretty stupid thing to do.
4. My nostrils actually froze,	which was no joke.
5. This motorcycle broke down,	which was no laughing matter.
6. The old lady didn't understand a word I said,	which was understandable.
	which is hardly surprising since my Russian's lousy.

CD2 44 Listen and check. Practice saying the comments with a partner.

2 Write sentences ending with a comment from **B**. Tell the class.

I missed the last bus home, which was no laughing matter.

1 What do you want from an airport or train station? Put these features in order for you.
(1 = the most important)

- [ ] a beautiful building
- [ ] a convenient location near the city center
- [ ] good shops and restaurants
- [ ] modern and efficient service
- [ ] a wide variety of destinations

Compare your answers with a partner then with the class.

2 Look at the photos of Grand Central Terminal. What can you see?

Does it look like ...?

a museum   a cathedral   a train station

3 Read the article and answer the questions.

PART 1

1. What *can't* you see when you go into Grand Central Station?
2. How do people react when they enter the main hall?
3. Find three adjectives in the second paragraph that mean *very big*.
4. Find the information booth in the photos.
5. In what ways does Grand Central look like a cathedral?
6. What do people do there that they usually do in a cathedral?

PART 2

Use these prompts to summarize the paragraphs.

original	north	steam	inadequate
demolished	electrified	1913	
start 20th century		French influence	
public architecture		white and classical	
Beaux-Arts	station facade		
arches and columns		sculptures	

PART 3

1. Where could you travel to from Grand Central before the 1950s?
2. When and why did train travel lose its popularity?
3. How was the building saved?
4. What was wrong with the building in the 1976?
5. What did the station symbolize in the early 20th century?

THE WONDER THAT'S NEW YORK'S GRAND CENTRAL

Don't go to Grand Central Terminal just to catch a train, says MAURICE STANOVIC. Go for the experience.

PART 1   OVERVIEW

When the light shines through the arched windows on all sides of the main hall, New York's Grand Central Terminal looks like a cathedral. It certainly doesn't resemble anything as ordinary as a train station. To start with, there aren't any trains to be seen (its 44 platforms are all underground). The hall is an awe-inspiring sight. Visitors stop, stand, and stare. They gaze open-mouthed and speechless and marvel at its size. They experience the kind of silent wonder more often found in an historic church or monument.

The hall is enormous—470 feet long and 125 feet wide. At both ends there are marble steps, modeled after the staircase in the Paris Opera House. In the middle there is a four-sided brass clock on top of an information booth, a popular meeting point. Balconies with huge, square columns run on either side. But it is the height of the ceiling, as high as a 12-story building, which takes your breath away. Visitors feel small and insignificant (as they do in a cathedral). The vast, blue-green ceiling is decorated with lights that depict all the stars of the zodiac with the heavens behind.

PART 2 EARLY HISTORY

The current Grand Central Terminal was not the first train station at 42nd Street and Park Avenue. The original station was built in 1871 at a cost of $6.4 million. At that time this was north of the main city, not yet central to anything. Trains were steam-powered, noisy, smelly, and dirty. As New York City grew in size and importance it soon became obvious that this station was inadequate, and it was demolished. The trains were electrified, and a new station was built. This opened in 1913 and cost $80 million.

At the start of the 20th century, there was a strong French influence in public architecture in America. Dark brownstone was no longer popular. Shining white and classical was the new fashion. This style was called Beaux-Arts. Grand Central's facade on 42nd Street has a true beaux-arts design. Large arches with columns are topped by a sculpture of Mercury, the god of commerce, next to Minerva and Hercules, representing wisdom and strength.

PART 3 LATER HISTORY

For many years Grand Central Terminal was the busiest railway station in America. Trains crossed the continent on their way to Los Angeles, New Orleans, and the Rocky Mountains via Chicago. This was the golden age of American train travel, and the trains were elegant and luxurious. One famous line, the 20th Century Limited from Grand Central to Chicago, actually rolled out a red carpet for passengers boarding and leaving the train! But by the early 1950's, post-war America was becoming a nation of suburbs and automobiles, with less demand for long-distance train travel. The station faced the threat of destruction yet again, and city leaders fought to save it. In 1976, it was declared a National Historic Landmark. The building had been saved, but it was old and in bad condition. The roof leaked, and the steel was rusty. There was pollution and dirt everywhere.

Huge renovations began. In 1998, at a cost of $200 million, the station was reborn. In the early 20th century it symbolized the growth and energy of industrial America. Now, in the 21st century, it excites and enthralls a new generation.

PART 4 THE STATION TODAY

Today the terminal serves only as a station for the local subway and for commuter trains to the suburbs, bringing 125,000 people per day down to the city from Connecticut and New York State. Destination boards announce trains to places with exotic names like Poughkeepsie, Breakneck Ridge, Cold Spring, Peekskill, Chappaqua, Tuckahoe, and Cos Cob. Grand Central has also become a tourist destination. Half a million visitors per day come to admire the building, to eat in one of more than 25 restaurants, to shop, or to visit an exhibition. Others come just to watch the hurry and buzz of the crisscrossing crowds in a great city space, the modern equivalent of an ancient town square. And, if you want, you can even catch a train.

PART 4
1. Where can you travel to now from Grand Central?
2. What do people do when they visit?

4 Here are some numbers from the article. What do they refer to?

44	470	four	12	42nd
$6.4 million		$80 million		$200 million
125,000	500,000			

CD2 45 Listen and check.

What do you think?
- What does the writer think is best about Grand Central Station?
- How does Grand Central rate according to the features in Exercise 1?
- What buildings is your town or capital city famous for? When were they built? Why are they famous?
- What's your favorite building? What building would you like to knock down?

VOCABULARY AND PRONUNCIATION
Adverb collocations

Extreme adjectives

Work with a partner.

1 Look at the adjectives in the box.
Find some with similar meanings.

good   bad   marvelous   huge   nice
wet   clever   enormous   fabulous
excited   surprised   valuable   small   silly
funny   interesting   thrilled   delighted
priceless   amazed   tiny   hilarious
wonderful   fanastic   ridiculous   awful
brilliant   pleased   fascinating   gorgeous
big   soaking   excellent   beautiful

Which adjectives go with which of
these adverbs? Why?

very   absolutely

2 Complete the conversations with suitable
adverbs and adjectives from Exercise 1.
Practice them with your partner.

1. **A** Did you get very cold in that snowstorm?
   B Snowstorm! It was a blizzard! We were . . . !

2. **A** I bet you were pretty excited when your
   team won.
   B Excited! We were . . . !

3. **A** I thought she looked kind of silly in that
   flowery hat, didn't you?
   B Silly! She looked . . . !

4. **A** Come on, nobody'll notice that tiny
   pimple on your nose.
   B They will, I just know they will! It's . . . !

5. **A** I thought that movie was absolutely
   hilarious.
   B Mmm. I wouldn't say that. It was . . . but
   not hilarious.

6. **A** Len left early. He wasn't feeling well.
   B I'm not surprised. When I saw him this
   morning he looked . . . !

3 **CD2 46** Listen and check. Practice again.
Make similar conversations with your
partner. You could talk about movies,
people you know, the weather …

Pretty

4 **CD2 47** The adverb *pretty* has different meanings. Listen and repeat
these sentences. Which in each pair is more positive?

1. a. She's pretty smart.   **2. a.** He's pretty nice.
b. She's pretty smart.   **b.** He's pretty nice.

5 Read these sentences aloud according to the meaning.
1. The movie was pretty interesting. You really should go and see it.
2. The movie was pretty interesting, but I wouldn't recommend it.
3. I'm pretty tired after that last game. Should we call it a day?
4. I'm pretty tired, but I'm up for another game if you are.

CD2 48 Listen, check, and repeat.

A night at the Oscars

6 Read the speech. Who is speaking? Why? Rewrite the speech and make it
sound more extreme by changing and adding adjectives and adverbs.

" I am very surprised and pleased to receive this award. I am grateful
to all those nice people who voted for me. *Red Hot in the Snow* was a
good movie to act in, not only because of all the smart people involved
in the making of it but also because of the beautiful, exciting, and often
pretty dangerous locations in Alaska. None of us could have predicted
that it would be such a big success. My special thanks go to Marius
Aherne, my director; Lulu Lovelace, my costar; Roger Sims, for writing a
script that was both interesting and funny; and last but not least to my
wife, Glynis, for her valuable support. I love you all."

7 **CD2 49** Listen and compare your choices.

EVERYDAY ENGLISH
The world around you

1 Look at the signs. Where could you … ?

- … borrow money to buy a house?
- … buy a hammer, a screwdriver, and some glue?
- … go to exercise?
- … get rid of your newspapers and bottles?
- … get an inexpensive bed for the night?
- … get help if you have car trouble?
- … get your driver's license?
- … have your car repaired?

2 **CD2 50** Listen to five conversations. Where are they taking place?

3 In pairs, write similar conversations that take place in two or three of the other places. Read them out to the rest of the class. Where are they taking place?

▶▶ **WRITING** Describing places—My favorite part of town *p. 115*

9 Changing times

Grammar: Expressing habit
• used to do/doing
Vocabulary: Homonyms and homophones
Everyday English: Making your point

TEST YOUR GRAMMAR

1 Match a line in **A** with a line in **B**. Underline the words that express habit. Which are past and which are present?

2 Choose the correct ending for these sentences.

| He used to work hard, | because he's a mover. |
| He's used to hard work | but now he's retired. |

A	B
1. A reliable friend	a. my dad would read me a story at bedtime.
2. In the 1960s, hippies	b. are always talking about themselves.
3. I think my sister's in love.	c. will never let you down.
4. When I was a kid	d. She'll spend hours staring into space.
5. My first girlfriend was Alice.	e. used to wear flowers in their hair.
6. Bigheaded people	f. We used to go to the movies on a Friday, and then we'd go for a pizza afterwards.

FRIENDS REUNITED
Expressing habit—*used to do/doing*

1 Read the e-mail from Alison to an old friend from school. Complete it with the lines a–l.

a. used to sit	g. went
b. 'd get	h. was
c. got	i. used to call
d. 's always talking	j. used to calling
e. used to go	k. were always giggling
f. 'd go	l. 'll always end up

CD3 2 Listen and check.

2 Which actions in the e-mail happened again and again? Which only happened once?

From: Alison Wright <AliWright72@yoohoo.com>
Subject: Springfield East
Date: Mon, Sep17 6.36 PM
To: sallydavis@yoohoo.com

Dear Sally,

Do you remember me? We ¹ _e_ to Springfield East together. You were the first person I ² ____ to know when I started there.

We ³ ____ next to each other in class, but then the teachers made us sit apart because we ⁴ ____ so much.

I remember we ⁵ ____ back to your house after school every day and listen to music for hours on end. We ⁶ ____ all the Beatles records as soon as they came out. Once we ate all the food in your fridge, and your mother ⁷ ____ furious.

Do you remember that time we nearly blew up the science lab? The teacher ⁸ ____ crazy, but it wasn't our fault. We ⁹ ____ him "Mickey Mouse" because he had sticky-out ears.

I still see Penny, and she's still as wild as ever. We meet up every now and then, and we ¹⁰ ____ chatting about old times together. She ¹¹ ____ about a class reunion. So if you're interested, drop me a line.

Looking forward to hearing from you.

Your old friend,

Alison Wright

PS I'm not ¹² ____ you Sally Davis! To me, you're still Sally Wilkinson!

3 Look at these two sentences.

> We used to go to school together . . .
> We'd go back to your house . . .

Which sentence is more factual?
Which is more nostalgic?

4 Match a line in **A** with a line in **B**. Practice saying them. Pay attention to contracted forms and weak forms.

A	B
we used to go	him "Mickey Mouse"
we used to sit	to school together
we were always giggling	you Sally Davis
we'd go back	so much
we used to call	to your house
I'm not used to calling	next to each other

CD3 3 Listen and check.

GRAMMAR SPOT

1 Look at the sentences that express present habit.
   a. *My sister **works** in a bank.*
   b. *She's **always borrowing** my clothes without asking me.*
   c. *She'**ll go out** on a Friday night and **won't be back** till morning.*

Which sentence expresses . . .
   • my attitude to this habit of hers? (I find it annoying.)
   • a simple fact about her?
   • characteristic behavior? (This is typical of her.)

2 Put sentences *a–c* into the past. Express sentence *a* in two ways.

3 Look at these sentences.
   a. *I've lived next to the airport for years, so I'**m used to** the noise.*
   b. *I **used to** live in Rome, but now I live in Paris.*
   c. *I'**m getting used to** traveling on the Metro.*

In which sentence is *used* a verb? In which is *used* an adjective?

Which sentence expresses . . .
   • a past habit now finished?
   • a situation which is familiar and no longer strange?
   • a situation which is still strange but becoming easier?

▶▶ **Grammar Reference 9.1 p. 146**

PRACTICE

What's she like?

1 Choose an adjective from the box to describe the people in the sentences.

> easygoing   clumsy   stingy   absentminded
> argumentative   sensitive   sensible   stubborn

   1. He's always losing things or forgetting where he's put things.
   2. She'll always cry at the end of a sad movie.
   3. Nothing ever upsets her or annoys her or worries her.
   4. I'm always dropping things or bumping into things.
   5. She's ruled by her head not her heart. She'll always think things through before she acts.
   6. He just won't listen to anyone else's suggestions.
   7. I remember Dave. He never tipped at restaurants.
   8. And he'd pick a fight with anyone about anything.

2 Add similar sentences to support these statements.
   1. My roommate is the messiest person in the whole world.
      He'll leave his dirty clothes everywhere.
   2. My boyfriend is insanely jealous.
   3. Marc is just the coolest guy I know.
   4. My mother really gets on my nerves.
   5. But my grandma was so sweet.
   6. My dog Bruno was my best friend.
   7. Your problem is you're self-centered.
   8. My sister's so nosy.

Discussing grammar

3 In pairs, decide which line in **B** best continues the line in **A**.

A	B
1. My friend Joe buys and sells cars. 2. He's always buying new things for himself—an iPhone, a laptop. 3. He'll buy a shirt and only wear it once.	He's a real techno-geek. Don't you think that's wasteful of him? He makes tons of money.
4. When I was young, we used to take vacations by the seaside. 5. My dad and I would build sandcastles and go swimming together. 6. One year we went to East Africa.	What an adventure that was! We'd go to the same place year after year. I remember those days with such fondness!
7. John usually does the cooking, 8. He used to do the cooking, 9. He's used to doing the cooking 10. He's getting used to doing the cooking,	because he's been doing it for years. but he still burns things. Maybe one day he'll get it. but then he stopped. but he isn't tonight. I am.

Parents

4 (CD3 4) Listen to four people talking about their relationship with their parents. Is it a good relationship?

5 (CD3 4) Listen again. These lines are similar to what they say. What are their actual words?

1. . . . she talked to me very openly . . .
   . . . we used to go out shopping . . .

2. My wife always asks me questions . . .
   . . . we didn't talk very much . . .
   . . . every week he took me to the barber.

3. . . . she always tells me to pick things up . . .
   She goes on for hours . . .

4. We did a lot together as a family.
   . . . he brought us each a treat . . .

6 Write a few sentences about the relationship between you and your parents. Tell your partner about it.

Answering questions

7 Answer the questions with a form of *used to*.

1. **A** You don't like your new teacher, do you?
   B Not a lot, but __we're getting used to her__.

2. **A** How can you get up at five o'clock in the morning?
   B No problem. I __'m used to it__.

3. **A** How come you know Mexico City so well?
   B I _____ live there.

4. **A** How are you finding your new job?
   B Difficult, but I _____ it bit by bit.

5. **A** Do you read comics?
   B I _____ when I was young but not anymore.

6. **A** You two argue so much. How can you live together?
   B After 20 years of marriage we _____ each other.

(CD3 5) Listen and check.

LISTENING AND SPEAKING
A teacher I'll never forget

1 Look at the pictures. What are the teachers doing? What are the students doing? How have teaching styles changed over the years?

2 [CD3] [6] Listen to four people talking about a teacher they'll never forget. What characteristics of a good and a bad teacher do they mention?

3 Discuss the questions.
1. Why did Alan like his teacher? What are some of the things he'd do?
2. Why didn't John like his teacher? What are some of the things he used to do?
3. What does Liz say about her teacher? What will she never forget?
4. Why does Kate have two opposing views of Mr. Brown?
5. What comments do they all make about their teacher's name?

What do you think?

Who is a teacher you'll never forget? Why? What was/is she/he like?

SPOKEN ENGLISH Adjective intensifiers

Look at these lines from the audio script.

> All the kids were **scared stiff** of him.
> . . . your answer was **dead wrong**.

These are compounds that intensify the meaning of the adjective. Complete the sentences with a word from the box.

brand	stiff	freezing	tiny	wide	great	boiling	fast

1. They live in this _____ big house in the center of Philadelphia.
2. I made one _____ little mistake on my driver's test, but I still failed.
3. Careful with the soup—it's _____ hot. Don't burn yourself.
4. It's _____ cold in here. Can't we turn up the heat?
5. Do you like my car? It's _____ new.
6. Don't worry. You won't wake the children. They're _____ asleep.
7. I take a cold shower every morning. After that I feel _____ awake.
8. "I'm fed up with this class." "Me, too. I'm bored _____."

READING AND SPEAKING
The man who planted trees

The man

Work in small groups.

1 Read the following quotation. What does it mean?

"Only when the last tree has died and the last river has been poisoned and the last fish has been caught will we realize that we can't eat money."

2 Who do you think said it? (The answer is on page 153.)

1 A political leader.
2 An African fisherman.
3 A French farmer.
4 An ancient Chinese philosopher.
5 A Native American.

3 The extracts are from a story called "The Man Who Planted Trees," by the French writer Jean Giono (1895–1971). In the story, Giono describes his meetings with a solitary shepherd who plants trees while the rest of the world is at war.

Read the extracts and answer the questions after each one.

Part 1

About 40 years ago I was taking a long trip on foot over mountain heights unknown to tourists. All around was bare and colorless land. Nothing grew there but wild lavender.

5 After five hours walking I had still not found water. All around me was the same dry grass. Suddenly, in the distance I saw a small black silhouette. It was a shepherd. Thirty sheep were lying about him on the baking earth. He gave me a drink and took me to his cottage in the plain.

I felt peace in the presence of this man. I asked if I could rest here for a day. He found the question quite natural. He gave me the impression that nothing 10 could surprise him. I didn't actually need to rest, but I was interested in this man and wished to know more about him.

1. Jean Giono wrote the story in 1953. In which year is the story set? What was happening in the world then?

2. What was Giono doing when he met the shepherd?

3. The story takes place in the south of France. What is the countryside like?

4. Why is the writer interested in the shepherd? What do you think he likes about the man and his lifestyle?

Before going to bed, the shepherd puts a large sack onto the table. From it he carefully removes a hundred perfect acorns. The writer is curious. The next day, when he goes out with the shepherd into the hills, he discovers what the acorns are for. What do you think the acorns are for?

Part 2

I noticed that he carried for a stick an iron rod as thick as my thumb and about a meter and a half long. He began thrusting his iron rod into the earth, making a hole in which he planted an acorn; then he would refill the hole. He was planting oak trees.

5 I was insistent in my questions; he answered every one. For three years he had been planting trees in this wilderness. He had planted one hundred thousand. Of the hundred thousand, twenty thousand had sprouted. Of the twenty thousand, he still expected to lose half. There remained ten thousand oak trees to grow where nothing had grown before.

10 That was when I began to wonder about the age of this man. He was obviously over 50. Fifty-five he told me. His name was Elzéard Bouffier. I told him that in 30 years his ten thousand oaks would be a magnificent forest. The next day we parted.

5. What did Elzéard do with the acorns? What did he use as a tool?

6. How many had he already planted? How many were growing?

7. How old was Elzéard at the time? How old do you think the writer was?

8. What do you think Elzéard's ambition is? What is his vision of the future?

9. Draw a sketch of the landscape around his home at the time of Parts 1 and 2. Draw a sketch of how you think it will look in 30 years.

who planted trees

For the next five years the writer is a soldier and fights in World War I. The war ends in 1918, and his thoughts turn again to the tree-planter in the mountains. He returns to look for him.

The writer returns for a final visit in 1945 after World War II. Elzéard is still alive. The writer is amazed at what he sees. Not only is there the forest, but houses and even villages have been rebuilt.

Part 3

I had seen too many men die during those five years not to imagine that Elzéard Bouffier was dead. He was not dead. As a matter of fact, he was extremely well. He had changed jobs. He had gotten rid of the sheep because they threatened his young
5 trees. He told me that the war had not disturbed him at all. He had continued to plant.

The oaks were then ten years old and taller than both of us. It was an impressive spectacle. I was literally speechless, and, as he did not talk, we spent the whole day walking in silence
10 through his forest. It measured eleven kilometers in length and three kilometers at its greatest width. When you remembered that all this had come from the hands of this one man, you understood that men could be effective in other ways than destruction.

10. Why did the writer think that Elzéard might have died?

11. How had the war affected Elzéard?

12. Why is the writer speechless?

13. What thoughts about human behavior does he have in the last sentence?

Part 4

The bus put me down in Vergons. Thirty-two years ago this village of ten or twelve abandoned houses had three inhabitants. Now everything had changed. Even the air. It was filled with scents from flowers. Where there used to be
5 harsh dry winds, a gentle breeze was blowing. A fountain had been built. Five houses had been restored. Now there were 28 inhabitants, four of them young married couples. It was a village where one would like to live. A sound like
10 water came from the mountains: it was the wind in the forest.

When I think that one man was able to cause this to grow from wasteland, I am convinced that in spite of everything, humanity is good.

Elzéard Bouffier died peacefully in his sleep in 1947.

14. What did the village use to be like? How had it changed?

15. Is the writer an optimist or pessimist at the end of the story? Why? What has happened in the writer's life that could have made him pessimistic?

16. How old was Elzéard when he died? Why was it important that he had a long life?

What do you think?

• How would you describe the personality of Elzéard Bouffier? Do you know any people like him?

• How does the context of two world wars help strengthen the author's message of the importance of nature and individual human beings?

VOCABULARY AND PRONUNCIATION
Homonyms and homophones

1 Work on your own. What do these words mean?

> fine   match   park   book   cross   mean

2 **CD3 7** Write down the words you hear.

3 Work with a partner. Compare your answers to Exercises 1 and 2. Do you have any differences? What are they?

Homonyms

4 Homonyms are words with the same spelling and more than one meaning.

> a **bank** on Main Street
> the **bank** of a river
> I've supported you up till now, but don't **bank** on it forever.

Complete the pairs of sentences with the same word used twice.

1. You'll like Paul. He's a really _____ guy. Easygoing and very good looking.

   There was a lovely _____ breeze coming off the sea.

2. "What's today's _____?" "The third."

   I've got a _____ tonight. I'm going out with Carol.

3. The movie was _____ in New York.

   My wife bought me a chess _____ for my birthday.

4. He goes to the gym every day. He's very _____.

   The pants are too small. They don't _____ you.

5. I can't _____ people who never stop talking about themselves.

   My four-year-old son won't go anywhere without his teddy _____.

5 Think of two meanings for these words.

> wave   suit   fan   miss   type
> point   train   right   mind   fair

Homophones

6 Homophones are words with the same pronunciation, but different spellings and different meanings.

> the **road** to the town center
> She **rode** a horse.
> I **rowed** across the river.

Write in the correct word.

1. hole/whole   the _____ world
   a _____ in the ground

2. piece/peace   a _____ of cake
   war and _____

3. flour/flower   a rose is a _____
   _____ to make bread

4. sale/sail   a yacht has a _____
   buy clothes on _____

5. sell/cell   salespeople _____ things
   a prisoner lives in a _____

7 Think of a homophone for these words.

> bored   war   hire   pair   plain   waist   seas   aloud

8 A lot of children's jokes are made with homonyms and homophones. Here are two! Which word makes the joke?

A How do you keep cool at a football game?
B I don't know.
A Sit next to a fan.

A Why did the teacher wear sunglasses?
B I don't know.
A Because her students were so bright.

CD3 8 Listen to some more jokes. Which word makes the joke? Practice telling them to each other.

EVERYDAY ENGLISH
Making your point

1 **CD3 9** Listen to Al, Vicky, and Brian talking about whether people should pay more tax on fast food. Who is for it, who is against it, and who is undecided?

2 Match a line in **A** with a line in **B** as they appear in the audio script on page 131.

A	B
What really	ask me . . .
But the main	I'm concerned . . .
If you	is that . . .
Another thing	the point.
If you want	the problem is that . . .
As	was saying . . .
To tell	my opinion . . .
That's not	I understand it . . .
The point	you the truth . . .
Anyway, as I	point is that . . .
As far as	I'm trying to make is that . . .
I suppose	worries me is that . . .

CD3 10 Check your answers. Listen carefully and practice the lines.

3 Write the adverbs that end in *-ly* in **CD3 9**.

firstly   secondly   personally

4 Match a line in **A** with a line in **B**.

A	B
1. First of all,	there are problems with the cost.
2. In addition to this,	I'd like to give my conclusion.
3. Finally,	I'd like to look at the general problem.
4. In my opinion,	how do you educate people to have a better diet?
5. Generally speaking,	fast food should be totally banned.
6. The problem is,	as a nation we don't get enough exercise.
7. As far as I know,	I don't know the answer to this problem.
8. To be exact,	there are five others like this.
9. To be honest,	this problem is quite common.

5 Have a class debate. Choose a topic you feel strongly about, something important to your community or one from this list.

- Being vegetarian
- Diets for children
- The effects of tourism
- Experiments on animals

Divide into groups to prepare your ideas. When you're ready, conduct the debate.

▶▶ **WRITING** Writing for talking—What I want to talk about is . . . *p. 116*

10 Dangerous living

Grammar: Modals and related verbs (2)
Vocabulary: Synonyms
Everyday English: Metaphors and idioms—the body

TEST YOUR GRAMMAR

1 All modal verbs can be used to express degrees of probability. Which of these sentences do this? Put a (✔). Which don't? Put a (✗).

1. She must be very rich.   ✔
2. I must do my homework. ✗
3. I can't sleep because of the noise.
4. They can't be in. There are no lights on.
5. I think that's Jane, but I might be wrong.
6. You should see a doctor.
7. I could swim when I was five.
8. Cheer up! Things could be worse.
9. The train may be late due to bad weather.
10. May I make a suggestion?

2 Put sentences 1–6 in the past.

ÖTZI THE ICEMAN
Modal auxiliary verbs in the past

1 A 5,300-year-old body was discovered in the Italian Alps in 1991. It had been preserved in ice. The man was named Ötzi after the Ötz Valley, where he was found. Look at the pictures.

What do you think ...
  ... he was?
  ... he wore?
  ... he ate?
Where did he live?
How did he die?
How old was he when he died?

> He was probably a hunter.

> He could have been a warrior.

2 **CD3 11** Listen to two people, Ann and Bill, discussing the questions in Exercise 1. Give one of their answers to each question.

3 Answer these questions about Ötzi using the words in *italics*.

1. What was he?

   a hunter/shepherd   *could*

2. What was he doing in the mountains?

   looking after his sheep/gotten lost   *might*

3. Where did he live? What did he wear?

   a cave   animal skins   *must*

4. How did he die?

   asleep/cold and starvation   *may*

5. Was it a good idea to go so high?

   so high on his own   *shouldn't*

   protective clothing   *should*

6. What did he eat?

   a lot of meat and berries   *must*

   crops like grains to make bread   *might can't*

   meat   *'d have thought*

7. Did they travel much?

   (not) much at all   *wouldn't have thought*

   stayed in the same area   *must*

8. How old was he when he died?

   between 40 and 45   *could*

   pretty old in those days   *must*

4 **CD3** **12** Listen and check. Practice the sentences, paying attention to contracted forms and weak forms.

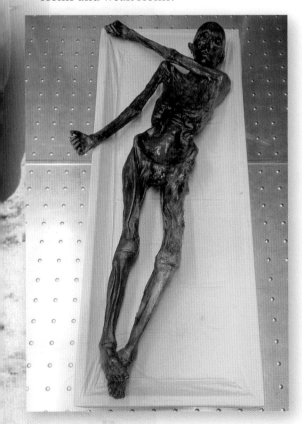

5 Here are some more things found on or near Ötzi's body. How can you explain them?

> I bet he used it to ...

> That must have/might have/could have been for ...

> I think/guess ...

> I'd have thought ...

> I wouldn't have thought ...

6 Read the results of recent tests done on Ötzi on page 154. Were Ann and Bill right or wrong in their assumptions? Were *you* right in *your* assumptions?

GRAMMAR SPOT

1 Write *certain* or *possible* next to these modal auxiliary verbs according to the degree of probability they express.

They must have		
They might have They could have They may have	arrived.	
They can't have		

2 What concept do these modal verbs express? Choose a definition on the right.

You shouldn't have told a lie.
You idiot! You could have killed yourself!

This was possible, but it didn't happen.
You did this, but it was wrong.

▶▶ **Grammar Reference 10.1 pp. 146–147**

PRACTICE

Discussing grammar

1 Circle the correct answer.

1. Sorry I'm late. I *should have gone/had to go* to the post office.

2. I looked for Pearl, but I *couldn't find/couldn't have found* her.

3. I don't know where Paul is. He *had to go/must have gone* home early.

4. I *had to work/must have worked* hard when I was in school.

5. You *can't have said/shouldn't have said* anything to Pam about her birthday party. It was going to be a surprise.

6. You *shouldn't have bought/couldn't have bought* a new vacuum cleaner. I managed to fix the old one.

7. You *should have asked/must have asked* me earlier. I *might have given/would have given* you a ride.

8. You *can't have done/shouldn't have done* your homework already! You only started five minutes ago.

9. You *could have told/must have told* me class had been cancelled! If you had, I *shouldn't have gotten/wouldn't have gotten* up so early.

10. You were lucky to get out of the car unhurt. You *would have been/could have been* badly injured.

2 Complete the sentences with a modal verb in the past.

1. I *did* tell you about Joe's party. You <u>must not have</u> been listening.

2. Thanks so much for all your help. I _____ managed without you.

3. Flowers, for me! Oh, that's so nice, but you really _____.

4. Come on! We're only five minutes late. The movie _____ started yet.

5. I don't believe that Kathy's going out with Mark. She _____ told me, I know she would.

6. We raced to get to the airport on time, but we _____ worried. The flight was delayed.

7. We've got a letter here that isn't for us. The mailman _____ delivered it by mistake.

8. You _____ gone swimming in such rough seas. You _____ drowned!

CD3 13 Listen and check. Practice the sentences with a partner.

Making assumptions

3 **CD3 14** You will hear one half of a telephone conversation. Who are the people? What are they talking about? Make assumptions.

> They must be divorced.

> They might just be separated.

4 Work with a partner. Look at the audio script on page 132. Write what you think is the other half of the conversation. Compare with other students.

There are many fixed expressions with modal auxiliary verbs often found in spoken English. Match a line in **A** with a line in **B**.

A	B
1. "That exam was totally impossible!" 2. "You might as well apply for the job, even though you're too young." 3. I know I shouldn't have eaten a whole tub of ice cream, . . . 4. "I'm going to tell her exactly what I think of her." 5. "You should have told me that Jackie and Dave broke up!"	a. "Sorry! I thought you knew." b. "You can say that again!" c. but I just couldn't help it. d. "Yes, why not! After all, I've got nothing to lose." e. "I wouldn't do that if I were you."
6. "I think you should forget all about her and move on." 7. "You should have been here yesterday! You'd have died laughing!" 8. "Then I found out that Annie's been going out with . . . guess who? Dave!" 9. I'd known this guy for five minutes when he asked me to marry him! 10. "I could use a break."	f. "Me, too. I'm dying for some coffee." g. "Believe me, I would if I could." h. "Why? What was so funny?" i. "Duh! I could have told you *that*." j. I just couldn't believe it!

CD3 **15** Listen and check. What extra lines do you hear? What are the contexts? Practice the conversations with a partner.

It all went wrong!

6 Write some notes about an occasion in your life when everything went wrong. Tell the class. They can comment and ask questions.

Couldn't you have ...

Why didn't you ...?

You must have been terrified!

Don't you think you should have ... ?

You can say that again!

I know I shouldn't have ... , but I couldn't help it.

I couldn't believe it!

▶▶ **WRITING** Formal and informal letters and e-mails—Do's and don'ts *p. 117*

READING AND SPEAKING
A story from New York

1 Write down three things you know about New York City. Share ideas with the class.

2 You are going to read about a young man, Bob Redman, who lives in New York City. Read the final paragraph of his story.

> This story just goes to prove that the U.S. is still a land of opportunity, where dreams can become reality. And, in the hectic, competitive world of New York, it is comforting to know that a man like Bob Redman exists.

What do you think?

- Is the U.S. "a land of opportunity?" What does this mean?

- Why is New York called "hectic and competitive?"

- Could Bob Redman be a successful businessman?

- Can you guess why his story might be comforting?

3 Now turn to page 86 to read Bob Redman's story.

Reading

4 Work with a partner. Read the title and the first paragraph. Answer these questions.

1. Who was Tarzan?
2. What advice is given about where to stay in New York? Why should you stay there?
3. What are the "enormous cliffs of stone and cement?"

5 Read the paragraph headings. What can you guess about Bob Redman? Is he a businessman? Where does he live?

He can't be a businessman

He could be a ...

He might live ...

6 Read the article. Are these statements true (✔) or false (✗)? Correct the false ones.

1. ☐ People near the park thought that someone might be living among the treetops.
2. ☐ Bob Redman was raised among trees in the countryside.
3. ☐ He built 14 tree houses altogether.
4. ☐ He gave an interview to the *New York Times*.
5. ☐ Bob felt lonely sometimes, especially at night.
6. ☐ He rented his final house to some friends.
7. ☐ He was pleased to see friends as long as they behaved well.
8. ☐ Bob's tree houses were usually detected very quickly.
9. ☐ The Park Director was very impressed with Bob's workmanship.
10. ☐ Unfortunately, Bob had to go to jail.

7 Read again about his final tree house. Try to draw it on a piece of paper. Comment on each other's pictures. Ask the student with the "best" one to draw it on the board.

Role play

Work in pairs. One of you is Bob Redman. The other is a journalist from the *New York Times*. Conduct an interview about Bob's past and present life. Begin like this.

Journalist Tell me about yourself, Bob. When and why did you build your first tree house?

Bob Well, I was just 14 and my mother and I ...

What do you think?

- Why is it comforting to read about a man like Bob Redman in New York?
- Look at this saying: "Find a job you love to do and you'll never have to work again in your life." What does it mean? Do you agree? How does it relate to Bob Redman's story?

THE TARZAN OF CENTRAL PARK

ANYBODY visiting New York for the first time should get a room high up in one of the hotels at the southern end of Central Park. The view is extraordinary. The park extends northwards until it is lost from sight in a sea of treetops with enormous cliffs of stone and cement on each side.

Life among the treetops

During recent years legends have grown up among people who live near the park, legends of life among the treetops. One story was of a young, handsome man who had been spotted from time to time among the branches. This rumor turned out to be true. There was a handsome young man who had been living in the treetops for eight years until he was discovered by the city authorities.

"I like the solitude."

It is a touching tale. Bob Redman, brought up by his mother in a tiny Manhattan apartment, had always been addicted to trees. When he was 14, he went into the park and built himself a tree house. It was the first of 13 houses, each one more elaborate than the last. "I like to be in trees," Redman explained to a reporter from the *New York Times*, "I like to be up, away from everything. I like the solitude. I love most of all to look at the stars. The view at night of the city lights and stars is beyond description."

A five-room split level home

His final house was the grandest of them all. Constructed at the top of a huge beech tree, it was what a real estate agent would describe as a "five-room split level home commanding spectacular views of the city skyline and Central Park." It included ladders and rope bridges leading to an adjacent tree as well as wooden benches and tables. Who can imagine what the rent might be for such a house?

Friends came to visit

Redman went to great pains to hide his tree houses, building them in neglected corners of the park and camouflaging them with branches and green paint. Friends used to come to visit him, sometimes as many as 12 people at a time, bringing sandwiches and radios and books and flashlights. Certain rules had to be obeyed: no breaking branches, no litter, no fires, and no loud noise—except his brother Bill, who sometimes brought a set of conga drums to the tree houses and played them very late at night, giving rise to rumors of a tree-dwelling tribe.

The party's over!

The park authorities quickly became aware of his activities. However, the houses were often not detected for long periods of time. Some lasted as long as a whole year before they were found and destroyed by officials with a mournful Bob Redman watching from a distance. His magnificent final house went unnoticed for four months before Bob was awoken one morning with the words: "Come down! The party's over!" He climbed down and was met by Frank Serpe, Park Director, and 10 officers of the Parks Enforcement Patrol. Mr. Serpe had been hunting Redman for years. But he was generous in his praise for the houses. "We marveled at the spectacular workmanship," he said. "The floors were strong enough to hold a truck, and not one nail was hammered into the tree."

The perfect job!

Mr. Serpe concluded that rather than lock him up in jail, perhaps they should offer Redman a job. He is now a professional pruner and tree climber for the Central Park Conservancy. However, he has had to promise not to build any more tree houses. He says he cannot believe that a job so perfect for him could possibly exist.

I suppose this story just goes to prove that the U.S. is still a land of opportunity, where dreams can become reality. And, in our hectic, competitive world, it is comforting to know that a man like Bob Redman exists.

LISTENING AND VOCABULARY
Synonyms—the story of Jim and the lion

In 1907 Hilaire Belloc published *Cautionary Tales for Children*. They are humorous verses with a moral.

1 Look at the title of the poem and the pictures. Guess the answers to these questions.

1. Where did his nurse* take him?
2. Was Jim a well-behaved little boy who always did what he was told, or was he naughty?
3. How far did he get when he ran away?
4. How did the lion go about eating him?
5. Who tried to help Jim? Did this work?
6. How did his parents react?

*Nowadays we would say *nanny*, not *nurse*.

2 **CD3 16** Listen and check.

3 Complete the lines with a word on the right. Think of style, rhythm, and rhyme. It might help to say the poem out loud. Do the first verse.

4 **CD3 16** Listen and check your answers to the first verse. Then do the same for the rest of the poem.

5 What is the moral of this poem? What is the tone?

Jim's parents, we are told, were "concerned" about their son. Why is this funny?

What do you think?

• What were your favorite stories as a child? Tell the class about one of them.
• Were they scary? Funny?
• Who were the main characters? Were the stories based on real life or fantasy?
• Did they have a moral? A happy ending?

Jim, who ran away from his nurse, and was eaten by a lion

There was a boy whose name was Jim;
His _____ were very good to him.
They gave him tea, and cakes, and jam,
And slices of _____ ham,
And read him _____ through
  and through,
And even took him to the zoo—
But there it was the _____ fate
Befell him, I now _____.

buddies / friends

delicious / tasty
novels / stories

dreadful / appalling
describe / relate

You know—at least you ought to know,
For I have _____ told you so—
That children never are _____
To leave their nurses in a crowd;
Now this was Jim's especial foible,
He ran away when he was able,
And on this _____ day
He slipped his hand and _____ away!

frequently / often
allowed / permitted

unlucky / inauspicious
hurried / ran

He hadn't gone a yard when—bang!
With open jaws, a lion _____,
And hungrily began to eat
The boy: _____ at his feet.
Now just _____ how it feels
When _____ your toes and then
  your heels,
And then by gradual degrees,
Your shins and ankles, calves and knees,
Are _____ eaten, bit by bit.

sprang / leapt

beginning / commencing
imagine / guess
initially / first

gradually / slowly

No wonder Jim _____ it!
No wonder that he _____ "Hi!"
The honest keeper heard his cry,
Though very _____, he almost ran
To help the little gentleman.
"Ponto!" he cried, with _____ frown
"Let go, sir! Down, sir! Put it down!"
The lion having reached his head,
The _____ boy was dead!

loathed / detested
shouted / screamed

fat / overweight

furious / angry

miserable / unfortunate

When nurse _____ his parents they
Were more _____ than I can say.
His mother, as she dried her eyes,
Said, "Well—it gives me no _____,
He would not do as he was told!"
His father, who was _____,
Bade all the _____ round attend
To James' miserable _____,
And always keep a-hold of nurse
For fear of finding something worse.

told / informed
concerned / upset

shock / surprise

reserved / self-controlled
kids / children
fate / end

EVERYDAY ENGLISH
Metaphors and idioms—the body

1 Complete the sentences with a part of the body.

> Your _____ is associated with intelligence.
> Your _____ are associated with manual skills.
> Your _____ is associated with emotions.

2 In which one of these sentences is the word in *italics* used literally? Rephrase the words used metaphorically.

1. Can you give me a *hand* with this sofa? It's so heavy.
2. She's so smart. She's *heading* for great things in life.
3. But she's not at all *bigheaded*.
4. We shook *hands* and introduced ourselves.
5. My daughter has a very good *head* for business.
6. I'd offer to help, but I've got my *hands* full at the moment.
7. I know she shouts a lot, but she's really got a *heart* of gold.
8. We had a *heart-to-heart* talk, and things are much clearer now.
9. My parents wanted me to be a lawyer, but my *heart* wasn't in it. Now I'm a journalist.

3 Complete the sentences with one of these expressions.

> face the fact   putting a brave face   on its last legs   goes to their head
> pulling your leg   getting back on his feet   a sharp tongue

1. My car's been driven over 200,000 miles. It's _____ now. I'll have to buy a new one.
2. With so many celebrities success _____, and they start to believe they're really special.
3. She's being very courageous and _____ on it, but I know she's in a lot of pain.
4. He lost everything when his business failed, but he's got a new job now and he's _____.
5. I'm almost 75. I simply have to _____ that I'm not as young as I was.
6. "Oh no! I forwarded your e-mail complaining about work to the boss!" "Are you serious?" "No, I'm just _____."
7. "Sue says some really cruel things." "Yes, she's got _____."

4 Look up another part of the body in your dictionary. Find one or two useful idioms or metaphorical uses. Explain them to the rest of the class.

In your dreams

Grammar: Hypothesizing • Expressions with *if*
Vocabulary: Word pairs
Everyday English: Moans and groans

TEST YOUR GRAMMAR

1 Helen is feeling very sorry for herself. Read column **A**. What are her problems?

2 Join a line in **A** with a wish in **B**.

3 Write down one thing you're not happy about. Tell the class what you wish.

A		B
1. It's raining again. 2. I'm not going out tonight. 3. There's nothing good on TV. 4. I don't like my job. 5. My girlfriend and I broke up last week. 6. I know he won't call me. 7. I feel really depressed. 8. I can't talk to anyone about it.	I wish	I was. I did. I didn't. I could. he would. there was. it wasn't. we hadn't.

IF ONLY...
Hypothesizing about the past and present

1 Look at the photos. Each one illustrates someone's regret or wish. What do you think the regret or wish is?

2 **CD3** **17** Listen to the people talking. Who says what? Number the pictures in the order you hear.

c.

a.

b.

3 **CD3** **17** Listen again and complete the lines. Who is speaking?

1. I shouldn't have …
   If only I hadn't …
   I wouldn't worry …

2. If only we could …
   That would …
   I'd just …
   Sometimes I wish …

3. What would you give … ?
   Which one would you choose if … ?
   . . . if I won the lottery, I'd …
   I wouldn't—I'd …

4. Don't you wish you … ?
   But *you* could have …

5. I shouldn't have …
   Come on, couldn't you … ?
   Supposing you …

4 Work with a partner. Use the lines in Exercise 3 to help you remember the conversations. Practice them.

5 What are the facts behind some of the wishes and regrets?
I shouldn't have gone out last night.
She did go out last night. She went to a party.

d.

e.

GRAMMAR SPOT

Hypothesizing—past and present

1 All of these sentences are hypothetical. That is, they imagine changing certain facts. What are the facts?
   a. *I wish I* **knew** *the answer.* **I don't know the answer.**
   b. *If only I* **could come** *to the party.*
   c. *If only I'***d told** *the truth.*
   d. *If I* **didn't get** *so nervous, I'***d get** *better results.*
   e. *If you'***d helped** *us, we'***d have finished** *by now.*
   f. *I* **should have listened** *to your advice.*
   g. *I wish I* **spoke** *French well.*
   h. *I wish you* **would speak** *to him.*

2 Which of the sentences are about present time? Which are about past time?

3 Look at sentences c, d, and e. What are the full forms of the contractions *I'd*, *you'd*, and *we'd*?

4 Other expressions are also used to hypothesize. Complete the sentences with the facts.

   It's time you **knew** the truth. The fact is that you . . .
   I'd rather you **didn't eat candy**. The fact is that you . . .
   I'd rather they **hadn't come**. The fact is that they . . .
   Supposing you'**d fallen** and **hurt** yourself! Fortunately, you . . .

▶▶ Grammar Reference 11.1 p. 147

PRACTICE

1 Express a wish or regret about these facts. Use the words in parentheses.

1. I don't speak English fluently. (*wish*)
   I wish I spoke English fluently.

2. You speak very fast. I don't understand. (*if*)

3. I'm an only child. (*wish*)

4. We don't have enough money to go on vacation. (*if only*)

5. I get up at six o'clock every morning. I have to go to work. (*wouldn't/if*)

6. I didn't learn to ski until I was 40. I'm not very good. (*if*)

7. My 13-year-old sister wants to be older. (*she wishes*)

8. My best friend always borrows my things without asking. (*I'd rather*)

9. I don't know anything about computers. I can't help you. (*if*)

10. We want to take a break. (*it's time*)

Broken dreams

2 Read Marty and Carrie's sad story. Explain the title.

If only they'd known!

CARRIE AND I were on vacation in Vanuatu in the South Pacific. It's really beautiful there, and one day we went for a walk and saw this house for sale. It was on a cliff overlooking a bay, and you can imagine, the views were absolutely fantastic. We just fell in love with it. We had to have it—so we bought it then and there, and the next day we hired an architect to redesign our dream vacation home. That evening we celebrated, and in the middle of the night, we were fast asleep when suddenly we were thrown from our beds. The room was shaking—it was the biggest earthquake that had ever hit the region. But the worst was still to come, because the next morning when we drove out to check our newly bought house, we found that the whole cliff had fallen into the sea. We lost every cent we had.

3 Use these words to form sentences about Marty and Carrie's story.

1. Marty and Carrie shouldn't/buy the house/that day.
2. If they/not buy/the house/their life/very different.
3. If they/contact the owner of the house/he might/give them/money back.
4. What/happen/if they/wait a few days more?
5. Supposing they/not go on vacation/to Vanuatu?

4 Work with a partner and complete these sentences about Marty and Carrie.

1. If they'd known that ...
2. They should have ...
3. They shouldn't have ...
4. If they hadn't ...
5. They wish they ...

Compare your answers with the class.

5 Form the question and answer it.

What/happen/if there/not be/earthquake?

Talking about you

6 What do you wish was different about your life? Make a wish list about some of these things and discuss it with other students.

My wish list			
• home • social life • money	If only	I you he	was/were . . . wasn't/weren't . . . did/didn't . . .
• family • work • relationships	I wish	she we	had/hadn't . . . could . . .
• friends • vacations		they	would/wouldn't . . .

SPOKEN ENGLISH Expressions with *if*

There are many fixed expressions with *if* often found in spoken English. Match a line in **A** with one in **B**.

A	B
1. Would it be OK if	if you've got a minute?
2. Win? What do you mean? If you ask me,	I'd never forgive myself.
3. If you knew what I know,	If anything, he's a little shy.
4. Could I have a word with you	I left a little early today?
5. If anything went wrong,	we can always postpone it.
6. If all goes well,	you'd never go out with him again.
7. It was a Thursday, not a Tuesday,	if any.
8. Well, if worse comes to worst,	they don't stand a chance.
9. You haven't made much progress,	we should be finished by Friday.
10. I don't think he's cold or arrogant.	if I remember correctly.

CD3 18 Listen to the conversations and check. What extra lines do you hear? What are the contexts? Practice with a partner.

VOCABULARY AND PRONUNCIATION
Word pairs

> There are many pairs of words joined by a conjunction.
> The order of the words is fixed.
>
> **1** Read these sentences aloud.
> **Each and every week** he bought a ticket.
> To his **shock and horror** he saw her on TV.
>
> **2** Complete these well-known ones.
> Life's full of **ups and** _____.
> There are always **pros and** _____ in any argument.
> We'll find out the truth **sooner or** _____.

1 Match a word pair with a definition.

A	B
1. off and on	a. compromise/be flexible
2. wait and see	b. occasionally
3. ins and outs	c. be patient and find out later
4. give and take	d. generally speaking
5. by and large	e. exact details
6. grin and bear it	f. accept it or refuse, I don't care.
7. odds and ends	g. tolerate it as best you can
8. take it or leave it	h. things

2 Complete the sentences with a word pair from above.

1. In any relationship you have to be prepared to _____.
   You can't have your own way all the time.
2. I didn't buy much at the mall. Just a few _____ for the kids.
   Socks for Ben and hairbands for Jane.
3. I'd been visiting Florida _____ for years before I finally moved there.
4. It's difficult to explain the _____ of the rules of baseball. It's so complicated.
5. "What did you get me for my birthday?" "You'll have to _____."
6. "Oh, no! The Burtons are coming for lunch! I hate their kids!"
   "I'm sorry, but you'll just have to _____. It's only for an hour or so."
7. OK, you can have it for $90. That's my final offer, _____.
8. California has lots of faults, of course, but _____, it's a nice place to live.

CD3 19 Listen and check.

3 Work with a partner. Match a word in **A** with a word in **B** and a word in **C**. Look for synonyms and antonyms.

A			B	C		
now	sick	more	and	tired	quiet	sound
touch	peace	safe	but	surely	then	go
slowly	then		or	there	less	

Try to put each pair into a sentence. Read the sentences aloud to the class.

4 **CD3 20** Listen to a conversation between two friends. What are they talking about? Write down all the word pairs you hear.

5 Look at the conversation on page 153. Practice it with your partner.

READING AND SPEAKING
Have you ever wondered?

1 As you go through your day, do you ever wonder about things? Have you ever puzzled over these questions? Discuss them in groups. Which can you answer? Make notes of your ideas.

1. **Why do we dream?**
2. **Why are some people left-handed?**
3. **Where do the oceans come from?**
4. **Is time travel possible?**
5. **What would happen if there was no dust?**
6. **What is the origin of the @ symbol ?**

2 Read the answers to the questions on pp. 94–95. Check your ideas and discuss them with your group.

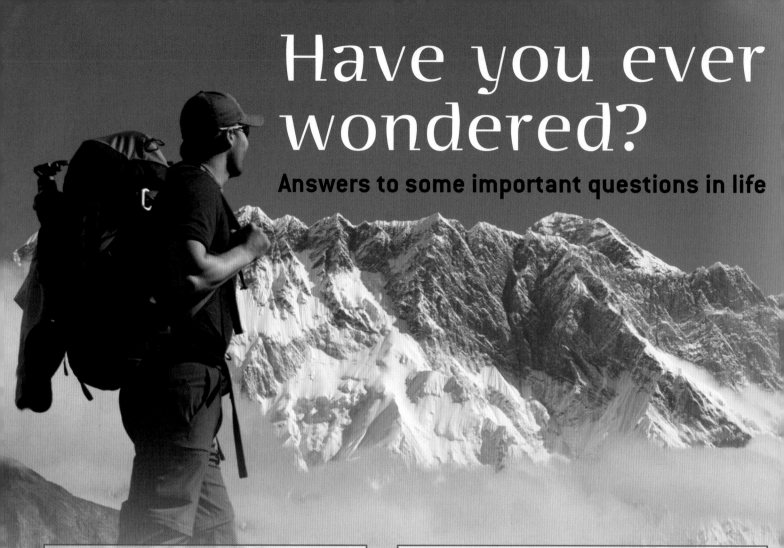

Have you ever wondered?

Answers to some important questions in life

1 Why do we dream?

Two different schools of thought exist as to why we dream: the physiological school and the psychological school. Both, however, agree that we dream during the REM, or rapid eye movement, phase of sleep. During this phase of sleep, our closed eyes dart rapidly around and our brain activity peaks.

The physiological theory centers upon how our brains function during the REM phase. Those who believe this theory say that we dream to exercise the brain cells. When awake, our brains constantly transmit and receive messages and keep our bodies in perpetual motion. Dreams replace this function.

Psychological theorists of dreams focus on our thoughts and emotions and say that dreams deal with immediate concerns in our lives, such as unfinished business from the day. Dreams can, in fact, (1)___. Connections between dreams and the human psyche have been made for thousands of years. The Greek philosopher Aristotle wrote in his *Parva Naturalia*, over 2,200 years ago, of a connection between dreams and emotional needs. Sweet dreams!

2 Why are some people left handed?

About 10% of the population is left-handed, and it seems to run in families. The cause, therefore, seems obvious: genetics. However, identical twins, who have identical genetic blueprints, aren't necessarily both left-handed or right-handed. This would appear to disprove the theory that being left-handed is inherited.

Even at birth, most babies tend to move one arm, usually the right, more than the other. Some scientists believe that the use of the left hand or the right hand is a result of the baby's environment. Most children (2)___ the right hand for any activity. However, the wisdom of this training is questionable.

3 Where do the oceans come from?

While the world's seas and oceans have been home to life for over 3 billion years, the origin of the 1.4 billion tons of water that they contain remains a mystery. It seems to have condensed out of the earth's atmosphere, (3)___.
One possible theory is that it was dropped on our planet by comets. These gigantic chunks of frozen vapor and dust are rich in water. According to some scientists, satellite pictures have shown that tiny comets continue to hit the earth, filling up our oceans all the time.

4 Is time travel possible?

Amazingly, there is nothing in the known laws of physics to prevent us from zooming off into the past or future. Exactly how one would build a time machine is anyone's guess, but many scientists have a bigger worry—paradoxes such as killing your mother before she gave birth to you. Maybe Nature has a clever way (4)___, but just think! If at any time in the future time travel becomes possible, then time travelers are with us now! And if this is the case, then they've always been with us!

5 What would happen if there was no dust?

Most of us who have ever cleaned a house would be much happier if there was less dust. However, without dust there would be less rainfall, and sunsets would be less beautiful. Rain is formed when water molecules in the air collect around particles of dust. When the collected water becomes heavy enough (5)___. Thus water vapor would be much less likely to turn to rain without the dust particles.

The water vapor and dust particles also reflect the rays of the sun. At sunrise and sunset, when the sun is below the horizon, the dust and water vapor molecules reflect the longer, red rays of light in such a way that we can see them for more time. The more dust particles in the air, the more colorful the sunrise or sunset.

6 What is the origin of the @ symbol?

The most common theory that the little @ in e-mail addresses, commonly referred to as the "at sign," stemmed from the tired hands of medieval monks. During the Middle Ages, before the invention of printing presses, every letter of a word had to be painstakingly transcribed by hand in Latin for each copy of a book. The monks that performed these tedious copying duties looked for ways to reduce the number of individual strokes for common words. Although *ad*, a Latin word for *at*, is quite short, it was so common that the monks thought it would be quicker and easier to shorten it even more. As a result, they looped the "d" around the "a" and eliminated two strokes of the pen.

With the introduction of e-mail the popularity of the @ symbol grew. (6)___. For instance, *joe@uselessknowledge.com*. There is no one universal name for the sign, but countries have found different ways to describe it. Several languages use words that associate the shape with some type of animal. These include:

snabel—Danish for "elephant's trunk"
klammeraffe—German for "hanging monkey"
papaki—Greek for "little duck"
kukac—Hungarian for "worm"
dalphaengi—Korean for "snail"
grisehale—Norwegian for "pig's tail"
sobachka—Russian for "little dog"

Reading

3 Read the texts again. These lines have been removed from them. Which text does each come from?

   a. but how it got there in the first place isn't known

   b. It separates a person's online user name from their mail server address.

   c. can be trained to use and prefer

   d. the water droplets fall to the earth as rain

   e. teach us things about ourselves that we are unaware of

   f. of getting around these

4 Answer the questions.

1. What does REM stand for?
2. What kind of things do dreams deal with?
3. Why could genetics explain left-handedness? What is the reason against this explanation?
4. What do comets consist of?
5. According to the laws of physics, is it possible to travel in time?
6. What worries many scientists about time travel?
7. What would happen to rain and sunsets if there was no dust?
8. Why did the monks invent the @ symbol?
9. What is the @ symbol called in different languages?

Vocabulary work

Find the highlighted words in the texts. Try to figure out their meaning from the contexts.

What do you think?

- Which questions did you find most interesting?

- Which facts were new to you? Which did you already know? Use some of these phrases to express your reactions.

I already knew that . . .	Did you know that . . .?
What surprised me was . . .	Everyone knows that . . .
I don't believe that . . .	I had no idea that . . .

- What do *you* call the @ sign? Which language's animal words do you think best describe it?

- Small children often ask lots of "Why" questions.

  Why is the grass green?   Why doesn't our cat talk to me?

Think of some good "Why" questions about the world. In pairs, try to answer them as if you were talking to a child. (Kids will often answer with another "Why?" question!)

Why doesn't our cat talk to me? — Because cats can't talk.
Why can't cats talk? — Because . . .

LISTENING AND SPEAKING
The interpretation of dreams

1 Everybody dreams, but some people remember their dreams better than others. Discuss these questions in groups.

1. Did you dream last night? Can you remember anything about it?
2. What often happens when you wake up from a dream and try to describe it to someone?
3. What do you think are common themes in dreams?

2 Read these descriptions of dreams. Discuss what you think each dream might mean.

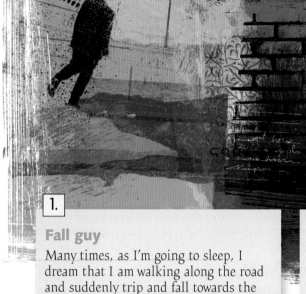

1.

Fall guy
Many times, as I'm going to sleep, I dream that I am walking along the road and suddenly trip and fall towards the pavement. I always wake up before I hit the ground. Why do I dream this?

J.H., SEATTLE, WASHINGTON

2.

Underneath it all
My dreams are often set in a small decaying cellar. I always wake up feeling bad about life when this happens. What does this dream mean?

D. J., WINNIPEG, CANADA

3.

Hidden treasure
I am digging in the garden of my childhood home and uncover a box of treasure. My life has been pretty bad lately. Does my dream indicate a change for the better?

P.T., SWINDON, UK

3 Read the interpretations of the dreams on page 154. Which do you think goes with each dream? Why? Compare them with your ideas.

4 **CD3 21** Listen to Paul describing a dream. What is really strange about the dream? Are these statements true or false? Correct the false ones.

1. Paul describes himself as a sensible, rational person.
2. The dream took place in his hometown.
3. In the dream, he and his girlfriend had arranged to meet in front of the station.
4. His girlfriend had a similar dream.
5. His girlfriend had never visited his hometown.
6. He believes their dreams were the result of a TV program they'd been watching.

Language work

Read the audio script on page 133.

1. Find four things in the story that Paul describes as *strange*.
2. Find other words which are similar in meaning to *strange*.

What do you think?

- Discuss Paul's dream in your groups and try to interpret it. Share your ideas with the class.
- Describe any memorable dreams that you have had.
- Do you ever have the same dream or dreams with common features?

▶▶ **WRITING** Narrative writing 2—Linking words and expressions *p. 118*

EVERYDAY ENGLISH

Moans and groans

It's not fair!
What a pain!
I don't believe it!

1 Read the complaints in **A**. Match them with a response in **B**. Which of the items in the box do they refer to?

> a leather jacket   e-mail   boots   ordering by phone
> a bookcase   a TV program   a package   a test

	A		B
1.	*e* I could kick myself. As soon as I'd handed it in, I remembered what the answer was. *a test*		a. What a pain! Have you tried calling the computer helpline?
2.	☐ I can't believe it! I've spent all morning trying to send this, and *all I get* is, "Ooops! Your message wasn't sent. Try again later."		b. Go easy on me! I was in a hurry. Anyway, they're not *that* muddy.
3.	☐ These instructions don't make any sense to me at all. If you can follow them, you're a genius.		c. I'm very sorry, sir. I'm afraid there's nothing I can do about it. It's out of my hands.
4.	☐ It's not fair. I'd been looking forward to watching it all day and then the phone goes and rings!		d. I know, it drives me crazy. But worse still is that you never get to speak to a real person anyway!
5.	☐ How many times do I have to tell you? Take them off *before* you come into the house!		e. Oh, I hate it when that happens! But do you think you still passed?
6.	☐ You've got to be kidding. You promised you'd deliver it by Thursday at the latest. Now you're saying next week!		f. It's such a shame. It would have gone so well with your white jeans.
7.	☐ I went away to think about it, and of course, when I went back it was gone. I wish I'd just bought it then and there.		g. Don't ask me! I had exactly the same trouble trying to put together a nightstand.
8.	☐ What a waste of time! Ten minutes listening to music and, "All our lines are busy. Thank you for waiting."		h. Typical! And who was it? Anyone interesting?

2 **CD3 22** Listen and check your answers. Read them aloud with a partner and add another line.

> **A** I could kick myself. As soon as I'd handed it in, I remembered what the answer was.
> **B** Oh, I hate it when that happens! But do you think you still passed?
> **A** Who knows? I'll just have to wait and see.

Music *of* English ♪♪

When people moan about something, there is an exaggeration on the rise and fall of the word with the main stress.

I don't believe it!   *It's not fair!*

CD3 23 Listen and repeat.

3 What are some of the events in a typical day in your life? For each event think of something to moan about.

What a pain! I got up and had to wait forever before the shower was free. But worse still, the water was freezing cold!

4 Do you have any moans and groans about anything that's happened recently in your country or in the world?

"Press 1 for classical, press 2 for easy listening, press 3 for jazz."

12 It's never too late

TEST YOUR GRAMMAR

1 Tell the story of Mary's grandfather, matching a line from **A** with a line from **C**. Use the correct article from **B** to connect the lines. Tell the story to a partner.

My grandfather used to be a judge. He retired ...

2 **CD3 24** Listen and check. What extra information do you hear?

A	B	C
1. My grandfather used to be		dinner with him.
2. He retired		captain of the ship.
3. He decided to go on		ocean cruise.
4. He enjoyed	a/an	cruise very much.
5. He sailed all around	one	year before last.
6. He met	the	judge.
7. He invited her to have	*no article*	love at any age.
8. They got along really well with		another.
9. My grandfather says you can find		world.
10. They were married by		attractive widow.

THE PACE OF LIFE
Articles and determiners

1 Take the quiz about your pace of life. Discuss your answers with a partner. Turn to page 154 and find out what kind of person you are. Do you agree?

2 Find these highlighted words in the quiz. Underline the nouns that follow. Which are followed by *of*?

enough	the whole	all	each	plenty
a great deal	hardly any	several	none	
no	(a) few	(a) little	most	every

3 These lines are similar to those in the quiz, but not the same. Find them in the quiz. What are the differences?

1. I leave sufficient time for relaxation.
2. Nonstop all of the time.
3. More than enough things.
4. Lots of enthusiasm.
5. Very few, just a couple of minor things.
6. There aren't any uncompleted projects.
7. I see every one of my projects through to the end.
8. I don't have any patience.
9. I have hardly any hobbies or leisure time.
10. In quite a few ways.
11. In all kinds of ways.
12. Nearly all of the time by e-mail.

How well do you

1 **How would you describe the pace of your life?**
   a. Easygoing. I just take life as it comes.
   b. Pretty fast, but I leave enough time for relaxation.
   c. At times frantic, at times relaxed.
   d. Nonstop the whole time, but I like it that way.

2 **How do you tackle all the things you have to do each day?**
   a. I do the things I feel like doing, but there aren't many of those.
   b. I prioritize. I do the important things and put off all the other stuff.
   c. There's either not enough time to do every little thing or too much time with nothing to do. I find this difficult.
   d. I have a daily "to do" list that I check off after each item is completed.

3 **How many things have you begun and not finished in the last few years?**
   a. Plenty of things. I begin with a great deal of enthusiasm but then get bored.
   b. Hardly any, just one or two minor things.
   c. Several things. Sometimes I get distracted and move from one thing to another.
   d. None. There are no uncompleted projects in my life. I see each of my projects through to the end before I start the next.

4 When do you switch off your cell phone?
a. Do most people have cell phones these days? I haven't gotten around to getting one yet.
b. In some public places and when I need some peace and quiet.
c. Not as often as I should.
d. Only if I have to.

5 How punctual are you?
a. I don't waste time worrying about it.
b. Being late is impolite and inefficient, so I try to be punctual.
c. I like to be on time in theory, but in practice I'm often late.
d. I'm always on time. I have no patience with people who are late.

use your time?

6 How do you spend your leisure time?
a. Doing a little of this and a little of that. I don't know where my time goes.
b. I recharge my batteries with a few hobbies and by being with friends.
c. I keep trying different things that people suggest, but nothing really grabs me.
d. I have few hobbies and little leisure time. I try to put all of my time to good use.

7 How do you keep in touch with friends?
a. I wait for them to get in touch with me.
b. In several ways—e-mails, text messages—but I also like to call them for a nice chat.
c. In any way I can—but it can be difficult. I think, "I must contact X," but time passes, and I realize I haven't.
d. Most of the time by e-mail. It's quick and efficient.

8 Which of these is closest to your philosophy on life?
a. Whatever will be will be.
b. Life is not a dress rehearsal.
c. There is a season for everything.
d. Seize the day.

4 What is the difference between these pairs of sentences?

| I have a few hobbies. | I have a little leisure time. |
| I have few hobbies. | I have little leisure time. |

5 Is there a difference in meaning between these sentences?

| I completed **each** project. | I completed **every** project. |

Which can mean you had only two projects? Which *can't* mean you had only two projects? Which can mean you had lots of projects?

GRAMMAR SPOT

Determiners

Determiners help identify nouns and express quantity.

1 Look at the examples. Which determiners go with which nouns? Which group expresses quantity?

the other another many other his only such a what a	book books good book

both neither each/every little all the whole no	book books time

2 Determiners can join a noun using *of + the/my/ our/ this/that*, etc. What expressions can you make from these examples?

both neither each all some none	of	the my those	book books time

▶▶ **Grammar Reference 12.1 p. 148**

PRACTICE

Talking about you

1 Complete the sentences with determiners which make them true for you.

1. I have _____ time to relax.
2. _____ my friends think I work too hard.
3. _____ my teachers think I work hard.
4. I spent _____ weekend relaxing.
5. I have _____ interests and hobbies.
6. _____ my hobbies are sports.
7. _____ my parents look like me.
8. _____ my relatives have fair hair.
9. My aunt gives _____ us birthday presents.
10. My grandparents watch TV _____ time.

Discussing grammar

2 Work with a partner. What is the difference in meaning between these pairs of sentences?

1. I spoke to all the students in the class.
   I spoke to each student in the class.
2. None of them knew the answer.
   Neither of them knew the answer.
3. The doctor's here.
   A doctor's here.
4. There's a man at the door.
   There's some man at the door.
5. There's a pair of socks missing.
   There's a couple of socks missing.
6. Whole families were evacuated from their homes.
   All the families were evacuated from their homes.

3 Match a line in **A** with a line in **B**.

A	B
Would you like Do all birds lay Where did I put	eggs? the egg? an egg?

A	B
I have two cars. Borrow It was great to see I have five nieces. I gave $10 to	each one. everyone. either one.

A	B
Love A love The love	I have for you is forever. is everything. of animals is vital for a vet.
Both All Every	my friends like dancing. person in my class is friendly. my parents are Canadian.

4 **CD3 25** Listen and respond to the lines with a sentence from Exercise 3.

> Do any of your friends like dancing?

> What do you mean, "any?"
> All my friends like dancing!

CD3 26 Listen and check. Pay particular attention to stress and intonation. Look at the audio script on page 134 and practice the conversations with a partner.

SPOKEN ENGLISH Using demonstratives and determiners

Demonstratives and determiners are often found in idiomatic language. Look at these examples of the demonstratives *this*, *that*, *these*, and *those* from the quiz on page 98.

> (I like) doing a little of *this* and a little of *that*.
> Most people have cell phones *these days*.
> . . . but there aren't many of *those*.

Find examples of the determiners *each*, *every*, and *all* in the quiz.

5 **Demonstratives—*this / that / these / those***
Complete the sentences with the correct demonstrative.

1. What's _____ song you're singing?
2. Look at _____ ladybug on my hand!
3. Did you hear _____ storm in the middle of the night?
4. Mmm! _____ strawberries are delicious!
5. Take _____ dirty shoes off! I've just cleaned in here.
6. I can't stand _____ weather. It's really getting me down.
7. Who was _____ man you were talking to _____ morning?
8. Do you remember when we were young? _____ were the days!
9. Children have no respect for authority _____ days, do they?

CD3 27 Listen and check.

6 **Determiners—*each, every,* or *all***
CD3 28 Listen to some short conversations. What is each about? Complete the replies. They all contain expressions with *each*, *every*, or *all*. Practice the conversations with a partner.

1. **A** What was the meal like?
   B _____
2. **A** Did you apologize to all the guests?
   B _____
3. **A** They didn't all pass, did they?
   B _____
4. **A** Sorry, I only have 50 cents on me.
   B _____
5. **A** When do you think you'll get there?
   B _____
6. **A** Want to grab a bite to eat?
   B _____

 WRITING Adding emphasis in writing—People of influence *p. 119*

LISTENING AND SPEAKING
Happy days

1 Work in small groups. What is the average life expectancy in your country? Suggest ages for these stages of life. What is typical behavior for each stage? Give examples and discuss with the whole class.

0	–	☐ infancy
☐	–	☐ childhood
☐	–	☐ teenage years
☐	–	☐ young adulthood
☐	–	☐ middle age
☐	–	☐ old age

2 You are going to listen to Bernie, Hayley, Tony, and Tommy talking about themselves. Here are some of the things they said (two for each person). Which stage of life do you think they are at?

1. I want to see the world, meet lots of people, get a good career before I settle down.
2. This time though, after the operation I knew right away it would be OK.
3. We have buckets and shovels.
4. Lizzie and I are content just to putter in the vegetable garden, or cut the grass, or weed the flower beds.
5. Most of us just go for the dancing.
6. I think the world has gone to pot.
7. It's got big, big wheels, hugest wheels ever.
8. These days the only thing that makes me unhappy is meeting people who don't realize what a gift life is.

3 **CD3 29** Listen to the four people. After each one discuss these questions.

1. At which stage of life is the person?
2. Which lines in Exercise 2 did he or she say?
3. What does the person do or say that is typical or not typical for their age?
4. What makes the person happy or unhappy?

What do you think?

- Which stage of life do you think is the best or worst? Why?
- Are there advantages and disadvantages for each stage? Discuss.
- Do you know people who you think are typical or not typical for their age? Are you?

READING AND SPEAKING
You're never too old

1 What age do you consider to be old? Think of some "old" people you know.

> How old are they?
> What are they like?
> What do they do every day?
> Which of these are typical for old people?
> - having trouble sleeping
> - liking routine
> - going to college
> - studying foreign languages
> - going to church
> - talking about the past
> - losing your memory
> - using the Internet
> - living in the center of a city
> - watching TV

2 Read the text quickly. Which of the activities in Exercise 1 are part of Mary Hobson's life? Explain the title, "A Life in the Day."

3 Read the text again. Find the highlighted lines and answer the questions about them.

1. l.04 What is "it?" Why does "it" do this?
2. l.10 What is "it?" How did Marcus Aurelius help Mary?
3. l.22 What does she work at for nothing? What does this imply about Mary's lifestyle?
4. l.24 Who is "he?" Who is "some old bat?"
5. l.30 What was hell for who? What did Mary do about it?
6. l.35 What was the session? What did Mary do in it?
7. l.47 Is "the time of your life" a good or bad time? What was the time of Mary's life?
8. l.55 Why do they think this?
9. l.65 What is "it?" What does Mary mean by this?
10. l.67 What is "it?" Why does she sleep so badly?

A life in the day

Mary Hobson, 77, gained a degree in Russian in her sixties and a PhD at 74. A mother of four, she lives in south London.

I've started to learn ancient Greek. It doesn't urge you to
05 communicate, only to learn, and I find the early hours of the morning the perfect time for that. I love ritual and routine. I wait until 6 a.m. to have tea; at 7 a.m. I phone my youngest daughter, and we start the day with a chat. At 7:30 I make breakfast—All-Bran, wholewheat toast, and a pot of black
10 coffee—and I take it back to bed along with the Roman emperor Marcus Aurelius.

I am a dedicated atheist. I regard religion as complete lunacy. You've got only one opportunity to be alive: for goodness' sake don't waste it waiting for an afterlife. I read Marcus Aurelius every
15 day; it was his philosophy that got me through my son Matthew's death four years ago in a motorcycle accident. Aurelius said: "What we cannot bear removes us from life." Matthew's death was such a waste. At first I would rather have been dead too, but then I thought: "No. I mustn't do less. I must do more!"

20 After a bath I spend the morning translating. A special committee was convened to organize the translation of the works of Pushkin for his centenary. Unpaid, of course. I'm an expert at working for nothing. Poor old Pushkin: some of his letters were scandalous. Really very rude indeed. How was he to know that, 200 years
25 later, some old bat would be poring over every line?

I am what you might call a late developer. I was 40 before I wrote my first novel, 62 when I went to college. My husband, Neil, was a talented jazz musician, but at 25 he developed a cerebral abscess, losing his speech and the use of the right side of his
30 body. It was hell for him and a nightmare for us. We were so broke we lived on government assistance for ages. When things got really bad, I'd collect up old china and give it to the children to smash out their frustrations on the wall outside.

I wrote my first novel while Neil had his weekly music therapy.
35 That 50-minute session was all I had. I used to sit in the ABC cafe in Earls Court and write and write while couples had life-and-death quarrels around me. Neil was terribly difficult. None of it was his fault, of course, but after 28 years I thought: "It's not my fault either." I was going down with him. I left, and Matthew stayed
40 with him to stop me from going back—I was very grateful for that.

Having snatched a bit of life back, I had to do something with it. My daughter Emma gave me *War and Peace*, and I loved it so much. Then it hit me: I hadn't read it at all, I'd only read a translation, and I so longed to read the actual words. A marvelous elderly
45 Russian lady taught me the basics, and I enrolled in the Russian-

Mary Hobson

by Caroline Scott

WINNER OF THE PUSHKIN GOLD MEDAL FOR TRANSLATION

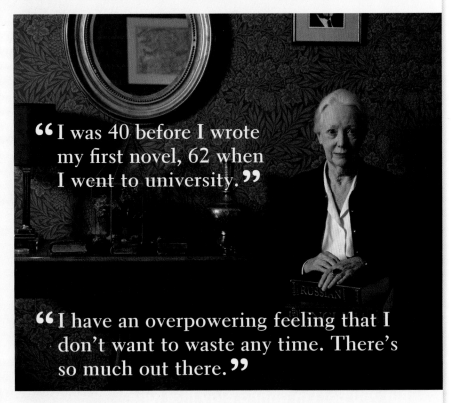

" I was 40 before I wrote my first novel, 62 when I went to university. "

" I have an overpowering feeling that I don't want to waste any time. There's so much out there. "

language degree course at the University of London. People talk about "the time of their lives." Well, that was mine. Don't let anyone tell you your memory goes with age. It's there if you want it enough. Gradually I forced it into action—it was such
50 an exhilarating experience. Oh, the joy of learning!

I have such good friends. After a late lunch, I might go and play Scrabble with a Russian lady. I write poetry en route, on buses and trains. I love London. Give me the town over the country any day. I try to go to Moscow every year in the coldest weather.
55 My Russian friends think I'm mad; it hits minus 40 and they find it hellish. I adore lying in bed listening to snow being scraped from the pavements.

I have an overpowering feeling that I don't want to waste any time. There's so much out there. I won't be able to get
60 around forever, so when I can't stagger down my front steps, I'll perfect my Greek. I order my groceries on the Internet, so I have everything sent. As long as I have my books I'll be happy.

If I'm not going out, I make supper and get into bed, simply because my feet are awful. Then I phone everyone I can think of.
65 I can't bear TV—it makes me feel as if everyone else is living and I'm only watching. I don't have a newspaper; I get my news through the radio. I sleep rottenly, so I have it on all night. Dreams are horrendous. Mine are all about anxiety and loss. I much prefer the day—at least you know you're in charge. "

Language work

There is *one* mistake in each of these sentences. Find it and discuss why it is wrong with a partner. Check your answers in the text.

1. I make breakfast and I take it back to the bed.
2. I am a dedicated atheist. My husband was talented jazz musician.
3. You've got only an opportunity to be alive.
4. I enrolled in the Russian-language degree course at University of London.
5. I try to go to Moscow every year in coldest weather.
6. Having snatched a bit of the life back, I had to do something with it.
7. Give me the town over a country.
8. I make supper and get into bed, simply because the feet are awful.

What do you think?

- It's easy to think of all the advantages of being young and the disadvantages of being old. But try it the other way around. Work in two groups.

  Group A List all the disadvantages of being young.

  Group B List all the advantages of being old.

- Find a partner from the other group and discuss your lists.
- Discuss as a class. What do you think is the best age to be in life?

VOCABULARY AND LISTENING
Hot words—*life* and *time*

1 Work with a partner. Complete the expressions below with either the word *life* or *time*. Use a dictionary to help.

Having the **time** of your **life**!	
not on your _____	you can bet your _____
take your _____	better luck next _____
get a _____	get a new lease on _____
kill _____	third _____'s the charm
it's high _____	for the _____ being
no _____ to lose	stand the test of _____
that's _____	live _____
on _____	in the nick of _____
any old _____	right on _____
a cushy _____	make good _____

2 Complete these lines with an expression from Exercise 1.

1. No need to hurry. Take …
2. For goodness' sake hurry up. There's no …
3. The operation was so successful that Grandpa got a new …
4. Shakespeare's writing is still relevant today. It's really stood …
5. I got to the bank in the … It was just about to close.
6. You can give them back any … I'm not going skiing again until next year.

3 **CD3 30** Listen to the conversations. What are the people talking about? Which of the expressions from Exercise 1 do you hear? Turn to page 135 and practice the conversations with your partner.

A song

4 **CD3 31** Close your books and listen to a song called "That's Life," by Robbie Williams. Then read the words on this page. There are many differences. Listen again and note them all.

5 **CD3 31** Listen again and sing along!

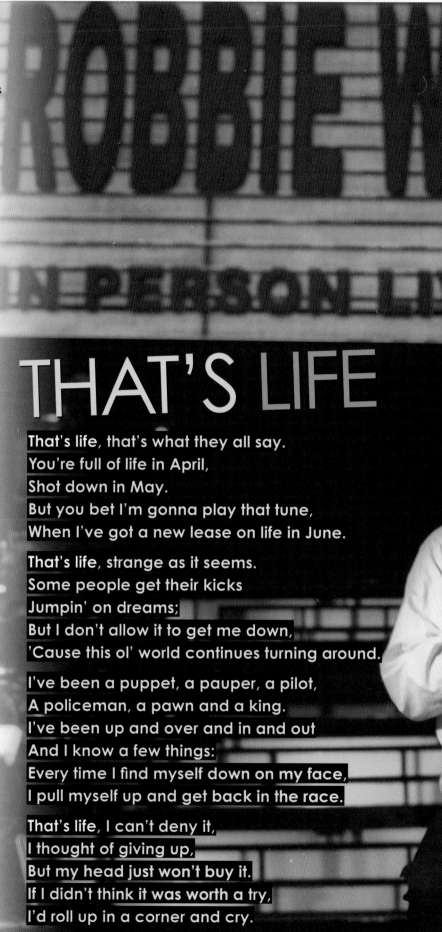

THAT'S LIFE

That's life, that's what they all say.
You're full of life in April,
Shot down in May.
But you bet I'm gonna play that tune,
When I've got a new lease on life in June.

That's life, strange as it seems.
Some people get their kicks
Jumpin' on dreams;
But I don't allow it to get me down,
'Cause this ol' world continues turning around.

I've been a puppet, a pauper, a pilot,
A policeman, a pawn and a king.
I've been up and over and in and out
And I know a few things:
Every time I find myself down on my face,
I pull myself up and get back in the race.

That's life, I can't deny it,
I thought of giving up,
But my head just won't buy it.
If I didn't think it was worth a try,
I'd roll up in a corner and cry.

EVERYDAY ENGLISH
Linking and commenting

1 Look at these lines from **CD3 29**. The expressions in **bold** link or comment on what has been said or what is going to be said. They are mainly adverbs.

Personally, I'm just happy to be alive. **Anyway**, I had some tests . . .
You see, I'd recently gotten married . . . **In fact**, my body rejected . . .

Find other examples from the audio scripts on pages 134–135.

2 Read these conversations. Choose the correct linking or commenting expression.

1. **A** Did you see the game last night?
   B No, but *apparently / obviously* it was a good one. We won, didn't we?
   A *Probably / Actually*, it was a tie, but it was really exciting.

2. **A** What do you think of Claire's new boyfriend?
   B *Personally / Certainly*, I can't stand him. I think he'll dump her like all the rest. *Ideally / However*, that's her problem, not mine.
   A Poor old Claire! She always picks the wrong ones, doesn't she? *Anyway / Honestly*, we'll find out soon enough.

3. **A** I don't know how you can afford to buy all those fabulous clothes!
   B *Still / Hopefully*, I'm going to get a bonus this month. My boss promised. *After all / Presumably*, I did earn the company over $100,000 last year. *Basically / Absolutely*, I deserve it.

4. **A** She said some terrible things to me. I hate her!
   B *Generally speaking / All the same*, I think you should apologize to her. *If you ask me / Apparently*, you lose your temper too easily. You're being very childish. It's time you both grew up!
   A What? I never thought I'd hear you speak to me like that.
   B *Still / Honestly*, I'm not taking sides. I just think you should make up.

5. **A** So, Billy. You say that this is the last record you're ever going to make?
   B *Surely / Definitely*.
   A But *surely / actually* you realize how upset your fans are going to be?
   B *Obviously / Hopefully*, I don't want to hurt anyone, but *certainly / basically*, I'm fed up with pop music. I'd like to do something else. *After all / Ideally*, I'd like to get into movies.

CD3 32 Listen and check your answers. Practice some of the conversations.

3 Complete these with a suitable line.
   1. They had a dreadful vacation. **Apparently, …**
   2. It should have been a happy marriage. **After all, …**
   3. I know you don't want to go to Harry's party. **All the same, …**
   4. I had the interview yesterday. **Hopefully, …**
   5. I'd rather you didn't let this go any further. **Obviously, …**
   6. I couldn't believe it, he just walked out and left her. **Presumably, …**
   7. I don't like flying very much. **As a matter of fact, …**
   8. So that's that. All's well that ends well. **Anyway, …**

Writing

1 What is a resume? What is the aim of one? Have you ever written one? What information did/would you include?

2 What is the purpose of a cover letter?

3 Write the headings from **A** in the correct spaces in the resume in **B**.

A

Achievements	Skills
Education	Work experience
References	Interests
~~Objective~~	

4 Answer the questions.

1. Where did Kate go to school?
2. What did she study in college?
3. Who is Prof. Jane Curtis?
4. Does she have a lot of work experience?

5 How is a resume different in your country?

B

Kate Henderson

132 Williams Street
Jamaica Plain, MA 02130
(617) 858-5366
katehenderson@yoohoo.com

Objective _____

A position at a school or camp that combines my experience working with children, my love of travel, and my degree in education and psychology.

_____

Boston University
BA, Psychology and Education
Summa cum laude

_____

March–June 2010
Teaching assistant, East Boston High School

June–August 2008
Swimming coach, KLC Swim Center, Boston

June–August 2007
Lifeguard, KLC Swim Center

_____

Dance, cooking, volleyball, travel, movies

_____

Boston University Honor Roll, 2007–2010
KLC Employee of the Month, 2007
Performed in regional dance festival, 2006

_____

Work well with children
Fluent written and spoken Spanish
Can use basic office software
Able to adapt to foreign cultures

_____

Prof. Jane Curtis
Dept of Education
Boston University
(617) 879-6875

Mike Benson
Manager
KLC Swim Center
(617) 355-7028

6 This is the job that Kate is applying for. Is she well qualified for it?

> **SPORTS CAMP COUNSELOR IN THE CANARY ISLANDS, SPAIN**
>
> *Are you …*
> - age 18–30?
> - energetic?
> - good at organizing people?
>
> *Do you …*
> - like kids?
> - like sports?
>
> **Then come and join us as a camp counselor for a spring break of fun, supervising groups of kids at sports camp!**
>
> **Send your resume to** Mark Smith at 106 Broadway, New York, NY 10005

7 Read Kate's cover letter. Which parts sound too informal? Replace them with the words on the right.

132 Williams Street
Jamaica Plain, MA 02130

Mark Smith
106 Broadway
New York, NY 10005

June 17, 2010

Dear Mark,

I am applying for the position of camp leader which I saw advertised somewhere recently. Here's my resume.

I guess I have just about everything needed for this job. I have worked lots with kids, doing all kinds of stuff. They generally do what I tell them, and we manage to have a great time together. Having studied psychology and education in college, I know quite a bit about the behavior of kids.

I am really into sports and have lots of experience organizing sporting events. I am a very practical person, easygoing, and it's no problem for me to make friends. I've been all over the place and enjoy meeting new people.

I can't wait to hear from you.

Your friend,

Kate Henderson

Kate Henderson

---

extensively with young adults

respect my leadership abilities

I find it easy

very interested in

have a strong understanding of

Enclosed please find

look forward to hearing

considerable

many of the relevant
   qualifications

have traveled widely

Mr. Smith

Sincerely,

in this Sunday's *Boston Globe*

feel

organizing a variety of activities

establish a good working relationship

Is this how a formal letter is laid out in your country? What are the differences?

8 Write your resume and a cover letter for a job that you would really like to do and are well qualified for.

1 Teachers sometimes use these symbols when correcting written work.

Correct the mistakes in these sentences.

1. I ∧ born in 1971 in <u>one</u> [WW] small town in Mexico.
2. My father is ∧ diplomat, so <u>my all life</u> [WO] I <u>live</u> [T] in <u>differents</u> [Gr] countries.
3. After t<u>he</u> [P] school, I went <u>for four years in</u> [WO] [T] a <u>busyness</u> [SP] college.
4. <u>I'm married</u> [T] <u>since</u> [Prep] five years. I <u>knew</u> [WW] my wife while I was a student.
5. My town <u>isnt</u> [P] as exciting <u>than</u> [WW] Miami. ∧ Is very <u>quite</u> [SP] <u>at</u> [Prep] the evening.
6. I <u>study</u> [T] English for five years. I <u>start</u> [T] when I <u>had</u> [WW] eleven years.
7. My father <u>wants that</u> [Gr] I work in a bank <u>becaus</u> [SP] ∧ is a good <u>work</u> [WW].
8. I <u>do</u> [T] <u>a</u> [Gr] evening course in English. I enjoy <u>very much</u> [WO] <u>to learn</u> [Gr] languages.

WW	Wrong word
SP	Spelling
T	Tense
Gr	Grammar
∧	Word missing
P	Punctuation
Prep	Preposition
WO	Word order
/	This word isn't necessary

2 Read the letter. Answer the questions.

1. Where was the letter written?
2. Who is the guest? Who is the host?
3. Which city is described? What is it like?
4. What season is it?

3 Work with a partner. Find the mistakes and put the symbols on the letter. Then correct the mistakes. The first line has been done to help you.

4 Write a letter (about 250 words).

Either …

You are going to stay with a family in an English-speaking country.

Or …

An English-speaking guest is coming to stay with you.

Give some information about yourself—your family, interests, school, town.

Check your work carefully for mistakes!

Avenida Campinas 361 ap. 45
01238-000 São Paulo SP Brasil

December 23

Dear James,

Thank you ∧ [T] your letter. I receive [Gr] it the last week. Sorry I no reply [T] you before ∧, but I've been very busy. It's Christmas soon, and everyone are very exciting!

In two weeks I am with you in California. I can no belief it! I looking forward meet you and your familly very much. I'm sure we will like us very well.

My city, São Paulo, is biggest and noisyest city in Brasil. Is not really for tourist. Is a center commercial. Also, it have very much pollution and traffic. But there is lot of things to do. I like very much listen music. There are clubs who stay open all night!

My friend went in Los Angeles last year, and he has seen a baseball game at Dodger Stadium. He said me was wonderfull. I like to do that also.

My plane arrive to LAX at 6:30 a.m. in Janury 3. Is very kind you meet me so early morning.

I hope very much improve my english during I am with you!

See you soon and happy New Year!

Fernando

1 Have you ever been in a dangerous situation? Write some notes about when, where, who you were with, and what happened. Discuss your notes with a partner and compare the situations.

2 Put the adverbs or adverbial phrases in the correct place in these sentences. Sometimes more than one place is possible.

1. I used to go skiing.	*in the winter, frequently*
2. I enjoyed going to Colorado.	*with my family, especially*
3. I had a bad accident.	*two years ago, then, really*
4. I skied into a tree.	*headfirst*
5. I broke my leg.	*in three places, unfortunately,*
6. I'd like to go skiing again.	*definitely, one day*
7. But I don't feel confident.	*yet, enough*
8. My family goes skiing.	*however, still, every February*

Read the completed story aloud with your partner.

3 Read through the story of two British mountain climbers, Rachel Kelsey and Jeremy Colenso. Where were they? What went wrong? How were they saved? What does the text message mean?

4 Place the adverbs on the right of the story in the correct place in the same line (sometimes more than one place is possible). Add punctuation where necessary.

5 What background information are you given in the article? When does the actual story of what happened start?

6 Using the notes you made earlier, write the story of your dangerous experience (about 250 words).

- Begin with background information.
- Describe the events in the order they happened.
- Make sure you use plenty of adverbs to describe people's feelings and actions.

Share your stories as a class, reading some of them aloud.

TEXTING TO THE RESCUE

On a mid-September day, British climbers Rachel Kelsey and Jeremy Colenso were climbing in the Swiss Alps.	several years ago high / with great confidence
They were both experienced climbers, and when they left their base the weather was good. They reached the summit, but as they started the climb down a severe storm struck the mountain. Snow began to fall, making it difficult to see where they could put their hands and feet on the rock. After several frightening minutes they found a narrow ledge and climbed onto it, hoping the snow would stop and they could continue their descent.	relatively easily suddenly / heavily / extremely safely luckily / desperately
The snow did not stop and the temperature dropped to 14°F. "We had to stay awake," said Rachel, "because it was so cold that we would have died. So we told stories and rubbed our fingers and toes to keep them warm."	however / dangerously afterwards / undoubtedly continuously
They decided that they had to get help. But what could they do? Rachel had brought her cell phone with her, but the only phone numbers she knew were in London. She sent a text message at 1:30 A.M. to get help. She sent the same message to five friends in the UK. It read: "Need heli rescue off north ridge of Piz Badile, Switzerland!" They were all asleep, so nothing happened.	eventually /possibly / fortunately unfortunately in fact urgently for hours then
At 5:00 A.M., one friend, Avery Cunliffe, got the message. He jumped into action, called the rescue services in Switzerland, and called Rachel to tell her that help was coming.	immediately / quickly then
The weather was too bad for the helicopters to operate, but Avery kept sending text messages to the climbers. At about 10:00 P.M. they were lifted off the mountain. "We owe our lives to Avery," they said when they were back at the base.	for the next 24 hours finally / safely exhaustedly

Need heli rescue off north ridge of Piz Badile, Switzerland!

Send   Cancel

1 Use the conjunctions *but*, *although*, and *however* to join these two sentences.

He's rich and famous.   He's unhappy.

2 Conjunctions can join sentences to express **contrast**, **reason and result**, **time**, and **condition**. In each group complete the sentences with suitable conjunctions.

Contrast	however	although	despite	even though

1. _____ I can't speak much Spanish, I can understand a lot.
2. I can't speak Spanish well. _____, I can understand most things.
3. He can't speak Spanish well, _____ he lives in Mexico.
4. _____ living in Mexico, he can't speak Spanish.

Reason and Result	such ... that	so	as	since	because	so ... that

1. I didn't sleep well last night, _____ I'm tired.
2. I'm tired _____ I didn't sleep well last night.
3. I wanted to go, but _____ it was late I decided not to.
4. _____ John can't be here today I've been asked to chair the meeting.
5. He always looks _____ innocent _____ he gets away with murder.
6. He's _____ a terrible liar _____ no one belives him.

Time	when(ever)	while	as (soon as)	until	after	since

1. I called you _____ I could.
2. He refused to talk to the police _____ his lawyer arrived.
3. I feel sad _____ I hear that song.
4. Their house was robbed _____ they were on vacation.
5. I've known her _____ I was a small child.
6. I'll help you with this exercise _____ I've had dinner.

Condition	if	as long as	unless	in case

1. _____ I'm going to be late, I'll call you.
2. You won't pass _____ you work harder.
3. Take an umbrella _____ it rains.
4. You can borrow my car _____ you drive carefully.

3 Discuss what you know about the politician John F. Kennedy.

4 Read about Kennedy's life and death. Choose the correct conjunctions to join the sentences.

5 Research and write about someone famous who interests you. Use the plan below to help you.

Paragraph 1: Introduction and your interest in this person
Paragraph 2: Early life
Paragraph 3: Career
Paragraph 4: Later life (and death)

JOHN F. KENNEDY
The Youngest Elected President of the U.S.A.

It is over 45 years (1) (*since / after*) John F. Kennedy, the thirty-fifth President of the United States, was assassinated. (2) (*Although / However*), theories concerning his death still fascinate the world.

On November 22nd, 1963, (3) (*when / while*) he had been in office just one thousand days, he was shot (4) (*as / while*) being driven through the streets of Dallas, Texas. Lee Harvey Oswald was charged with the killing, but (5) (*before / when*) he was put on trial, he was also murdered.

John Fitzgerald Kennedy, known simply as JFK, was born in Brookline, Massachusetts, on May 29th, 1917, the second of nine children of the millionaire Joseph P. Kennedy and Rose Fitzgerald.

(6) (*Since / After*) graduating from Harvard University in 1940, he entered the navy. In 1943 he was seriously injured (7) (*when / while*) his boat was sunk, but (8) (*despite / even though*) his injuries he rescued many of his crew, showing (9) (*so / such*) bravery that he was awarded the Purple Heart medal.

After the war, he became a Democratic congressman, joining the Senate in 1953. That same year he married Jacqueline Bouvier, the daughter of a wealthy Wall Street broker. She was stylish, attractive, and very popular, (10) (*so / as*) much so that her husband once said (11) (*during / while*) addressing an audience in France: "I am the man who accompanied Jacqueline Kennedy to Paris!" The couple had three children, Caroline, John Junior and Patrick, who lived only two days.

From 1956 (12) (*until / when*) he became President in 1961, his family worked tirelessly to support him. (13) (*During / While*) the election campaign millions watched his television debates with Richard Nixon, the Republican candidate. Kennedy won and his inaugural address is best remembered for the line: "Ask not what your country can do for you—ask what you can do for your country."

(14) (*Despite / Even though*) his term in office was short, there were many major events, including the Cuban missile crisis, the building of the Berlin Wall, and the space race. His death shocked the world. Subsequent presidents have employed more and more bodyguards (15) (*in case of / unless*) assassination. JFK was much loved. The NASA Space Center and New York's main airport were renamed after him.

1 How does writing an e-mail differ from writing letters? List some differences.

2 E-mails to friends are usually very informal, and grammar words are often left out. How could you express these typical e-mail phrases more formally?

> Glad you're OK.
> Great news—got the job!
> Sorry, can't make next Sat.
> You still OK for Friday?
> Sounds fantastic.
> Can't wait to see you.

3 Read the e-mail and note features that are typical of e-mails. What changes would you make if it were a letter? Go through and discuss with your partner.

4 Read the letter from Jane to a friend. What is her main reason for writing? What parts of the letter give extra information?

Work with a partner and discuss how to make it more like an e-mail.

5 Write an e-mail in reply to Jane (about 250 words).
- Begin by reacting to her news
- Reply positively to her invitation
- Suggest arrangements for meeting her
- End by giving some news about yourself

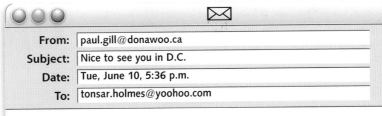

From: paul.gill@donawoo.ca
Subject: Nice to see you in D.C.
Date: Tue, June 10, 5:36 p.m.
To: tonsar.holmes@yoohoo.com

Hi Tony and Sarah,

GREAT to see you in D.C. last week and catch up on what's new with you. Wasn't the Old Church Hotel nice? (Hey, but what about the lousy breakfast service!). The party seemed to go OK. Wonder what the group photo will be like this year? Also, the coffee and cupcakes in the cafe after—MOST enjoyable!

Got back to Montreal after a 2 day drive—stopped off at nice 3 star hotel outside of New York. Kids loved the indoor pool and jacuzzi. Came as a welcome break from driving for us.

Hope all is well with you. Pam is off with kids to the lake, swimming. Remember when we went up there with yours once—many moons ago?

Keep in touch. Would be great if you could get out here to visit us.

Lots of love
Paul & Pam
& Hannah and Freddie

July 8th

Dear Rob,

It was so good to see you and Jenny a few weeks ago. We really must get together more often—we always have so much to talk about.

On the subject of get-togethers, I just got a postcard from—guess who? Graham Pellowe. Do you remember "gorgeous" Graham who was studying zoology? Well, he's in town. Apparently he's a real big shot these days. He works for an international environmental agency, believe it or not. Anyway, he's coming to Cleveland next Thursday, and he really wants to meet up and discuss old times. He's staying with friends downtown, close to where I used to live. I know a great restaurant there called the Green Olive, or else there's the Red Pepper—both are excellent. Anyway, I am assuming and desperately hoping that you can come that evening—I'm not up for a whole evening with old Graham on my own. I finish work at about six, and he can't make it to the restaurant until 8:30, which gives us some time to catch up. Let me know if any of this is possible.

Please call me or e-mail when you can, and I'll book a table.
It could be a fun evening.

Love,
Jane

1 What does the term "fast food" mean to you? What fast food outlets are popular in your country? What does the term "organic food" mean to you? Do you ever buy it?

2 A company called The Organic Burger Company has commissioned a consumer survey to find out who their customers could be in the future. The results of the survey are presented to them as a report. Here are some headings from the report.

TO: ⎯

RE: ⎯

Background and objectives ⎯ ⎯ ⎯

Research and findings ⎯ ⎯ ⎯ ⎯

Summary and recommendations ⎯ ⎯

Action points ⎯ ⎯

Match these expressions with the headings.

a. In conclusion,
b. CEO
c. The purpose of this report
d. two main findings
e. The history of this issue
f. Survey into potential demand for organic burgers
g. We recommend that
h. The results
i. We propose that
j. were asked to say what they thought
k. within the next six months
l. We were asked to investigate
m. not enough evidence

3 Read the report based on the consumer survey conducted for The Organic Burger Company and complete it with the expressions from Exercise 2.

The OrganicBurger Company

TO:	(1)_____, Organic Burger Company
RE:	(2)_____
Date:	November 30

Background and objectives

(3)_____ is that there has recently been a drop in customers at traditional fast food outlets such as McDonald's. The Organic Burger Company wants to fill the growing gap in the market.

(4)_____ is to survey consumer attitudes by doing preliminary research with the young people of Cincinnati, a medium-sized American city.

(5)_____ what the customers would want from the experience of buying and eating a high-quality organic burger.

Research and findings

We surveyed 120 people. The age range was:

16–19: 31%   **20–24:** 34%   **25–35:** 19%
36–50: 12%   **51+:** 4%

They (6)_____ about the following statements:

1. I prefer to eat organic meat in my burger.
SA A DK D SD

2. I prefer to have a restaurant interior that is tasteful and modern.   SA A DK D SD

3. I prefer my food to be grown with respect for the environment.   SA A DK D SD

4. I prefer all the other ingredients to be fresh and organic.   SA A DK D SD

5. I am prepared to pay more than I pay now.
SA A DK D SD

(SA = Strongly Agree, A = Agree, DK = Don't Know, D = Disagree, SD = Strongly Disagree)

WRITING A SURVEY AND A REPORT

4 You work for a marketing firm. Your client is a supermarket chain. Your job is to find out if shoppers in your town would be prepared to buy more "fair trade" products in the local supermarket. Fair trade products cost more because producers in developing countries are paid a better price for their products.

- Think of four or five statements like the ones used in the survey for The Organic Burger Company.

  I want to know where the things I buy come from.

  SA A DK D SD

- Ask at least 20 people, either in your class or outside your class.
- Take data about age. Possibly also male / female.
- Add up the statistics.

5 Write the report (about 250 words). Use expressions from Exercises 2 and 3, and use the structure of the report as a model.

(7)_____ are as follows:

1. 46% agreed or strongly agreed
2. 47% agreed or strongly agreed
3. 77% agreed or strongly agreed
4. 39% agreed or strongly agreed
5. 22% agreed or strongly agreed

The (8)_____ are:

1. There is a growing preference for organic food.
2. There is (9)_____ that there is a large market yet.

Summary and recommendations

(10)_____ we believe that our survey showed that:

- the tastes of young people in a typical midwestern city are changing.
- demand exists for more stylish fast food and this demand is growing.

(11)_____ the company loses no time in preparing for a push into all midwestern markets.

Action points

(12)_____ further research be carried out on a larger scale and in other regions. This should be completed (13)_____.

1 Think of one good experience and one bad experience you've had with e-mail. What happened? Who sent the e-mails to whom? Discuss with a partner, then with the class.

2 Almost everyone uses e-mail, but has it truly improved our lives? Is is a good or bad thing? Brainstorm ideas as a class. Divide the blackboard into two. Appoint two students to take notes, one for each column.

PROS (+)	CONS (−)

Discuss your results. On balance, which side wins? What's your opinion?

3 Read through the article quickly. How many of the points you made are mentioned?

4 Study the article more carefully.
1. How is the topic introduced?
2. What personal examples does the writer include?
3. For each point on the plus side, <u>underline</u> the words and expressions used to connect the ideas.
   <u>First of all</u>, e-mail is easy.
4. Compare the words and expressions used to connect the ideas on the minus side. Which are similar?
5. How is the article concluded? How does the writer express his opinion?

5 Brainstorm the arguments for and against one of the topics below. Then write an introduction, the pros, the cons, and your conclusion (about 250 words).
- The cell phone
- Traveling the world in your 20s
- Adult children living at home

Subject: E-mail—a good thing or a bad thing?

In recent years e-mail has become an increasingly important means of communication. However, in my opinion, like most things it has both advantages and disadvantages.

On the plus side:
- First of all, e-mail is easy. All you need is the appropriate software on your computer. There are no stamps to stick and no trips in the freezing cold to mailboxes.
- A second point is that e-mail is fast. No matter where you're sending your message, whether it's to the next street or to the other side of the planet, it takes only seconds to reach its destination. Nowadays, whenever I send regular mail (or "snail mail," as e-mail users call it), I can't believe that it's actually going to take days to reach its destination. How primitive!
- E-mail is not only fast, it is also cheap. Unlike long distance telephone calls, you pay no more for messages sent from the U.S. to London, Ohio, or London, Ontario, or London, England.
- Also, e-mail messages are easily stored. Because they're electronic, saving an e-mail message you've received (and calling it back up again later) is a breeze.
- In addition to this, e-mail is environmentally friendly because, being electronic, it saves natural resources such as paper.
- Last but not least, e-mail is practically universal. Even my great-aunt in rural Canada is using it these days.

On the minus side:
- Firstly, e-mail is impersonal. Unlike when face to face or in telephone conversations, it's difficult to get across subtle meanings in e-mail prose with no visual or voice clues.
- Secondly, it can be argued that e-mail is in fact too easy. You can write a message in a few seconds and send it off with one click. And once it's sent, you can't get back a message that may have been written in a fit of irritation or anger.
- Another point is that e-mail security is lax. As your e-mail message makes its way to its destination, it has to pass through other, public, systems. Anyone with the right technical know-how can intercept it without you knowing.
- Although, as stated above, it is an advantage that e-mail messages are easily stored, this can also be a disadvantage. If you say nasty things about your boss in a message, a saved copy can come back to haunt you in the future.
- A final and very important point is that e-mail can take over your life. Because it is so easy, you start getting more and more correspondence, and you end up spending most of your day reading and responding to floods of messages.

Overall, however, in my mind the pros of e-mail easily outweigh the cons, and e-mail is a good thing. It has transformed the world of communication in largely beneficial ways, and alongside text messaging, is now a major way of keeping in touch.

---

1 What's your favorite town or city? Why do you like it? Which parts of it do you particularly like? Work with a partner and tell them about it.

2 Do the words in the box describe something positive, negative, or neutral?

Do they refer to a person, a place, or food? Or more than one?

> picturesque   intellectual   brand-new   snoring
> a down-and-out   a haven   twisting   boutiques
> mouth-watering aromas   a magnet   flock (v)

3 Read the description of Greenwich Village in New York City. Which parts of the Village do the pictures show?

4 Work with your partner and decide where you could divide the text into four paragraphs. What is the purpose of each paragraph? Think of a heading for each one and compare them with others in the class.

5 The description is part fact and part opinion. Find examples of both.

6 Underline examples of relative clauses and participles.

7 Write a description of your favorite part of town (about 250 words). Use the paragraph plan to help you.

Paragraph 1: General / personal impressions
Paragraph 2: Its history
Paragraph 3: Its character
Paragraph 4: Conclusion and/or final anecdote

I'm a New Yorker, and proud of it.

I live in Manhattan, in Greenwich Village, which is in the "downtown" (southern) part of the island and includes Washington Square Park, New York University, and a maze of picturesque little streets. It's my favorite part of town. So why do I like it so much? It's an artistic and intellectual neighborhood with people playing chess in the park, artists selling paintings on the sidewalk, and students discussing life in coffee shops. Life in "the

Greenwich Village: My favorite part of town

Village" is never dull. There's a surprise around every corner—maybe a brand-new restaurant that wasn't there last week, a snoring down-and-out sleeping in a doorway, or a celebrity being pursued by paparazzi and fans. A sense of history pervades Greenwich Village. It was first inhabited by native Americans, then Dutch settlers, and then the British, who in 1713 named it "Greenwich" after a town in England. The Village really was a small, rural village until the 1800s, when people escaping outbreaks of disease began moving there. Ever since the Village has been a haven for artists, writers, poets, and musicians. Many famous people have lived in Greenwich Village, including the writer Jack Kerouac, the singer Bob Dylan, and the actress Uma Thurman. The popular sitcom *Friends* is set here, and busloads of tourists looking for places mentioned in the show come here every weekend. The heart of the Village is an area of pretty, twisting streets west of Sixth Avenue, where there are endless theaters, used bookstores, coffee shops, trendy boutiques, and of course, restaurants. A large part of the Village experience has to do with food. The Village is packed with food shops and restaurants from every region of the world. Mouth-watering aromas are everywhere from first thing in the morning until late at night. The Village is a genuine 24/7 part of town. Washington Square Park is like a magnet for young people. They flock from every corner of the world to sit on the benches or beside the fountain, talking, playing musical instruments, and celebrating the freedom and friendship of youth. My mother, who grew up in New York City, used to say that Times Square is for tourists, but the Village is the *real* New York.

1 Think of *any* aspect of your life that you would like to tell other people about. It could be your job, a hobby, a person, a place, a special occasion, a news event. Write some notes about it. Ask and answer questions about it with a partner.

2 **CD3 33** Read and listen to someone talking about a man named Christopher and answer the questions.

   1. What is the speaker's relationship to Christopher?
   2. Why is he called "Cheap Christopher?" What does "stingy" mean?
   3. What do you learn about Christopher's work and family?
   4. Name some of the stingy things Christopher does.
   5. What's the stingiest thing he has ever done?
   6. What did he use to give his mother on Mother's Day?
   7. What is the speaker's opinion of Christopher?
   8. What does his wife say?

3 Now read the talk carefully and answer the questions.

   1. <u>Underline</u> the phrases that introduce each paragraph. Why are these words used?
   2. <u>Underline</u> *all* the questions in the text. These are *rhetorical questions*. What does this mean? Why are they used?
   3. Find examples of the speaker giving her personal opinion.
   4. Practice reading aloud the first paragraph with a partner.

Cheap Christopher

The title of my talk is "Cheap Christopher." That's what everyone calls my cousin. Why do they call him that? Well, simply because he's so stingy. He gets everything on the cheap. He's the stingiest person I've ever met, and that's why I want to talk about him today.

Let's start with some background. Christopher is intelligent. He's a part-time journalist, and he's not poor at all. I think he makes about $50,000 a year. He's married with two children, and his wife has a good job, too. So why is Christopher so stingy?

First, let me tell you just how stingy he is. He never spends money on himself. He never buys new clothes. He gets them secondhand from thrift stores for about $5 an item. He never eats out in restaurants. When his work colleagues invite him out to lunch, he stays in his office and says he's expecting a phone call. He hardly ever uses his car. He says he can live on $10 a week. Can you believe that?

Another thing, Christopher never, ever invites friends to dinner, but he doesn't feel guilty about accepting their invitations. Do you know what he says? He says that they invite him to dinner just to have someone interesting to talk to.

All these things are pretty bad, but in my opinion, the stingiest thing he's ever done is this. He went to a friend's wedding without a present. He just took some wrapping paper and a card saying "Love from Christopher" and put it on the table with the other presents. Afterwards he got a thank-you letter from the bride. She obviously thought she'd misplaced the present.

The obvious question is, "Why is he so stingy?" I asked him about it. He said, "I've always been stingy." When he was a child, he'd never buy his mother flowers on Mother's Day. He'd give her a bouquet from her own garden.

Finally, I'd like to say that Christopher may be the world's stingiest guy, but I still like him. Why, you may ask. Well, he's my cousin, and besides, he's got a lot of other good qualities like his sense of humor. His wife doesn't seem to mind that he's so cheap. She says he's just "being careful with his money."

Preparing your talk

4 Think of a title for the notes you made about your topic. Write a talk using these guidelines. Try to include some rhetorical questions.

   1. Give the title:
      The title of my talk is …

   2. Introduce your topic:
      I want to talk about X because …
      Today I'll be talking about X because …

   3. Give some background:
      Let's start with some background. …
      I've always been interested in …
      As you all probably know, …

   4. Hit your first point:
      First, …
      What happened was this, …

   5. Move to new points:
      I'd now like to turn to …
      Moving on, …
      Another thing is …

   6. Conclude:
      Finally, I'd like to say …
      Thank you all very much for listening to me.
      Are there any questions?

5 Mark pauses and words you want to stress. Practice reading it aloud to a partner. Give your talk to the class. Answer any questions.

1 You have looked at letters and e-mails in Units 1, 2, and 5. Are the following statements about **informal** letters and e-mails true or false? (Some are partly true.)

1. You can begin with *Dear Rob*, *Hi Rob*, or just *Rob*.
2. Use contracted forms such as *won't*, *I've*, and *couldn't*.
3. The way you end the letter depends on how well you know the person.
4. You can end with *Good-bye*, *Bye for now*, *All the best*, *Best wishes*, *Take care*, *Yours*, or *Love*.
5. Sign or write your full name, and print it out underneath.
6. If you have forgotten to write something important, you can add it at the bottom with *PS*, for example, *PS Say Hi to Ellie! Tell her I'll be in touch.*

2 Are these statements about **formal** letters and e-mails true or false? (Some are partly true.)

1. If you know the person's name, you can begin with *Dear Mr. Brown*, *Dear Robert Brown*, *Dear Brown*, *Dear Mr. Robert Brown*, or just *Brown*.
2. If you're writing to a woman, begin with *Dear Ms. Black*.
3. If you don't know the person's name, you can begin with *Dear Sir or Madam*.
4. Avoid contracted forms except *doesn't*, *don't*, or *didn't*.
5. If you begin with *Dear Sir or Madam*, end with *Yours faithfully* or just *Yours*. If you begin with the person's name, end with *Sincerely yours*.
6. Sign or write your full name.

3 Read the letter from Keiko to her friend Amber Jones. Which parts sound too formal? Replace them with words on the right.

4 Write an informal letter to another student in the class (about 250 words). Ask a few questions about the other person's life, and then give some news about yourself. Invite the other person out, and give some suggestions for a time and place to meet.

4-2 Nagayama 3-chome
Tama-shi, Tokyo 206

Dear Ms. Jones,

How are things with you? I trust you and your family are in good health, and that you benefited from an enjoyable holiday in France. I recently went on a school trip for a few days. Please find enclosed a photo of me and several acquaintances at an ancient temple. Hope you like it.

I was most delighted to hear that you are coming to Japan in the near future! You didn't specify the exact dates. I would be grateful if you could supply them to me. I will do my utmost to ensure I have some time free in order to be able to accompany you around Tokyo. I can assure you that there is a lot to see and do here. We'll have lots of fun! The shops here are of a very high standard too, so we'll no doubt end up buying excessive quantities of clothes!

In conclusion, I'm obliged to finish now. It's time for bed! Please contact me soon. I look forward to hearing from you.

Sincerely yours,

Keiko

PS Please give my sincere regards to your parents. Tell them I miss them!

Believe me,
had a great time
It's great news
hope
say when exactly
can't wait to hear
Anyway
Please let me know
Hi Amber!
get in touch
lots of
so I can show
soon
say hello
Love and best wishes
absolutely fantastic
a few friends
we're sure to
I'll do my best to make sure
I have to
I'm sending you
all well

1 Think of something that you looked forward to for a long time that finally happened.

- What was the occasion or event? Why did you want it so much?
- Did you have to make preparations for it? If so, what were they?
- What actually happened?
- Did it live up to your expectations or not?

Write some notes and then tell your partner about it.

2 Read these lines from Larry's story and reconstruct it with a partner.

> Larry's dream to fly airplanes /
> bought 20 balloons / a lawn chair /
> packed a few sandwiches and a BB
> gun / cut the rope / floated around /
> the winds were blowing / an American
> Airlines pilot at 11,000 feet /
> a helicopter / a TV reporter

3 Read the full story and compare it with yours. Match these five headings with the correct paragraphs.

- ☐ **Serious problems**
- ☐ **Preparing for takeoff**
- ☐ **Down to earth with a bump**
- ☐ **Larry and his dream**
- ☐ **Flying high**

4 Read the story again and complete it with a correct linking word or expression from the box.

first of all	Finally	Eventually	Next
However	All day long	Then, one day	
By this time	until	As soon as	
Right away	Fortunately,	just at that moment	
Unfortunately	in order to	so	because

5 Use your notes from Exercise 1 and write your story (about 250 words).

6 Read each other's stories and ask and answer questions about them.

Larry follows his dream

1. **Larry was a truck driver, but his lifelong dream was to fly airplanes.**

   (1)_____ he would watch the fighter jets criss-crossing the skies above his backyard and dream about the magic of flying. (2)_____, he had an idea. He drove to the nearest hardware store and bought 20 large balloons and five tanks of helium. (3)_____, they were not normal brightly colored party balloons but heavy three-feet weather balloons used by meteorologists.

2. Back in his yard, (4)_____, Larry used a rope to tie a chair to his car door. (5)_____ he tied the balloons to the chair and inflated them, one by one. (6)_____, he packed a few sandwiches and a bottle of Coke, loaded a BB gun, and climbed on to the chair. His plan was to float up lazily into the sky to about 200 feet and then to pop a few balloons with the BB gun (7)_____ descend to earth again.

3. His preparations complete, Larry cut the rope. (8)_____, he didn't float up, he shot up, as if he had been fired from a cannon! Not to 200 feet, but up and up and up, (9)_____ about 11,000 feet. If he had popped any balloons at this height, he would have plummeted to earth, (10)_____ he just had to stay up there, floating around and wondering what to do.

4. (11)_____, night was falling and things were getting serious. Winds were blowing Larry out to sea. (12)_____ an amazed airline pilot spotted him and radioed the airport saying he'd just seen a man with a gun, sitting on a lawn chair at 11,000 feet. (13)_____ a helicopter was sent to rescue him, but it wasn't easy (14)_____ the wind from their rotor blades kept pushing the homemade airship further away. (15)_____, they managed to drop a line down from above and pulled him to safety.

5. (16)_____ he was on the ground he was arrested. A TV reporter shouted, "Hey man, why did you do it?" Larry looked him in the eye and said, "A man's got to follow his dreams."

1 Who are the most influential people in the world today? And in the past? Share ideas as a class.

2 Compare the two texts about Michelangelo. Work with a partner and find differences in the way the same information is presented.

Find examples of how emphasis is added by:

1. Changes of word order.
2. Changes of words.
3. Sentences that begin with *It was . . .* and *What . . . .*
4. The use of *this* to refer back.

Which text sounds better? Why?

3 Rephrase these sentences in different ways to make them more emphatic.

1. I love my grandfather's kind, wrinkly smile.
   What I love about …   *The thing I love about …*
   What I love about my grandfather is his kind, wrinkly smile.
   The thing I love about my grandfather is his kind, wrinkly smile.

2. They don't understand the president's policies.
   It's the president's policies …   *What they …*

3. The softness of Norah Jones's voice makes it special.
   What makes …   *It's the …*

4. I admired Mother Teresa's courage.
   What I admired about …   *It was …*

5. The way Pele could head a soccer ball was amazing.
   What was …   *What amazed me …*

4 Research the career of someone you consider influential, e.g., an athlete, artist, singer, actor, writer, or businessperson.

Using some of the structures for adding emphasis, write (about 250 words) about:

- their early life
- how their career grew
- why he/she is/was a person of influence
- the high points of their professional life

MICHELANGELO (1475–1564)

TEXT A

1. Michelangelo had a great influence on the world of art. He was a sculptor, an architect, a painter, and a poet.

2. He was born near Arezzo, but he considered Florence to be his hometown. He loved the city's art, architecture, and culture.

3. He concentrated on sculpture initially. He began to carve a figure of David from a huge block of marble in 1501. He finished it in 1504, when he was 29.

4. Pope Julius II asked him to paint the ceiling of the Sistine Chapel later. He worked at this every day for four years from 1508 until 1512. He lay on his back at the top of high scaffolding.

5. He designed many buildings. His greatest achievement as an architect was his work at St Peter's Basilica. Its revolutionary design is difficult to appreciate nowadays.

6. Michelangelo belongs to a small group of artists, such as Shakespeare and Beethoven, who have been able to express humanity's deepest experiences through their work.

TEXT B

1. Michelangelo, sculptor, architect, painter, and poet, had a tremendous influence on the world of art.

2. Although he was born near Arezzo, it was Florence that he considered to be his hometown. What he loved above all about the city was its art, architecture, and culture.

3. Initially, he concentrated on sculpture. In 1501 he began to carve a figure of David from a huge block of marble. This he finished in 1504, when he was 29.

4. Later, he was asked by Pope Julius II to paint the ceiling of the Sistine Chapel. To do this, every day for four years, from 1508 until 1512, he worked lying on his back at the top of high scaffolding.

5. He designed many buildings, but it was his work at St Peter's Basilica that was his greatest achievement as an architect. What is difficult to appreciate nowadays is its revolutionary design.

6. There is a small group of artists, such as Shakespeare and Beethoven, who, through their work, have been able to express the deepest experiences of humanity. Michelangelo belongs to this group.

Audio Scripts

UNIT 1

CD1 2

1. Where is Tyler spending his junior year?
   In London.
2. Is this his first trip abroad?
   No, it isn't. He's been abroad once before. Last year he went to Mexico.
3. Where does Dave live?
   In north London.
4. How long is Tyler going to stay with Dave?
   A few days.
5. Why did the guy say "cheers" to Tyler?
   Because he held the door open for him.
6. Does he like his host family?
   Yes, he does. They seem very nice.
7. What are they doing on Sunday?
   They're visiting Shakespeare's hometown.

CD1 3

1. How long has Teresa been in Africa?
   Since last September.
2. What time does she start work?
   Early, at seven o'clock.
3. What did she just buy?
   A "piki-piki." It's a little motorcycle.
4. Where did she go last Sunday?
   To a really awesome beach.
5. What is she going to bring home?
   Her collection of shells.
6. How many shells has she collected already?
   Hundreds.
7. What did they do at the beach?
   They barbecued fish and swam until the sun went down.
8. What is she sending to her parents?
   A photo of the sunset.

CD1 4

1. A Are you being helped, sir?
   B Just looking, thank you.
2. I heard that she's been seeing a lot of Patrick recently.
3. I'll be seeing Bill this afternoon—I'll tell him the good news then.
4. Apparently, he was doing 70 miles per hour around a curve when they stopped him.
5. I hadn't seen her since she was a little girl, and she'd completely changed.
6. Nobody will listen to him. He's the kind of guy who isn't believed by anyone.
7. I haven't been told yet if I've got it. I'll be told in writing sometime next week.
8. Do you have any idea which address it was sent to?

CD1 5

1. A On weekends I often don't bother getting up till lunchtime.
   B Absolutely! Why bother if you don't have to?
2. A My parents have never ever had an argument.
   B Really? Mine are at it all the time.
3. A I don't think I'll ever master this DVD player.
   B Well, don't ask me. I can't even find the on/off button.
4. A I was saying to a friend just the other day that I hadn't seen you for ages.
   B I know. How long has it been?
5. A I hate Mondays because nothing ever goes right on a Monday.
   B Just Mondays, eh? Aren't you the lucky one!

6. A I'd just returned home last night when I realized I'd left my briefcase on the bus.
   B Well, you won't see that again.
7. A I was just getting ready to go out today when my grandmother called to chat. It's so frustrating!
   B I know, and you feel really bad if you say it's not a good time.
8. A I've been told that our teacher wears purple pajamas in bed!
   B Who on earth told you that?
9. A In my very first English class I was taught to introduce myself and say "hello."
   B I was taught to say "the cat runs after the mouse" and stuff like that—useful, huh?
10. A The reason I'm studying English is because it's spoken all over the world.
    B True. But isn't Chinese spoken by more people?

CD1 6

1. A Heard about Jane and John splitting up?
   B No! Really? I always thought they got along really well.
   A Apparently not. John's been seeing his ex-girlfriend.
2. A Leaving already? What's wrong?
   B I just have a headache, that's all.
3. A Failed again? How many times is that?
   B OK, OK. You don't have to rub it in! They say the *best* drivers fail three times.
4. A Sorry I'm late. Been waiting long?
   B No, I just arrived myself. Got caught in traffic.
5. A Doing anything interesting this weekend?
   B Yeah, if you call housework interesting. I've just *got* to clean my apartment this weekend.
6. A Like the car! When did you get it?
   B Had it a while, actually. Runs pretty good.
7. A Bye, Joe! See you tonight.
   B OK. I'll come over about eight!
8. A Just coming! Hang on!
   B Get a move on, or we'll go without you.
9. A Want a ride? Hop in.
   B Great. Can you drop me off downtown?
10. A Seen Jim lately?
    B No, I haven't. I wonder what he's up to these days.

CD1 7 A long-distance phone call

D Hello?
C Dad! It's me, Cara.
D Cara! How are you? How's it all going?
C I'm fine but still a bit jet-lagged.
D I can imagine. What exactly is the time difference over there?
C It's 16 hours ahead. I just can't get used to it. Last night I lay awake all night, and then today I nearly fell asleep at work in the middle of a meeting.
D You poor thing. And what's work like?
C It's early, but I think it's going to be really good. It's a big company, but everybody's being so kind and helpful. I've been trying to find out how everything works.
D And what about Seoul? What's it like? Have you seen much of the city yet?
C I've seen a bit. It just seems like such a big, busy city. I don't see how I'll ever find my way around it.
D I know. Big cities can seem really strange and frightening at first. Is it anything like Denver?

C No, it's nothing like Denver. It's like nowhere else I've ever been—huge buildings, underground shopping centers, lots of buses, taxis, and people—so many people—but it's so clean. No litter on the streets or anything.
D And where are you living? What kind of housing do you have?
C Well, for the time being I've been given a tiny apartment, but it's in a great part of town.
D What do you mean "for the time being?" Will you be moving somewhere else?
C That's right. I won't be living here for long. I'll be offered a bigger place as soon as one becomes available, which is good 'cause this one really is tiny. But at least it's near where I'm working.
D How do you get to work, then? Do you walk?
C Walk! You're kidding! It's not *that* close. It's a short bus ride away. And the buses and trains come so regularly—it's a really easy commute, which is good 'cause I start work very early in the morning.
D It all sounds really interesting, but are you enjoying yourself?
C Again, it's too early to say. I think I really will be enjoying it all soon. I'm sure it's going to be a great experience. It's just that I miss everyone at home so much.
D Oh, we miss you too, very much. Make sure you e-mail us regularly—it's the best way to keep in touch.
C I will. I promise. And you e-mail me back with all your news. I just love hearing from home. Give everyone my love. Bye.
D Bye, sweetheart. It's been great talking to you.

CD1 8

1. A I'm going away for two weeks. Do you think you could possibly water my houseplants for me?
   B No problem. I'd be glad to. I'll keep an eye on your whole house if you like.
   A That would be great. You're sure it's not too much work for you?
   B Don't worry, I'll make sure everything stays clean and tidy. I don't mind doing housework. In fact, I sort of like it!
   A I'll do the same for you any time, you know.
   B Thanks.
2. A Julie, have you heard? Anna's just been made manager of the New York branch of her firm, so she's coming back to the U.S.!
   B Oh, that's great news. Let's give her a spectacular homecoming party when she gets back from Hong Kong. Hmmm. She's certainly the career girl of the family.
   A Doing really well, isn't she?
   B I know, and I'm happy for her. Me? I'm just a homemaker. Four kids, homemade pies, and homegrown vegetables!
   A And how *are* my wonderful grandchildren?
3. A We're having a housewarming party on the 12th. Can you come? I'll give you our new address.
   B Yes, you bet. We'd love to! But I didn't know you'd moved.
   A Yeah, two weeks ago. It's much bigger than the old one. Huge kitchen and three big bedrooms.
   B Sounds great.
   A Yeah. The problem is, with the place being much bigger, there's much more housework to do!
   B That's a pain!

4. **A** Hey, you going to Carly's on Saturday?
    B I dunno.
    A She's got the house to herself. It'll be great.
    B Cool. Where are her parents, then?
    A Carly says they're visiting her relatives. Her grandmother's sick and homebound, so they have to go and help.
    B OK. Count me in. I'll be there.

CD1 9

1. I'm going away for two weeks. Do you think you could possibly water my houseplants for me?
2. I'll make sure everything stays clean and tidy. I don't mind doing housework.
3. Let's give her a spectacular homecoming party when she gets back from Hong Kong.
4. Me? I'm just a homemaker. Four kids, homemade pies, and homegrown vegetables!
5. We're having a housewarming party on the 12th. Can you come? I'll give you our new address.
6. The problem is, with the place being much bigger, there's much more housework to do!
7. Her grandmother's sick and homebound, so they have to go and help.

CD1 10 Things I miss from home

Andrew
Well, I travel a lot for my job—uh, too much, actually. And what I really hate is how it's so hard to eat healthy. You know? At home I eat tons of fresh fruit and vegetables I get from the corner market, but that's, like, practically impossible on a business trip. I mean, I know it's not like other cities don't have fresh fruit or grocery stores. It's just that you never know where they are. So what I do now is, uh, before I go on my trip, I google supermarkets near the hotel. And then, as soon as I'm checked in, I go straight there and pick up lots of fresh fruit to keep in the hotel fridge.

Gabriele
Short trips—you know, weekends away, whatever—I don't miss anything. But when I'm away for longer, uh, what I do miss are my two cats. Mickey, that's the older one, he's always getting into trouble out in the yard, and C.J., he's just a kitten, just a few months old. He does the most adorable things with a ball of string and… well, anyway. What I do when I have to leave them is I set up a webcam at my house so I can watch them online. Oh, and I keep a photo of them in my bag to look at if I don't have Internet access. That sounds very silly, but I like to see them every once in a while.

Paul
Uh, if I'm away from home for a while, what I usually miss most is a pillow that I like. Hotels have this incredible knack for providing pillows that you just can't sleep on—either they're too soft, or they're too firm. You know what I mean? So I started taking my own pillow on trips. I know it sounds crazy, but this one I take is just the way I like it, you know, soft but not too soft. And it doesn't take up much room in your suitcase if you pack it right.

Anna
There's not a lot that I actually miss but—oh! Pizza! It's a little weird, since I don't eat much of it at home, but whenever I go abroad I really miss American pizza. Pizza's, like, universal, of course, but in other countries they always put weird stuff on it like fish. Or corn. And there's not enough cheese. But what can you do? I just eat it anyway. It's funny, I was having this pizza in Italy last year and thinking, "Hey! Where'd the cheese go? This isn't *real* pizza!" But, you know, they *invented* pizza in Italy!

Sylvia
Well, when I'm out of the country, there are lots of things I miss—my kids and stuff—but what I really miss is the news. I mean, obviously other countries have news. But I'm a big fan of this one specific anchor lady, and if she's not there to tell me the news, I can't quite believe what I hear. Strange, right? It doesn't happen with newspapers. I'm happy to read any newspaper, but on TV, um, I like to see a familiar face. But now I sometimes watch her on my laptop, you know, online. It's still not the same, but, uh, it's better than nothing!

Chris
I think the thing I miss most when I go away on business, and especially if I go abroad, is probably Saturday morning. I mean a really lazy Saturday when I can get up late, get a bagel and the newspaper, make some coffee…. and, you know, I'll spend the morning just sitting around reading the paper, drinking coffee, and just relaxing. When I'm away on business it's not like that. Sometimes I'll order hotel room service on a Saturday, you know, to get the same feeling. And maybe check out some headlines on the Internet. But it just isn't the same.

CD1 11

1. **A** Great to see you. Come on in.
    B Thanks. I was just passing through and thought I'd drop by.
2. **A** Excuse me, don't I know you from somewhere?
    B No, I don't think so.
3. **A** What do you mean you're not coming to my party?
    B Well, I'm just not up for going out tonight.
4. **A** I think I'll have the chocolate cake. What about you?
    B Let me see. No, actually, I think I'll pass on dessert.
5. **A** My roommate can't make it to your party.
    B Really? That's too bad. I was hoping to meet her.
6. **A** How come you're not going on vacation this year?
    B Because we just can't afford it.
7. **A** You'll get yourself sick if you keep working at that pace.
    B That may be, but I have to get this finished by Friday.
8. **A** I got you the last two tickets for the show.
    B Fantastic! I knew you'd come through for us.

CD1 12 See p. 11

CD1 13 See p. 149

CD1 14

1. **A** Excuse me, don't I know you from somewhere?
    B Actually, I don't think so.
    A Weren't you at Gavin's party last week?
    B Not me. I don't know anyone named Gavin.
    A Well, someone who looked just like you was there.
    B Well, that may be, but it certainly wasn't me.
    A I am sorry!
2. **A** Tony! Hi! Great to see you!
    B Well, I was just passing through, and I thought I'd drop by and say "hello."
    A Come on in! Tell me what's new!
    B You're sure? You're not too busy?
    A Never too busy to talk to you.
    B Thanks. It'd be really nice to have a chat.
    A Fantastic! Let me take your coat.

UNIT 2

CD1 15 Marco Polo

Marco Polo was the first European to travel the entire 5,000-mile length of the Silk Route, the main trade link between Cathay (China) and the West for over two thousand years. He was born in Venice, the son of a merchant. In 1271, when he was 17, he set off for China. The journey took him four years. His route led him through Persia, Afghanistan, and Mongolia. He traveled by boat, but mainly on horseback, and he frequently got lost. He was met by the emperor Kublai Khan. He was one of the first Europeans to visit the territory, and he traveled extensively. He went over mountain ranges, down rivers, and across deserts. He stayed in China for 17 years. When he left, he took back a fortune in gold and jewelry. He arrived back home in 1295. He wrote a book called *The Travels of Marco Polo*, which gave Europeans their first information about China and the Far East.

Tommy Willis
Tommy Willis is in Fiji. He's on a nine-month backpacking trip around Asia. He flew into Bangkok five months ago. Since then, he's been to Vietnam, Hong Kong, South Korea, and Japan. He's visited royal palaces and national parks in South Korea and climbed to the summit of Mount Fuji in Japan. He's been staying in cheap hostels along with a lot of other young people. "I've met a lot of really great people, but it hasn't all been easy," said Tommy. "I've had diarrhea a few times, and I've been pickpocketed once. I've also been mugged, which was really scary." Apart from that, his only worry is the insects. He's been stung all over his body. He's been traveling mainly by public transportation—bus, train, and ferry—but when he's been able to afford it, he's also taken the occasional plane. He's looking forward to taking things easy for another week then setting off again for Australia. "Once you've got the travel bug, it becomes very hard to stay in the same place for too long," he said.

CD1 16

He's been stung all over his body.
He's visited royal palaces.
He's been staying in cheap hostels.
"I've been pickpocketed and mugged."
"I've met a lot of really great people."
He's been to Vietnam and Japan.

CD1 17

1. When and where was he born?
    In 1254 in Venice.
2. How long did it take him to travel to China?
    Four years.
3. How long did he stay in China?
    For 17 years.
4. What did he take back to Venice?
    Gold and jewelry.
5. What was his book called?
    The Travels of Marco Polo.
6. How long has he been away from home?
    For five months.
7. What places has he been to?
    Thailand, Vietnam, Hong Kong, South Korea, and Japan.
8. Where's he been staying?
    In cheap hostels.
9. How many times has he had diarrhea?
    A few times.
10. Has he been pickpocketed?
    Yes, once.

CD1 18

1. Alan
They are one of the most eerie and strange experiences you can possibly have. The first time I saw them, they appeared as a kind of shimmering curtain over the top of a ridge of mountains, and they went from a greenish color to a kind of purplish red. And they just stayed there. The second time I saw them, it was the most amazing sight because they were right above our heads, and they covered the whole sky. The other interesting thing is that not everybody hears it, but they sometimes make a sound, a kind of buzzing noise. It was a real sense of wonder and awe. I just kind of sat there with my mouth hanging open, just feeling kind of small.

2. James
You start at the bottom of the valley and slowly make your way up the hill, about a seven-hour hike until you get to a camp. Then you get up very early the next morning, about four o'clock, to get there for the sunrise. You walk for an hour or so, and suddenly you reach this point where you're looking down on this ancient city, just as the sun is breaking through the clouds. It's the most amazing sight. And you walk around in the total silence of a city that's more than five hundred years old. At that point it's invaded by thousands of tourists, and it's time to go.

3. Willow
We got up about five o'clock in the morning. We went to the site and set off. Because you're floating with the wind, there is no breeze on you, and it really was like flying like a bird. You could look down on everyone, and they were all so small, like ants. It was just amazing and so silent. And we landed about seven o'clock, and suddenly we were back with the rest of civilization. It was just the most beautiful experience.

CD1 19

1. When you go on a job interview it's important to make a good impression.
2. I think we're all getting tired. Can I make a suggestion? Let's take a break.
3. A lot of research has been done into the causes of cancer.
4. I think the CEO is basically doing a good job. He's reliable, he's honest, and he gets results.
5. I'd like to make it clear right now that I am totally opposed to this idea.
6. We can't make a profit in this business unless we raise prices.
7. I don't mind if we go now or later. It makes no difference to me.
8. Could you do me a favor and lend me some money till tomorrow?

CD1 20

1. I'm so thirsty. I could do with a glass of tea.
2. Your homework was full of mistakes. You'll have to do it over.
3. I think we should do away with pennies. You can't buy anything with them anymore.
4. I could never do without my assistant. She organizes everything for me.

CD1 21

1. Thieves broke into the mansion and made off with jewelry and antique paintings.
2. Jake's parents buy him lots of toys. They're trying to make up for always being at work.
3. What did you make of the lecture? I didn't understand a word.
4. You didn't believe his story, did you? He made the whole thing up.

CD1 22 **Tashi Wheeler – girl on the move**

I = Interviewer, T = Tashi

Part one

I Now, traveling. Um…when did you start traveling?
T When I was eight months old.
I And where did you go?
T Um, I think we did a lot of south … yeah, we did a lot of southeast Asia when I was younger. And the Galapagos Islands, Philippines, and stuff like that.
I And your first memories … OK, eight months, you started, but you presumably don't …
T … don't remember.
I What are your first memories of traveling?
T Um … airports. Um … what else? Beaches. It was a lot in Asia at the time, so it was always hot. Big fruit drinks, and … I don't know, lots of bus rides.
I Was there a time at which you sort of felt, "Yeah, I quite enjoy this traveling," or was it …? It sounds almost a bit of a chore, the way you describe it at the moment.
T No, it was never a chore. I always really enjoyed it. I think … I was quite comfortable. Mum used to say that when I was two years old she just put me down, and I just ran off. And she wouldn't see me, and then someone would pick me up and bring me back. I was quite happy fitting in everywhere.
I What do you think were your, your best memories of traveling? I mean, what can you actually remember that still stands out years on?
T From when I was much younger?
I Yes.
T Um … Africa, when I think I was around eight or nine. We had … we went on safaris there and got chased by an elephant, had lion cubs jumping around the … um … safari bus, monkeys swinging off the … um … rearview mirrors, and things. So that was … and trekking in Nepal is something I'll always remember. The getting up at like four in the morning and looking over all the mountains, and then just walking all day, talking to porters, and coming into villages, and all the kids running out and seeing you, and things. There's lots of amazing experiences.

CD1 23 **Part two**

I And when you were on these travels, I mean, did your dad sort of have a notebook, and he'd be sort of stopping everywhere …?
T Constantly.
I … and writing detailed notes of everywhere?
T Yeah, he's always got pen and paper and three or four guidebooks and other people's guidebooks and so on.
I And that must have made travel a lot slower for you as a family.
T Oh, no. He's hectic, Dad. He's … we land in a country, his feet hit the ground, and he takes off. We don't stop for two seconds. He gets up and goes out before we get up, comes back, gets us up, takes us to breakfast, we rush around all the sights, see everything, stop for one drink here, lunch somewhere else, dinner somewhere else, after-dinner drink somewhere else, takes us back to the hotel, then he goes out again, and goes on all night.
I Amazing! Exhausting!
T Ah, it is! It's really exhausting! It got to a point where me and my brother … what we really liked about traveling for a while was sitting at home watching movies and getting room service. That was quite exciting and different for us.
I This raises the question, of course, travel broadening the mind, as … as … as often said. Do you think it does?

T Yeah, definitely. I don't think you can travel and not have your mind broadened. We saw everything, we ran around, and it was hectic, but at the same time, you knew it was an experience while you were doing it, especially as you got older. And you value it. And still do.

CD1 24 **Part three**

I I was going to say, we've talked a bit about, you know, when you were really young. What about as you got older? I mean, how did the sort of experience and feel of it change as you became, say, a teenager, and … midteenage years and so on?
T You always wanted to stay home summer holidays. I mean, just before you go away … there'd be all your friends having parties and holidays and things, and you'd want to stay and hang out. But at the same time you knew you were doing something different, and everyone's always asking about where you've been, and what you're doing, so you know you … it's a privileged situation, and you're lucky to have it.
I Did that make it easier for you socially or … or not so easy?
T Um …
I Different in that way, in that you'd traveled sort of more than anyone, really, hadn't you?
T I think it had its pros and cons. I think for a number of years, especially around probably 13 to 16, I felt quite backward, I think, 'cause I didn't really know how to get along with kids my own age and my own culture and country and stuff. Um … just from traveling for so long in places, countries, cultures or whatever, where you can't talk to boys, or you can't look at people in a certain way, or you don't wear certain clothing, or something. And I think … I don't know … just the adjusting back and forth constantly did make it a little awkward. The kids at school seemed to be cool, and they had things going on, watch TV, and this program was good, and I was never up to date with all that stuff, so I was constantly being pulled out of it and brought back. But at the same time, I did have that, like I'd seen things, I knew things, and stuff—just a broader view of life, I guess.
I There is a view of traveling that you become a kind of world citizen, and the world is your home.
T Melbourne's definitely my home. But I do feel comfortable anywhere, particularly in Asia, I don't know … I think I'm a real … I just feel like I'm coming home when I go back to Asia. And after living for a year in Paris, I love going back there, but it's not really my home, I guess. No, Melbourne is definitely my home.
I Is there anywhere you fe … don't feel comfortable?
T Um … I haven't found that place yet! But you never know, I might. I haven't been everywhere.
I Your mother's not so long ago written a book about traveling with children, hasn't she? Is traveling … would … is that, is that something you'd sort of advocate, traveling with children? Would you travel with … will you travel with your own children?
T Yeah, definitely. I think … I mean … it's a time where your ideas, your personality, is being formed, and I think … it can only benefit you. Really. I think it's something … and you don't have as much time to do these things when you're older, so try to fit as much of it in as you can when you're younger. Definitely.
I So you'll continue traveling yourself, will you, do you think?
T I hope so. I really can't handle being in one place for too long. I get very itchy-footed.

1. How's your steak? Is it OK?
2. We were all going to go on vacation to Mexico next week. We were really looking forward to it, but my father's been sick, so we had to cancel the trip.
3. **A** Has Ann had the baby yet? It must be due any time now.
   B Oh, yes. Haven't you heard? She didn't have one baby. She had three! Tom's the father of triplets!
4. Watch your head as you come through this door. It's very low.
5. Do be careful. That bowl's really heavy.
6. You know what my favorite snack is? A peanut butter and mustard sandwich.
7. Look! Isn't that Peter over there, sitting by himself?
8. Sarah told me that you hated me. She said that you never wanted to see me ever again!
9. I saw Julie yesterday.
10. Tomorrow's test has been canceled.

1. **A** How's your steak? Is it OK?
   B Mmm! It's absolutely delicious! Just the way I like it.
2. **A** We were all going to go on vacation to Mexico next week. We were really looking forward to it, but my father's been sick, so we had to cancel the trip.
   B Ah! What a shame! You must be so disappointed!
3. **A** Has Ann had the baby yet? It must be due any time now.
   B Oh, yes. Haven't you heard? She didn't have one baby. She had three! Tom's the father of triplets!
   A Wow! That's unbelievable! How amazing! Triplets! That'll keep them busy!
4. **A** Watch your head as you come through this door. It's very low.
   B Ouch! That really hurt! I've got to watch where I'm going!
5. **A** Do be careful. That bowl's really heavy.
   B Whoops! Sorry about that! I dropped it! Don't worry. I'll get you a new one.
6. **A** You know what my favorite snack is? A peanut butter and mustard sandwich.
   B Yuck! That's disgusting! You wouldn't catch me eating that!
7. **A** Look! Isn't that Peter over there, sitting by himself?
   B Hey, Peter! Come over here and sit with us. Tell us what's new!
8. **A** Sarah told me that you hated me. She said that you never wanted to see me ever again!
   B Huh? That's nonsense! What a weird thing to say! You know it's not true.
9. **A** I saw Julie yesterday.
   B Oh, really? How interesting! I haven't seen her for weeks. How is she?
10. **A** Tomorrow's test has been canceled.
    B Phew! What a relief! Thank goodness for that! I hadn't done any studying for it at all.

 See p. 21

1. I just won $25,000 in the lottery!
2. Let's take a long coffee break.
3. Maria, you wrote "at Rome" instead of "in Rome."
4. We were stuck in a traffic jam for four hours!
5. Look at this kitchen! It hasn't been cleaned for weeks!
6. It's another rainy day. That's the fifth in a row!

7. The teacher told us to memorize the entire dictionary for homework!
8. We hadn't heard from our daughter for a month, then she called last night.
9. My sister says it's possible to learn French in three months!
10. Yesterday I got a tax bill for $20,000.

UNIT 3

1. **A** Did you read that story about the guy who jumped off Niagara Falls?
   B No. What happened to him? Did he die?
   A No, he survived, amazingly enough.
   B Really? I guess he was wearing some kind of protective clothing.
   A That's the incredible thing. He was just wearing ordinary clothes. He just jumped in, fell down 180 feet, and somehow managed to avoid hitting the rocks.
   B That's amazing! What did he do it for?
   A Apparently he just did it for a dare. He'd been talking about doing it for years. His friends had bet him he wouldn't do it.
   B What a crazy guy!
2. **A** There was a story the other day about this mountain climber. She was stuck on top of a mountain, and she only managed to escape by sending text messages.
   B No! Where did this happen?
   A In the Swiss Alps, I think. She was climbing with a partner, and they'd been climbing for three hours when they got trapped in a terrible storm.
   B You're kidding!
   A No. So they built a shelter or something, and they hid in that.
   B Then what happened?
   A She started sending text messages to friends in London, and one of them sent a message back saying that the mountain rescue teams in Switzerland had been contacted.
   B Amazing.
   A I know. Anyway, they were rescued the next night, and now they're safe and sound.
   B Unbelievable.
3. **A** I was reading in the paper the other day about this kid who hacked into these top-secret U.S. military computers. Incredible, isn't it?
   B Yeah. How old was he? 17? 18?
   A Actually, he was only 14.
   B Why did he do it?
   A Well, he'd developed his own software program, and he'd been using this to download movies and music from the Internet.
   B I don't get it. What's that got to do with the U.S. military?
   A Well, he'd figured that if he broke into these powerful military computers, he could use them to download stuff even faster.
   B Oh, so he wasn't a spy or anything.
   A No. But he still got in trouble. The military got in touch with the FBI, and this boy was tracked down to his house somewhere in Kansas or something.
   B And he's only 14? They should give him a job!

He was wearing ordinary clothes.
He'd been talking about doing it for years.
His friends had bet him he wouldn't do it.
She was climbing with a partner.
They were rescued the next night.

And now the latest headlines. Ten workers have been rescued from an accident 400 feet beneath the streets of New York. They had spent the past 36 hours trapped underground. They had been digging a tunnel for a new subway line when the roof of their tunnel collapsed. Sixty men managed to escape immediately, but two were fatally injured. Last night the ten men were recovering in the hospital. An investigation into the cause of the accident is due to start tomorrow.

Three children who had been missing for two days have been found safe and sound. The three ten-year-olds, two boys and a girl, disappeared after school on Wednesday. Police had released photographs of the three and had been searching nearby houses. They were eventually spotted by a neighbor, who alerted the police. The children said they had slept outside in a garden shed on a dare and hadn't realized the concern they had caused.

1.
Certainly one of my favorite movies is *Witness*. It's the one starring Harrison Ford where he plays a detective who's investigating a murder that an Amish child has witnessed, and he has to protect the child. And to do that at one point he has to go and spend some time living with the Amish community. Now, the Amish are that religious group in the U.S. who live a very old-fashioned lifestyle. They have no modern gadgets and no modern technology because their religion doesn't allow it. Now, Harrison Ford plays this very tough, hard-nosed city cop, and there are some wonderful scenes where his values and culture really clash with this very peaceful Amish community. It also has a love story in it because he falls in love with the boy's mother, who's Amish. It's a very, very intense and passionate love story. And it's a thriller because it deals with police corruption, and it's unbearably tense, and the buildup towards the end is incredible. It really, really does have you on the edge of your seat.

2.
I don't know if I'd say this is my favorite book, but this is certainly a book that made …um … quite an impression on me. The book is called, um, *The Secret History* by Donna Tartt, and without actually giving away entirely what happens in the story, um, *The Secret History* is about a group of students, and it's all about somebody's desire to belong to a group. And, in fact, the group of students, um, do something really, really terrible. Um, they are involved in a murder, and you know right from the beginning of the novel that this is going to happen. And so you would think that there isn't any element of suspense because you know that somebody's going to die, and you have some idea about how they're actually going to die. But, in fact, um, the whole story's very, very claustrophobic. You feel sort of trapped inside the group and trapped inside their situation. It's completely compelling to read. It's not a comfortable read, but it was about 600 pages long, and I read it in about a week, um, and I lived and breathed this book over that week. Um, I would recommend it to anybody who wants to read something that is really dramatic, you know, psychologically.

I = Interviewer, R = Rachel
I …And we're back! We've got Rachel Aumann in the studio. She's one of those girls you've been reading about in the papers who found *all* that torn-up money. Good morning, Rachel.
R Good morning.

I Now this is wild. You saw these bits of dollar bills just blowing in the wind?

R Yeah it was, um, like really bizarre. We were just walking to school, and there's ripped-up notes flying all over the street. And then we followed it to, like, a garbage can, and that's where the big bag was full of them.

I How big a bag?

R Um …

I Like a big garbage bag or something?

R No, actually not that big. Um, it's about—I think it was like a grocery store shopping bag, like one of those.

I And it was just jammed full of torn-up dollar bills—what, just fives and tens and that sort of thing?

R Yeah, just fives, tens, twenties.

I And how little were the pieces?

R Some were bigger than a postage stamp.

I That small?

R Yeah, some were smaller.

I And so what did you do? Did you take them to the police or something?

R Um, we had to go to school, so we went to school and then after school we were playing outside around on like the same road. And, um, when the police arrived we went over then and started talking to them and telling them when we found it.

I And they took them away at that stage, right?

R Yeah.

I And then what happened?

R They kept them for like a long time cause there's a certain number of months that they have to keep them before they can give them back.

I Right.

R And I think they went to the U.S. Treasury and to the Secret Service and um, when they said, "Yeah, its real money," they gave it back and we put it together.

I You say you put it together—but tiny bits of dollar bills! It must have taken you forever to do! What a jigsaw puzzle!

R Yeah, it's taking forever. It's been about a year, and we still haven't finished.

I So, how many have you got left now then?

R We have all the fives to do and just a few twenties, but the tens are all finished.

I Amazing! How much time do you spend doing this?

R Well, when we first got it we did like half an hour, an hour a day, but then as, like, time passed we just slowly, like, died down and didn't do as much.

I But I am trying to picture you doing this. What do you do, stick them to bits of tape or stick them to a piece of paper or what?

R Well, you get the two serial numbers, and then you have to get, like, a little bit from the middle of the bill. And so once you've got that you put a little bit of tape on the back of them so that they all stay together, and put it in a bag.

I Good heavens! And you're going to keep doing it, huh?

R Yeah, hopefully.

I $1200 so far?

R Um, yeah.

I And how much do you think you'll make in the end?

R I think if we stick to it, we will probably get about $2,000.

I Well, I think you've earned every penny of it, Rachel. Thank you very much for talking with us today.

R Thank you.

I And now here's this week's number-one smash hit…

CD1 **35**

A Jade's got a new boyfriend.

B A new boyfriend? Good for her!

A Apparently, he lives in a castle.

B He does? How amazing!

A I know. She met him in Slovenia.

B In Slovenia? That's interesting.

A Unfortunately, he can't speak much English.

B He can't? I thought everyone could these days!

CD1 **36** See p. 29

CD1 **37**

1. **A** Sam wants to apologize.
   B He does?
   A Yes. He's broken your mother's Chinese vase.
   B My mother's Chinese vase? Oh, no!
2. **A** We had a terrible vacation.
   B You did?
   A Yes. It rained all the time.
   B It did?
   A Yes. And the food was disgusting!
   B It was? What a drag!
3. **A** I'm broke.
   B You are? How come?
   A Because I just got a phone bill for $500.
   B $500? Why so much?
   A Because I have a girlfriend in Korea.
   B You do? How interesting!
4. **A** It took me three hours to get here.
   B It did?
   A Yes. There was a traffic jam ten miles long.
   B Ten miles long? That's awful!
   A Now I've got a headache!
   B You do? Poor thing. I'll get you something for it.
5. **A** I'm watching the sun set over the ocean.
   B You are?
   A Yes. And I've got something very important to ask you.
   B You do? What is it? I can't wait!
   A You'd better sit down. I'd like to marry you.
   B Marry me? Wow!

UNIT 4

CD1 **38**

a. Oh, dear! It's not that I *dislike* him, I just don't *love* him. How can I tell him I don't want to marry him without hurting his feelings? Trouble is, I'm actually interested in his best friend!

b. There's this group of guys, you know—they're always picking on me. But I can't tell my mom and dad—if they find out, they'll go to the principal and complain, and that would make everything much worse.

c. How do you tell someone when they look awful? That dress doesn't suit her at all. But I don't know how to tell her. She obviously thinks she looks great in it.

d. Me and Emma are going clubbing, but I could never tell my Dad—he'd kill me. I've got a big test next week, and I haven't done a thing for it. I've got no clue what time I'll be back.

e. I know I'm not really sick. But it's a beautiful morning, and I don't want to sit in a stuffy office all day. I'm playing golf. I never get any days off!

f. She looks like she doesn't want to be disturbed. I'd better take a message.

CD1 **39**

1. Who did she give it to?
2. What do you want to talk about?
3. Who did you dance with?
4. What do you need it for?
5. Who did you get it from?
6. Who did you buy it for?
7. What are you thinking about?
8. Where do you want a ride to?

CD1 **40** See p. 32

CD1 **41**

A Don't you like ice cream?

B No. I know it's weird, but I never have. Not even vanilla.

A Don't you have a computer?

B No, actually, I don't. I use one all day at work, and that's enough for me.

A Can't you swim?

B No, I can't. I never learned when I was a kid. But I'm starting lessons soon.

A Isn't it hot today?

B Yeah, I know. It's usually much cooler this time of year.

A Isn't this your pen?

B Actually, it isn't. Mine's blue. That one's black.

A Don't you live in New York?

B Yes, that's right. I have a tiny little apartment in Brooklyn.

CD1 **42** **My friend Norman**

Part one

My friend Norman is a funny guy. He's an insomniac, he's dyslexic, and he's an atheist. He's single, unemployed, and lives all alone in a tiny studio apartment without even a pet for company. He's also a vegetarian.

CD1 **43** **Part two**

I dropped by to see Norman last Sunday. As I walked up the driveway his dog started barking. His wife answered the door, and she called for Norman to come downstairs and join us in the living room. He was in a bad mood because he'd overslept that morning, and he'd been late for church. He said they'd had a wild party at his house the night before. All of his friends from his office were there. They'd had a barbecue in the backyard with steaks and burgers. One of his favorite pastimes is doing crosswords, and while he was talking to me he was doing one of those big puzzles from the newspaper. "So how are you, Norman?" I asked him.

"OK, my friend, OK. How about you?"

Anyway, as I said, Norman's an insomniac, dyslexic atheist. So the joke is that he lies awake all night wondering about the existence of dog. Get it?

CD1 **44**

1. **Andrew**

Oh, man, my most embarrassing lie was just last year. All my friends were bugging me to go to the beach with them, but it was a Tuesday and I had to work. So, uh, I called my boss and pretended to be sick, you know. And then I was hanging out at the beach all day, which was awesome, but, uh, like an idiot, I put pictures of it online on my Facebook page. So the next day my boss calls me into his office and he's like, "Hey, Andrew, you look pretty tan for someone who was home sick all day. You weren't at the beach, were you?" So of course I started denying everything, but then he shows me my own page on the Internet with the beach pictures. Ouch. I was totally busted. I had no idea my boss used Facebook—he's like 40 years old! Luckily, he didn't fire me. I just lost a vacation day. Oh, and I had to come in on a Saturday to make up the time I missed.

2. Paul

I have one memory of lying regularly as a child—actually, it was to a priest. Uh, I was brought up Catholic, and from the age of seven you had to go to confession every week and confess your sins. And when you're that age, uh, first of all you're not quite sure what a sin really is, you know? So you just make things up—like, you say, "I swore," or, "I stole some cookies from the cookie jar." And strangely, what you end up doing is lying to the priest so that you've got something to say in your confession.

3. Carolyn

Uh, I can think of a time recently when I had to tell a white lie which was, uh, basically when a friend of mine got married. Um, it, they actually got married in London because her husband's British, so I didn't go to the wedding. But they—they were showing me the photos and, well, basically she looked awful. She had a really frumpy dress on. It did nothing for her figure. But, you know, obviously you can't just say that when you see someone's wedding pictures. So I was like, "Hey, that's really pretty, you look really great."

4. Kiki

One lie I can remember telling was when I lost a necklace that my grandmother had given to me. And I know where I lost it, I lost it at a party because, uh, I was having a very good time and wasn't taking care of it, and I lied and told her it had been stolen in a robbery we had at our house. And to this day I've never told her what happened to it. But sometimes when she mentions things like, "Oh, I should get you another one," you know, it comes back to me.

5. Sean

One lie I can remember, uh, is when I was about five or six years old, and I was in the playground and I was just about to get into a fight and, uh, the only way I could think of to escape was to say, "You can't hit me, I know karate." I don't know where that came from. I'd never done karate in my life. But people left me alone because of it. Oh, but then the other kids wanted to take karate, too, and eventually somebody's mom called my mom to get all the details—which, uh, which was when I had to admit that it was all a lie.

6. Kate

I remember once, I was maybe five years old, and I had been playing with my toys in my room, and our pet cat was there, by the toy box, and for some reason I put him in the box and forgot about him. I was just a kid, you know? I just forgot! And hours later, uh, my mother asked me where the cat was, and suddenly I remembered. I felt awful, uh, so I lied and said that I hadn't seen him, hadn't played with him—and I probably said, "and I didn't put him in the toy box," because my mother went there and found him. Luckily, he was all right. Just a little hungry and scared.

CD1 45

1. **A** Well, Barnaby, how do you like the liver and onions?
   B They're, uh, very nice, thanks.
   A Here. You must have some more!
   B Uh, no thanks, Mrs. Wilson. They're really delicious, but I think I'm full now.
2. **A** And here he is! Little baby Alfred!
   B Oh! Uh, yes, there he is.
   A So what do you think? Isn't he gorgeous?
   B Well, uh, of course he is. He has his father's eyes.
3. **A** So, Emily, did you get my e-mail about going to the lake house?
   B Uh, well, actually –
   A Wouldn't it be great? Just you and me for two whole weeks! No TV, no DVDs, no e-mail, no other people!

B Oh, Aunt Trudy, it sounds really wonderful. But I'm afraid things are really busy at work, and my boss won't give me the time off. I'm really sorry.

CD1 46

1. I'm sorry to bother you, but could you possibly change a ten-dollar bill?
   Do you have change for a ten-dollar bill?
2. Where's the station?
   Could you tell me where the station is, please?
3. **A** This is a present for you.
   B For me? Oh, how nice! You shouldn't have, really. Thank you so much.
   C This is a present for you.
   D Thanks.
4. **A** Can you come to a party on Saturday?
   B No, I can't.
   C Can you come to a party on Saturday?
   D Oh, what a shame! I'd love to, but I've already made plans.
   C Oh, that's too bad!
   D But thanks for the invitation, anyway.
5. **A** Excuse me. Do you mind if I sit down here?
   B No, not at all.
   C Is anyone sitting here?
   D No.
6. **A** Can you give me a hand? I need to carry this box upstairs.
   B All right, if you want.
   C I wonder if you could possibly do me a favor. Would you mind helping me with this box?
   D No, not at all.

CD1 47 See p. 39

CD1 48

1. **A** Do you think you could give me a ride to the station?
   B I'm really sorry, but I can't. I have to be at work by 8:30. I'll call you a taxi, though.
2. **A** Could you possibly help me find my glasses? I can't find them anywhere.
   B Sorry! I've got to run, or I'll miss my bus. I'm no good at finding things anyway.
3. **A** Hi! Listen, would you like to come over for dinner tomorrow evening? I'm cooking Chinese.
   B Oh, I'd love to, but I've already got plans.
   A Oh, that's too bad. Maybe next time.
4. **A** Would you mind lending me your dictionary?
   B I would if I could, but I forgot to bring it with me today. Sorry.
5. **A** Would you like me to help you with this exercise? I think I know the answers.
   B That's really nice of you, but I want to try and work it out for myself. Thanks anyway.
6. **A** Excuse me. Would you mind *not* whistling?
   B I'm sorry. I didn't realize I was.
   A That's OK.

CD1 49 See p. 152

UNIT 5

CD2 2

1. I took the SAT a few months ago, and luckily I got a good score, so I'm going to study psychology at New York University. Classes start in September.
2. It's Sunday tomorrow, so I'm gonna see the game with my son. Chicago's playing St. Louis. It'll be a great game. It starts at 3 o'clock, so we'll have a little lunch before the game.

3. Marie's having a baby soon, so we're both very excited. The baby's due in five weeks. If it's a boy, we're going to call him Jamie. And if it's a girl, she'll be Heather.
4. What am I doing tomorrow, you say? Well, it's Thursday tomorrow, so I'll be doing what I always do on a Thursday. My daughter will come to see me, she'll be bringing the little ones, and we'll all have a cup of tea and a good old chat. And I'll bake some cookies. They like that.
5. Right now I'm packing because tomorrow I'm going to study in France for a year. My plane leaves at 10:30. My mom and dad are taking me to the airport. I have absolutely no idea how I'm going to carry all this stuff!
6. I play guitar in little coffee shops around town. I write most of my own songs, and I even have a few fans! In the next few years I'm going to be a lot more famous. I hope I'll be performing in much bigger places. My goal is that before I'm 25 I'll have made an album with all my own songs.

CD2 3

1. She's going to study psychology.
   They start in September.
2. He's going to a baseball game.
   The game starts at three o'clock.
3. Because they're going to have a baby.
   The baby's due in five weeks.
4. Elsie's daughter and grandchildren will be visiting.
   They'll have a cup of tea and a chat.
5. Because she's going to France for a year.
   Her mother and father are taking her.
6. He's going to be a lot more famous and perform in much bigger places.
   He'll have made an album with all his own songs.

CD2 4

1. Which university is she going to?
2. Who's he going to the game with? Who's playing?
3. What are they going to name the baby?
4. What is she going to bake?
5. What time does her plane leave?
6. Where will he be performing?

CD2 5

1. I'm very excited. I'm going to see my whole family this weekend.
   I don't know if I have time to come this evening. I'll see.
2. So you're off to Canada for a year! What are you going to do there?
   I'm sure you will pass your exams, but what will you do if you don't?
3. I'll come with you if you like.
   I'm coming with you whether you like it or not.
4. Your latest grades are terrible. What are you going to do about it?
   What are you doing this evening?
5. I've had enough of her lazy attitude. I'm going to give her a good talking-to.
   I'm giving a presentation at 3:00 this afternoon. I'm scared stiff.
6. John! Peter is leaving now. Come and say good-bye.
   The bus leaves at 8:00, so don't be late.
7. I'll see you outside the theater at 8:00.
   I'll be seeing Peter this afternoon, so I'll tell him the news.
8. You'll have seen enough of me by the end of this visit.
   I'm going to be a star one day. You'll see.

This is your captain speaking. Good morning, ladies and gentlemen. Welcome on board this United Airlines flight to Tokyo. In a very short time we'll be taking off. When we have reached our cruising speed of 550 miles per hour, we'll be flying at 35,000 feet. Our flight time today is about 12 hours, so we'll be in Tokyo in time for breakfast tomorrow! The cabin crew will be serving refreshments during the flight. If you need any assistance, just press the button, and a flight attendant will come to help you.
In just a few minutes the crew will be coming around with duty-free goods. We will also be giving out landing cards. When you have filled them in, place them in your passport. They will be collected as you go through passport control. In 20 minutes we will be landing at Narita Airport. Please put your seats in the upright position. You are requested to remain seated until the plane has come to a complete stop. We hope you will fly again soon with United Airlines.

1. Do you think you'll ever be rich?
   I hope so.
   I might one day.
   It's possible, but I doubt it.
   I'm sure I will.
   I'm sure I won't.
2. Are you going out tonight?
   Yes, I am.
   I think so, but I'm not sure.
   I might be.
3. Do you think the world's climate will change dramatically in the next 50 years?
   I don't think so.
   I hope not.
   Who knows? Maybe.

1. The wedding took place in an old country church. It was lovely, but it was miles away. It took forever to get there.
2. My son's always hanging out at the mall, but I'll put a stop to that. I won't give him any more pocket money.
3. Please don't take offense, but I don't think your work has been up to your usual standard recently.
4. I told you that boy was no good for you. You should have taken my advice and had nothing to do with him.
5. The older you get, the more you have to learn to take responsibility for your own life.
6. My boss is putting pressure on me to resign, but I won't go.
7. I tried to get the teacher's attention, but she took no notice of me at all.
8. Children never say "Thank you" or "How are you?" to their parents. They just take them for granted.

1. The store takes on extra workers every Christmas.
2. The lecture was too complicated, and the students couldn't take it all in.
3. My business really took off after I picked up six new clients.
4. You called me a liar, but I'm not. Take it back and apologize!

1. Put some music on! Whatever you want.
2. That article about factory farming has really put me off eating chicken.
3. Could you put away your toys, please? Your room's a mess.
4. The kitchen fire was scary, but luckily I put it out.

J = Jack   A = Amy
A Hello?
J Hi, Amy. It's Jack. Jack Cunningham.
A Jack! Hi! How are you? How are things?
J OK, not too bad. And you? How's the family?
A Oh, we're surviving! Busy, busy, busy, but what's new?
J Tell me about it! Listen, I'm calling about the class reunion. You're still going, right?
A Yeah, I'm actually going this time. I just hope I don't bump into anybody I don't want to see, you know what I mean?
J Don't worry. It'll be fun, I promise. Why don't we meet up somewhere beforehand?
A That's a great idea. Let's definitely do that.
J Cool, so maybe you, me, and Gabe? Gabe's coming too this time.
A Great! Do you have any ideas where we can meet? A restaurant somewhere?
J A restaurant sounds good. What are you into? Chinese? Mexican?
A Hmm, oh, there's that really good Indian restaurant we used to go to on Washington Street. Remember?
J Oh, yeah. What's it called again?
A Uh, it's Bombay House, right?
J That's it. Now, I'm driving up from New York, so I'll be coming into the city from I-90. Where can I park?
A There's a parking lot right across from the restaurant.
J Right, I remember now. I'll be leaving about one, so I should be in Boston about 5, 6 o'clock, depending on the traffic.
A Where are you staying?
J At the Boston Park Plaza.
A Wow! Big spender!
J I know, I know, but I got a really great deal online. What about you?
A I'm at The Back Bay Hotel. I think that's just around the corner from yours. We can meet up for coffee.
J Sounds great! When are you getting in?
A Well, I've got a direct flight from San Francisco, luckily. I think my plane takes off around seven in the morning and lands around 4 o'clock Boston time, and then I've got to get my bags and check in at the hotel. Why don't I come to the Park Plaza around 6:30? I'll meet you in the lobby.
J All right. That sounds great. Will you call Gabe, or should I?
A Uh … No, don't worry. I'll call him.
J OK. So I'll see you in the lobby of the Park Plaza on the fourteenth.
A Right. Around 6:30.
J Got it. Bye.
A Bye-bye. Take care.

A= Amy   G = Gabe
G Good afternoon, CompuCom Industries. Gabe speaking.
A Hello, Gabe. This is Amy Stevens. How are you?
G Amy! Hello! It's great to hear from you! How's everything with you?
A Oh, fine. Are you keeping busy these days?
G Too busy! But I can't complain.

A That's right. Business is business! Anyway, Gabe, I spoke to Jack yesterday, you know, about all of us meeting up before the reunion on the fourteenth, and I'm just calling to let you know what's happening.
G Great!
A We were thinking of meeting at Bombay House, the, uh …Indian restaurant …
G You mean the one that used to be on Washington Street?
A Yes. But "used to be?" What do you mean?
G It closed about three years ago.
A Oh, boy. Are you sure?
G Uh huh. Absolutely. But it doesn't matter. There's that other one, Curry Cafe .
A Now where is that? I've forgotten.
G It's over on Newbury Street.
A Oh, great. OK. Now, how are you coming in? You're coming from the suburbs, right?
G Right, from Newton. So I'll just take the train. I get off work at 6:30, and I'll go straight to the train station.
A So you'll be in Boston at about … what? Seven?
G Yeah, something like that.
A Well, OK. I'm meeting Jack at the Park Plaza before that because we both get in earlier than you. So why don't we all meet up at Curry Cafe between seven and seven-thirty?
G Fine. That should give me enough time. I'll call Jack and work it all out. Oh, and should I call and make a reservation?
A Good idea. By the way, where are you staying that night?
G I'm going to call a friend of mine to see if he can put me up for the night.
A Oh, good idea! Well, we'll see you at the restaurant on the fourteenth, then, around 7:15.
G At the restaurant, right. And you know where it is, don't you?
A Yeah, yeah, I've got it. Newbury Street. Bye, now, Gabe.
G Bye, Amy. Great talking to you!

1. A Hello. The Regent Hotel. Kathy speaking. How can I help you?
   B Hello. I was wondering if I could book a room …
2. A Hello?
   B Hey, Pat. It's me, Dave.
   A Dave! Hi! How are things?
   B Not bad. Busy, busy, busy, but life's like that. How's everything with you?
   A Oh, you know, we've all got the flu, and Mike's away on business, so I've got to do everything—cooking, cleaning, shopping…
3. Welcome to First Bank of America. To continue in English, press 1 now. To help us serve you better, please listen carefully, and select from the following options. For account information, press 1 now. If you have questions about your bank statement, press 2 now. For all other inquiries, press 3 now, or stay on the line.

A Hello. TVS Computer Services. Samantha speaking. How can I help you?
B Yes, could I speak to your customer service manager, please?
A Certainly. May I ask who's calling?
B This is Keith Jones.
A Thank you. One moment, please.
C Hello. Customer service.
B Hello, I was wondering if you could help me …

A So that's about all that's new here, Mom. It was good to talk to you.
B I know, we should do it more often. By the way, are you still seeing that nice guy from Boston? Brian, wasn't it?
A Mom. I told you, Brian's just a friend, not a boyfriend. I really don't have time to date right now. Anyway, Mom…
B What a shame! You know you should get out more, Lily. It's not good to…
A Don't worry, I get out pretty often, just not with Brian. Listen, Mom, I've got to run. I've got dinner on the stove.
B OK, don't want to keep you. Oh, one more thing, you're coming home for Thanksgiving, right?
A Of course.
B But have you booked your flight yet? You know it's a very busy time of year.
A I know, Mom, I know. Look, I'll book a flight right after dinner, I promise. All right. Love you, Mom. Love to Dad!
B Love you, too, honey! Thanks for calling! Bye now.

UNIT 6

CD2 16 Jamie Oliver

Jamie Oliver became an extremely successful and well-known chef at a very young age. He has a few restaurants in different parts of the world. He has written a lot of books and made quite a few TV series. He doesn't have many free days anymore. How did he make it big?
His rise to fame came early and swiftly. By the age of eight he had already started cooking at his parents' pub, earning a little money. After a couple of years in cooking school and a little time in France, he started working in restaurants. He worked with a few famous chefs in London before he was spotted by a TV producer at 21, and his life changed.
Even though he had hardly any experience, he had a lot of enthusiasm for cooking and was very natural in front of the camera. His first TV program featured him zipping around London on his scooter buying ingredients and cooking for his friends. His recipes were simple—they didn't involve complicated cooking techniques and used lots of fresh ingredients. That's why he is known as "The Naked Chef."
He opened a restaurant called Fifteen, where he trained a group of unemployed young people to work in the business. There are now similar restaurants in Holland and Australia. He also started a campaign to improve the meals children eat at school, trying to replace junk food with fresh, nutritious dishes.
So what is his recipe for success? "A little bit of luck and a lot of passion!" he says.

CD2 17

1. How much money do you have in your pocket? About $20.
2. How many cups of coffee do you drink a day? It depends. I have a cup for breakfast, sometimes another around mid-morning, then maybe one or two, black, after lunch and dinner.
3. How many times have you been on a plane? About five or six.
4. How much time do you spend watching TV? A couple of hours a night, just before I go to bed, I guess.
5. How much sugar do you have in your coffee? Just half a spoonful.

6. How many pairs of jeans do you have? Three. A black pair, a blue pair, and an old pair I wear when I do messy jobs like cleaning the car.
7. How many books do you read in one year? I honestly don't know. Ten? Fifteen? I read the most when I'm on vacation.
8. How much homework do you get in a night? Too much! About two hours, maybe? It depends.
9. How many English teachers have you had? Um … let me see … about ten, I guess.
10. How many movies do you watch a month? One or two in the theater and one or two on television.

CD2 18

1. There's no need to rush. We've got tons of time.
2. We've got mountains of food for the party. Don't buy any more.
3. I can't see you today. I've got millions of things to do.
4. She's got piles of money. I think she inherited it.
5. When my daughter comes back from college, she always brings heaps of laundry.
6. There were boatloads of people at the sale. I decided not to fight my way through them.

CD2 19

1. **S = Sarah M = Mommy**
Sarah is five, and this is her favorite T-shirt. It's pink with fluffy yellow ducks. Sarah loves her shirt.
S It's my favorite.
And she wears it to play in the garden.
S Look what I found, Mommy!
And you wash it at low temperature. And she wears it to play in the garden.
S Mommy! Look what I made!
And you wash it. And she wears it to play in the garden.
M Sarah! What on earth … ?
And after a while, the dirt builds up so the pink isn't quite as pink, and the yellow ducks aren't as fluffy. New System Sudso Automatic can help. Its advanced formula can remove ground-in dirt even at low temperatures. So the pink stays very pink, and the fluffy yellow ducks are happy again. Wash …
S Mommy! Look what I made!
… after wash …
S Look what I found, Mommy!
… after wash …
M Sarah! Don't you dare bring that in here!
New System Sudso Automatic. It's all you could want from a powder.

2. A Yo, Tony! C'mere! Get a load of this. Look! Look at that car trying to park!
B Ooh! You gotta be kidding me! Uh-oh! That's just gotta be a woman driver. You know it's gotta be.
A It has to be. Hey, need some help, sweetie? Hey, look! Look at her now! Look! Look!
B I don't believe it! She just whacked that BMW! You all right, honey?
A It's a guy.
B A guy. Oh. It was a tight space, though, wuddinit?
A Oh, yeah. Really.
B Yeah, that space, very tight space. Yeah.
A Complicated.
Since men are responsible for 81% of parking accidents and 96% of dangerous driving offenses, why should women have to pay the same for car insurance? At AllSmart we offer policies for women for up to 20% less. For a quote, contact your local branch, or call us at 1-800-689-4200.

3. **C = Child D = Daddy**

C Daddy! Daddy! Today I did a picture of you! And I got two stars! And Miss Lewis said I was the best in the class!
D You're a very naughty girl!
C Why, Daddy?
D Don't argue with your father, young lady! Now go to your room!
C But—
D It's no use crying about it! Come on, go! Get out!
Tuesday Night Football. Only on Channel 9. 9:00 p.m. Do not disturb.

4. **D = Daughter F = Father**
D Hey, Dad! I've decided which new car I'm getting.
F Oh, yeah? When I was your age…
D You counted yourself lucky to have a bike. And it was used. And you had to ride both ways uphill to school…
F Now, well, that's where you're wrong, Miss Smartypants. I was going to say that when I was a teenager, I couldn't have even afforded to pay these terrible gas prices!
D Neither can I.
F Well, don't expect me…
D …and I don't have to. 'Cause all new StarCars come with coupons for a free year's fill-ups. The offer's good for anyone between 18 and 80. Which rules you out, anyway.
See your tri-state StarCar dealer now. Offer ends soon. Coupons good for one tank of gasoline per month. Other terms and conditions apply.
F …just like your mother. Always have to have the last word.
D No, I don't.

5. Hi, this is Sue. Please leave a message.

Hi, Sue. Met you last night. Just wondering if you…uh, if you want to meet up sometime. Um, I'm going away soon, so maybe it could be soon. Uh, I don't want to sound too eager! Not that I'm not eager 'cause I am. Geez, I hope you don't think I'm desperate or something!
Anyway, maybe lunch, or maybe just some coffee? Not that you shouldn't do lunch, I mean, you're not fat. Um, you're not fat at all, actually, you've got a great…well. Not that that's important. It's—it's personality that counts. Um, anyway…
Give yourself a break. Have a smooth, rich Choco Crunch bar.

6. **P = Priest T = Tony**
P O-kay! Everyone! Welcome! We're gathered here today, in the presence of others, to marry Tony and Helen. Helen, do you take Tony to be your husband? Just nod. Tony, do you take her?
T I d—
P Great. Rings. Oops! Just leave it! Leave it! Kiss! Super. Husband and wife. Wife, husband. Right. You're married. Done. I'm outta here.
Come to Lee's Furniture after work. But don't rush! We're open till 10 p.m. weeknights.

CD2 20

	Nouns	Verbs
a.	'export	ex'port
b.	'import	im'port
c.	'decrease	de'crease
d.	'increase	in'crease
e.	'progress	pro'gress
f.	'record	re'cord
g.	'produce	pro'duce
h	'permit	per'mit
i	'insult	in'sult
j.	'protest	pro'test

CD2 21

1. Japan imports a lot of its oil from other countries. Its exports include cars and electronics.
2. I'm very pleased with my French. I'm making a lot of progress.
3. Government officials are worried. There has been an increase in the unemployment rate.
4. But the number of crimes has decreased, so that's good news.
5. How dare you call me a liar and a cheat! What an insult!
6. There was a demonstration yesterday. People were protesting about the price of gasoline.
7. He ran 100 meters in 9.45 seconds and broke the world record.
8. Don't touch the DVD player! I'm recording a movie.
9. Britain produces about 50% of its own oil.

CD2 22

	Nouns	Others
a.	'refuse	re'fuse
b.	'present	pre'sent
c.	'minute	mi'nute
d.	'desert	de'sert
e.	'content	con'tent
f.	'object	ob'ject
g.	'invalid	in'valid
h.	'contract	con'tract

CD2 23

1. Refuse.
2. An unidentified flying object.
3. A desert in northern Africa.
4. Presents!
5. The contents pages.
6. con'tent   mi'nute
   'contract   re'fuse
   in'valid

CD2 24

1. **A** Mike! Good to see you again! How's business?
   B Good, thanks, Jeff. Sales are up again. How about yourself?
2. **A** I'm afraid something's come up, and I can't make our meeting on the 6th.
   B That's OK. Let's try for the following week. Is Wednesday the 13th good for you?
3. **A** What are your travel arrangements?
   B I'm on flight UA 2762 at 6:45.
4. **A** Could you confirm the details in writing?
   B Sure. I'll e-mail them to you as an attachment.
5. **A** They want a deposit of 2½ percent, which is $7,500, and we ha… ge … t…
   B Sorry, you're breaking up. Can you repeat that last part?
6. **A** I'll give you $5,250 for your car. That's my final offer.
   B Great! It's a deal. It's yours.
7. **A** I don't know their number offhand. Bear with me while I look it up.
   B No problem. I'll hold.
8. **A** OK. Here's their number. Are you ready? It's 708-555-2200.
   B I'll read that back to you. Seven oh eight, five five five, twenty-two hundred.
9. **A** I got a pay raise, but I didn't get a better office.
   B You win some, you lose some.
10. **A** Did you apply for that job?
    B No. There's no point. I'm not qualified for it. I wouldn't stand a chance.

CD2 25 See p. 57

UNIT 7

CD2 26

1. If I were you, I wouldn't wear red. It doesn't suit you.
2. Is it OK if I make a suggestion?
3. You're allowed to smoke in the designated area only.
4. I'll be able to take you to the airport, after all.
5. You are required to obtain a visa to work in Australia.
6. It's always a good idea to make an appointment.
7. You're sure to pass. Don't worry.
8. You aren't permitted to walk on the grass.
9. I didn't manage to get through. The line was busy.
10. I refuse to discuss the matter any further.

CD2 27 See p. 58

CD2 28

1. **A** What the … where do you think you're going?
   B What do you mean?
   A Well, you're not allowed to turn right here.
   B Who says it's not allowed?
   A That sign does. "Do Not Enter." You ought to be able to read that.
   B Hey, it's impossible to see.
   A You'd better get your eyes tested. You're not fit to be on the roads.
2. **A** Promise not to tell anyone!
   B I promise.
   A It's really important not to tell a soul.
   B Trust me. I won't say a word.
   A But I know you. You're sure to tell someone.
   B Look. I really am able to keep a secret, you know, but is it OK if I tell David?
   A That's fine. He's invited too, of course. It's just that Ben and I want a really quiet affair, this being the second time around for both of us.

CD2 29

A I think you should swallow your pride and forgive and forget.
B Never! I will not.
A You'll have to in the end. You can't ignore each other forever.
B I might forgive him, but I can never forget.
A It must be possible to talk it over and work something out. You must for the sake of the children.
B Oh, I just don't know what to do!

CD2 30

A I don't know if I can come tonight.
B But you must. You said you would.
A Yeah, but I can't go out on weeknights. My parents won't let me.
B You could tell your parents that you're going over to the library to study.
A I can't. Somebody will see me and tell them.
B We'll have to cancel the party then. Lots of kids can't go out during final exams.

CD2 31

R Hello?
M Rebecca, Rebecca, is that you? I've got to talk to you.
R Maria, hi! Why all the excitement?
M Well, can you remember that quiz contest I entered, just for fun, a few weeks ago?
R Yes, I can. I remember you doing it in the coffee shop. It was the one in the *Post*, wasn't it? Didn't you have to name a bunch of capital cities?
M Yes, that's it. You've got it. Well, get this, I *won*! I came in first!
R No way! I don't believe it! What's the prize?
M A trip to New York.
R You must be kidding! That's great! For how long?
M Just three days—but it's three days in the Ritz Carlton, of all places!
R Well, you should be able to do a lot in three days. And the Ritz Carlton! I'm impressed! Doesn't that overlook Central Park?
M Yes, it does.
R I thought so. Can't say I've been there, of course.
M Well, you can now!
R What do you mean? How would I ever be able to?
M Well, it's a trip for two, and I'd really love it if you would come with me. Will you?
R You can't be serious! You know I'd love to! But why me? Surely you should be taking David.
M Haven't you heard? David and I broke up.
R Oh, I'm sorry! I didn't know. When did this happen?
M Well, a couple of weeks ago. We hadn't been getting along for a long time. Anyway, you've got to come with me!
R Well, what can I say? How could I possibly refuse an offer like that?
M You'll come then?
R I definitely will!

CD2 32

I = Interviewer   P = Pratima

I How old were you when you met your husband, Pratima?
P Mmm …. I was just sixteen.
I Were you still at school?
P No, I'd left school, but I was having private tuition at home to prepare me for some exams.
I And your father arranged your marriage, is that right?
P That's right.
I Could you tell me how he did that?
P Well, he looked around for a suitable husband. He asked friends and relatives if they knew anyone and found out about their education, their background, and, um, most importantly the family's background. He managed to get a lot of information about them, you know.
I And how long did this take?
P Not too long in my case, but, you know, sometimes a father can see up to a hundred men before he chooses one. For my sister, my elder sister, he saw over one hundred men before …
I He saw how many? Goodness. It must take up a lot of time.
P Yes, it can be difficult to decide, but for me he saw only two, um … one in the morning and one in the afternoon and, um, he chose the second one.
I What a day! Can you tell me about it?
P Yes … well, in the morning the first man was very wealthy, and he was well-dressed and had good manners, but he hadn't had a good education.
I Ah. And the other one?
P Well, he wasn't terribly wealthy, but he was well-educated, and he came from a good background. His family owned a village and were like princes. He was 22 and studying law.
I And this one your father chose?
P That's right. I think he thought money wasn't everything—for my father education was more important and anyway, if a man is well-educated, he will earn in the end. Actually, Shyam, that's my husband's name, Shyam didn't want to get married at all, but his father had told him he must, so when he came to my house to meet my father, he was very badly-dressed because he hoped my father would refuse him. But luckily for me my father did like him, and, uh, he had to say yes.

128   Audio Scripts

I He had to?

P Oh, yes, he had promised his father.

I And what about you? Did you meet both men?

P Yes, I met them that day. First my family spoke to them, and then they called me in and we spoke for four … four or five minutes.

I And did you prefer the second?

P Well, actually, I wasn't sure. I left it to my father.

I You must trust him a lot.

P Oh, yes.

I So what happened next?

P Well, after a while, there was a special day when I went to meet his family, and his family came to meet mine. It was kind of an engagement party. But we—you know—Shyam and me, we used to be on the phone every day and we'd meet regularly, but we always had to have a chaperone. And after ten months we got married.

I And how long have you been married?

P Nearly twenty-five years now.

I And ….it's been a successful marriage? Your father made a good choice?

P Oh… yes, of course, and we have two beautiful sons. They're twenty-two and seventeen now.

I And will you arrange their marriages?

P Oh, yes. My husband is planning them now. He's been asking families for some time already and …

I And your sons want it?

P Well, Krishna, he's the eldest, he's OK about it—he's studying hard and hasn't got the time to meet girls but…

I Yes, what about the youngest? Ravi, isn't it?

P Yes, um, well actually, Ravi's not so keen. It might be difficult to persuade …

I But you still believe that the system of arranged marriages is a good one?

P Oh, yes, I do, of course I do—but you know it depends on a lot, uh, especially on the family choosing the right person. But one main reason I think it does work, is that the couple enter the marriage not *expecting* too much, if you see what I mean. Actually, you know, there are many more divorces between couples who thought they were marrying for love. You know my mother, um, she had to marry at thirteen, but she's still happily married nearly fifty years later. Of course, nowadays thirteen is considered too young but you know… times change.

I Yeah, that's very true. Thank you very much indeed, Pratima.

CD2 33

1. **A** My friends went to Alaska on vacation.
   B They went *where*?
2. **A** I got home at 5:00 this morning.
   B You got home *when*?
3. **A** I paid $300 for a pair of jeans.
   B You paid *how much*?
4. **A** I met the president while I was out shopping.
   B You met *who*?
5. **A** He invited me to the White House for lunch.
   B He invited you *where*?

CD2 34

1. **A** I'm dying for a cup of coffee.
   B I wouldn't mind one myself.
2. **A** His parents are pretty well off, aren't they?
   B You can say that again! They're totally loaded!
3. **A** You must have hit the roof when she told you she'd crashed your car.
   B Well, yeah, I was a little upset.
4. **A** I think Tony was a little rude last night.
   B No kidding! He was completely out of line!
5. **A** I can't stand the sight of him!
   B I have to say I'm not too big on him, either.
6. **A** He isn't very smart, is he?
   B That's for sure. He's as dumb as dirt.

7. **A** I'm fed up with this weather! It's freezing.
   B I guess it is a little chilly.
8. **A** Well, that was a fantastic trip!
   B Yes, it was a nice little break, but all good things must come to an end.
9. **A** I'm wiped out. I've got to go to bed.
   B Yeah. I'm a little tired, too.
10. **A** They're obviously madly in love.
    B Yeah, they do seem to get along well.

CD2 35 See p. 65

CD2 36

1. **A** Is that a new watch? I bet that cost something.
   B Something? It cost a fortune!
2. **A** It's a little chilly in here, don't you think?
   B You can say that again. I'm absolutely freezing.
3. **A** These shoes aren't bad, are they?
   B They're *gorgeous*! I want them!
4. **A** Can we pull over at the next rest stop? I could use something to eat.
   B Me too. I'm starving. I didn't have breakfast this morning.

UNIT 8

CD2 37

Welcome to JUMBOLAIR, Florida—the world's only housing development where the super-rich can commute to work by jet plane from their own front doors.

Jumbolair's most famous resident is Hollywood movie star John Travolta, whose $3.5 million mansion is big enough to park a row of airplanes, including a Gulfstream executive jet, a two-seater jet fighter, and a four-engine Boeing 707, previously owned by Frank Sinatra. Travolta holds a commercial pilot's license, which means he's qualified to fly passenger jets. He can land his planes and taxi them up to his front gates. His sumptuous Florida home, which is built in the style of an airport terminal building, is the ultimate boys' fantasy house made real. As well as the parking lots for the jets, there is a heliport, swimming pool and gym, stables for 75 horses, and of course a 1.4-mile runway. Family man Travolta, who lives with wife Kelly and daughter Ella Bleu, flies daily from his home when filming. Walking out of his door and into the cockpit, he is airborne in minutes. His neighbors, most of whom share his love of aviation, don't seem to mind the roar of his jets. They say it's nice to meet a superstar who isn't full of himself. "He's just a regular guy, very friendly," says one neighbor.

CD2 38

1. The area of New York I like best is Soho.
2. My father, who's a doctor, plays the drums.
3. The book that I'm reading now is fascinating.
4. Paul passed his driver's test on the first try, which surprised everybody.
5. People who smoke risk getting all sorts of illnesses.
6. I met a man whose main aim in life was to visit every capital city in the world.
7. The Channel Tunnel, which opened in 1995, is a great way to get from England to France.
8. What I like best about work are the vacation days,
9. A short bald man seen running away from the scene of the crime is being sought by the police.

CD2 39

1. **A** How did you do on the math test?
   B Oh! Don't ask! It's too awful.
   A Oh, man. What did you get?
   B Twenty-two percent. I came in last, and I thought I was going to do really well.
2. **A** How was your vacation?
   B Great, thanks. Just what we needed.
   A Did you do much?
   B Not a lot. We just sat by the pool, read books, and took it easy for two whole weeks. Absolute bliss.
3. **A** Have you heard about Dave and Maggie?
   B No. Tell me, tell me!
   A Well, last week they went to a party, had this huge fight in front of all these people and … .
   B Did it get physical?
   A Oh, yeah! Maggie shoved Dave into a flowerpot, told him to get lost, and went off with another guy!
   B What? I'm amazed! I just can't believe Maggie'd do such a thing. It doesn't sound like her at all.
4. **A** Come on in. You must be exhausted!
   B Oof, I am. I've been traveling for the past 30 hours, and I haven't slept a wink.
   A I know—I can never sleep on a plane, either. Just sit down, take it easy, and I'll get you some water.
5. **A** How's the new job going?
   B Good, thanks, very good. But it's quite difficult. I have to deal with so many new things. Still, I'm enjoying it all.
   A Mmm – I know what you mean.
   B Yeah. It's great to be doing something that's so satisfying. And I love meeting so many people from abroad.
   A Absolutely.
6. **A** So, anyway, just to end the perfect evening, I had to walk back home because I'd lost the car keys, and I didn't have any money for a taxi. I didn't get home until three in the morning.
   B That's the funniest thing I've heard for ages. Poor you. Sorry I'm laughing.
   A Well, I'm glad you think it's so funny—I didn't think it was funny at the time.
7. **A** There is just nothing good on TV tonight!
   B What about that wildlife program?
   A Do you mean the one about the life of frogs?
   B Yeah, does it look any good?
   A You're kidding. It looks totally boring.
8. **A** What's the matter with you?
   B Oh, my gosh—I just put my foot right in my mouth.
   A What do you mean?
   B Well, I was talking to that lady over there, and I asked her when her baby was due, and, um, she told me she wasn't pregnant.
   A Oh, no! That's awful!

CD2 40

On a cold and rainy night, a mysterious young man wearing a rumpled suit walked nervously along a deserted street, carrying a briefcase full of $100 bills.

CD2 41

1. Lost in her thoughts, a beautiful young woman was sitting in her country garden, watching a bee lazily going from rose to rose gathering honey.
2. Peter, who's very wealthy, has a huge, 16th-century farmhouse, surrounded by woods in the heart of the English countryside.
3. Ann Croft, the world famous actress, who married for the sixth time only last month, was seen having lunch in a Los Angeles restaurant with a well-known European film director.

4. The trip to Hawaii, which we had looked forward to so much, was a complete and utter disaster from start to finish.
5. A ten-year-old boy, walking home from school, found an old, battered, wallet filled with $5,000 in $50 bills on Main Street.

CD2 42 Simone

Well, it was when I was living in Cairo. And it was the middle of the summer, so it was extremely hot, between 104 and 113 degrees Fahrenheit, and, um, stupidly we decided to go dancing. And, um, we went to this nightclub, and we must have danced for hours and hours. It was very hot inside, and we were sweating profusely, and by the time we came out it was about 5 o'clock in the morning, and we decided, "Ooh, wouldn't it be a great idea to go to the pyramids and see the sunrise?"
So we jumped in a taxi and the taxi was quite stuffy and hot, and we must have been starting to dehydrate at this point. Anyway, we got to the pyramids, and the sun was just starting to come up. And in Egypt, as soon as the sun comes up the temperature rises dramatically. But we were so excited at seeing the pyramids that we decided just to, um, to go and walk and see.
At this point, um, a man approached us and asked us if we wanted to borrow his motorcycle, or rent his motorcycle, and we said yes. So my friend and I, we jumped onto the motorcycle and raced out into the desert, only to find after about ten, fifteen minutes, that the motorcycle was pretty old and suddenly it broke down! So we were miles from anywhere and had to push this motorcycle to get back. I was the one at the back pushing the motorcycle, and of course I was using lots of energy. I was losing a lot of fluid. And it was getting hotter and hotter. Anyway, by the time we got home, um, I did start to feel a bit strange, I had a slight headache and, um, I decided to go straight to bed. Anyway, I woke up about half an hour later, feeling pretty confused and sick, a little nauseous. And I realized that my brain wasn't working properly, and that in fact I probably had heat exhaustion. Anyway, it wasn't very pleasant and, uh, it was a lesson in what not to do in temperatures like that. I've never done that again. And I always carry my salt tablets with me now.

CD2 43 Anna

The time that I was very, very cold, um, was a time when I was working in Russia, in a small town in central Russia, and I was going to see some friends who lived on the outskirts of the town. And they were worried about me getting lost, and they said that they'd come to meet me. But I wanted to be independent, so I told them, "Don't be silly, of course I'll find it."
And on the day of the visit, um, it was very, very cold. It might have been minus 30, but it might have been colder than that. And, um, it was so cold that at some of the tram stops and bus stops there were bonfires lit—special street fires, um, to keep people warm. And I think it was a day when the schools were closed, and the children didn't go to school because it was so cold. So I put on all the clothes that I had, all the scarves and sweaters, and I took the tram to the outskirts of the town where my friends lived. And I got off the tram, which was heated, into this cold white world. And, um, it was so cold that when you breathed in, little balls of ice formed in your nostrils. You had to keep your scarf over your mouth and nose.
About a minute, two minutes after getting off the tram my feet and hands were already hurting they were so cold. So I was walking around, trying to find the house, but it was completely anonymous this, this landscape. There were these huge snow-covered white blocks, these buildings, fifteen or sixteen floors, but they all looked exactly the same. And I couldn't find the name of the street either, and it was very, very quiet, and the tram had gone. Um… and I began, actually, to get very frightened because I was feeling so, so cold. Um, my feet and hands had gone beyond hurting almost, I couldn't feel them anymore. Um, it was pretty difficult to breathe because of the icy scarf over my mouth and nose. I just couldn't find where they lived! And I asked an old lady the way, but my Russian wasn't good enough. She didn't understand me. And I was beginning to really, seriously panic when suddenly, in the distance, I saw my friends. They'd come to find me, and they took me home.

CD2 44

1. We went dancing in temperatures of over 104°F, which was a pretty stupid thing to do.
2. My friends were worried I'd get lost, which was understandable.
3. We visited the pyramids at sunrise, which was just amazing.
4. My nostrils actually froze, which is hard to believe.
5. This motorcycle broke down, which was no joke.
6. The old lady didn't understand a word I said, which is hardly surprising since my Russian's lousy.

CD2 45

1. There are forty-four platforms at Grand Central Terminal.
2. The main hall is four hundred and seventy feet long.
3. The clock on top of the information booth has four sides.
4. The ceiling of the main hall is as high as a twelve-story building.
5. The station is located at 42nd Street and Park Avenue.
6. The original station built in 1871 cost $6.4 million.
7. The station that opened in 1913 cost $80 million.
8. The renovations in the 1990s cost $200 million.
9. One hundred and twenty-five thousand commuters use the station every day.
10. There are half a million visitors every day.

CD2 46

1. A Did you get very cold in that snowstorm?
   B Snowstorm! It was a blizzard! We were absolutely freezing!
2. A I bet you were pretty excited when your team won.
   B Excited! We were absolutely thrilled!
3. A I thought she looked kind of silly in that flowery hat, didn't you?
   B Silly! She looked absolutely ridiculous!
4. A Come on, nobody'll notice that tiny pimple on your nose.
   B They will, I just know they will! It's absolutely enormous!
5. A I thought that movie was absolutely hilarious.
   B Mmm. I wouldn't say that. It was pretty funny but not hilarious.
6. A Len left early. He wasn't feeling well.
   B I'm not surprised. When I saw him this morning he looked absolutely awful!

CD2 47 See p. 72

CD2 48 See p. 72

CD2 49

I am absolutely amazed and delighted to receive this award. I'm truly grateful to all those wonderful people who voted for me. *Red Hot in the Snow* was an absolutely fantastic movie to act in, not only because of all the totally brilliant and talented people involved in the making of it but also because of the fabulous, thrilling, and often extremely dangerous locations in Alaska. None of us could have predicted that it would be such a huge success. My special thanks go to Marius Aherne, my excellent director; Lulu Lovelace, my gorgeous costar; Roger Sims, for writing a script that was both fascinating and hilarious; and last but not least to my marvelous wife, Glynis, for her priceless support. I absolutely adore you all.

CD2 50

1. A Hello. Could I make an appointment for our golden retriever, Molly?
   B Sure. What seems to be the problem?
   A Well, she's stopped eating her food, which is very unusual for her, and she has no interest in going out for walks. She just lies around all day long …
2. A What have we got here?
   B All these old bottles, a washing machine that doesn't work anymore, and a whole bunch of cardboard.
   A All right, well, the bottles can go in there with the glass. And the washing machine—that would be metal, so it goes over there…
3. A Hello. I'd like to open an account, please.
   B Are you a student?
   A Yes, I am.
   B Well, we have a couple of special accounts for students. One gives you free checking and ATM access with a minimum balance of $1000. Another gives you up to ten transactions per month with no minimum balance and a monthly fee of …
4. A Yes, please. How can I help you?
   B Yeah, I'm driving cross-country this summer to help my grandma move, and I want some kind of coverage in case the car breaks down.
   A I see. Well, you could get a year's membership, and that includes free towing anywhere in the U.S. Just call this number if you have car trouble, and we'll send someone to tow you to the nearest garage.
   B Sounds good. How much does that cost?
   A It's $65 for a year, and your membership card can get you discounts on hotels, airfare, restaurants…
5. A Hello there, can I help you?
   B Yes, I'm looking for something for a leaky faucet? The water keeps drip, drip, dripping all night!
   A Aw, sounds terrible.
   B Yeah. My roommate said we need to replace some kind of seal or gasket? Some kind of rubber thing, I guess.
   A I know just what you need. Follow me and I'll show you…

UNIT 9

CD3 2

Dear Sally,
Do you remember me? We used to go to Springfield East together. You were the first person I got to know when I started there.

We used to sit next to each other in class, but then the teachers made us sit apart because we were always giggling so much.

I remember we'd go back to your house after school every day and listen to music for hours on end. We'd get all the Beatles records as soon as they came out. Once we ate all the food in your fridge, and your mother was furious.

Do you remember that time we nearly blew up the science lab? The teacher went crazy, but it wasn't our fault. We used to call him "Mickey Mouse" because he had sticky-out ears.

I still see Penny, and she's still as wild as ever. We meet up every now and then, and we'll always end up chatting about old times together. She's always talking about a class reunion. So if you're interested, drop me a line.

Looking forward to hearing from you.

Your old friend,

Alison Wright

PS I'm not used to calling you Sally Davis! To me, you're still Sally Wilkinson!

CD3 3

we used to go to school together
we used to sit next to each other
we were always giggling so much
we'd go back to your house
we used to call him "Mickey Mouse"
I'm not used to calling you Sally Davis

CD3 4

1. I got along very well with my mother. She was my best friend, still is. We had to get along, really. Dad left when I was three. I used to tell her everything, well, nearly everything. And she'd talk to me very openly, too. Sometimes she'd say to me, "Don't go to school today. Stay with me." And we'd go out shopping or something like that. It's a wonder I had any education at all, the number of days I missed from school.
2. I don't remember much about my childhood. My wife's always asking me questions like, "When you were a boy, did you use to …?" and I reply, "I don't know. I can't remember." We didn't … uh … really, we didn't use to talk very much. We weren't very close, or if we were, we didn't show it. I remember I used to have my hair cut every Friday. My father was in the Army, and he had a thing about short hair, so every week he'd take me to the barber. I had the shortest hair in the school. I used to hate it. And him.
3. I'm not a very neat person, but my mother's a real clean freak, so she's always telling me to pick things up and put them away and do this and do that. She'll go on for hours about how "Cleanliness is next to godliness," and that just makes me want to scream. My father isn't like that at all. He's much more laid back. I think he's just learned to tune out my mother.
4. I have very fond memories of my childhood. To me it represented security. We used to do a lot together as a family. I remember walks, and picnics, and going for car rides on a Sunday afternoon. Every Friday when my Dad came home, he'd bring us each a treat, just something little. My mother used to say he was spoiling us, but why not? It didn't do us any harm.

CD3 5

1. **A** You don't like your new teacher, do you?
   B Not a lot, but we're getting used to her.
2. **A** How can you get up at five o'clock in the morning?
   B No problem. I'm used to it.
3. **A** How come you know Mexico City so well?
   B I used to live there.
4. **A** How are you finding your new job?
   B Difficult, but I'm getting used to it bit by bit.
5. **A** Do you read comics?
   B I used to when I was young but not anymore.
6. **A** You two argue so much. How can you live together?
   B After 20 years of marriage we're used to each other.

CD3 6

1. **Alan**
I was very fortunate in high school to have a really good teacher for a subject called social studies, which combines history and geography. And I think the thing that made this teacher so good was that he not only had a terrific sense of humor, but he could also keep the class under control. We always paid attention when he wanted us to pay attention, but he could always get us to laugh at the same time. So he had a way of kind of being flexible in his teaching style. And he'd do crazy things like, you know, sometimes he'd stand on a desk and recite a poem, or he'd draw funny pictures on the blackboard. But I never forgot him. His name was Mr. Sparks, which I think is a fantastic name for a teacher. And he'd stand at the front of the class—he had this sort of funny beard—a short, pointy beard, and glasses. And this kind of graying, slicked back hair. And he'd stand there and look at us with this terrifying look on his face and then tell a joke! Just to make us all laugh!

2. **John**
I had a teacher at school who was just awful. He taught French and German, and his name was Colin Tivvy. I'll never forget that name. It sends shivers down my spine just to hear it. It wasn't that he was a bad teacher. In fact, he used to get very good results. It was the way he got those results. He taught out of pure fear. All the kids were scared stiff of him, so you'd do his homework first and best because the last thing you wanted was to make a mistake. If you made any mistake, in homework or in class, you had to write it out one hundred times that night. He'd been a soldier in the army, and he'd worked as an interrogator, and that was just how he taught. We had to stand in a line outside his classroom, and when he was ready, he'd shout, "Get in, men!," and we'd all march into class. And all through the class, he'd pace up and down the classroom, and he used to wear those kinds of shoes that didn't make a noise, you know? And the worst feeling in the whole world was when you knew he was just behind you. You were waiting for a smack on the back of the head. But the worst was when he picked you up by the hairs on the back of your neck. That hurt.

3. **Liz**
The teacher I remember most from my school days was a teacher named Miss Potts. She was a history teacher, and I was about thirteen or fourteen years old. We were all very interested in fashion, and Miss Potts used to wear the most amazing things to come in to teach. She was a very memorable teacher. Every day we'd be asking ourselves, "What's she gonna wear today?" She would wear blue tights with red skirts and very red sweaters and very bright red lipstick, and she'd come teetering into the classroom on very high heels, and we thought she looked wonderful. But the very best thing about Miss Potts was the way she actually taught history—it's what makes her most memorable. She not only brought history to life, but she made it seem easy. The way she described the characters from history made us feel as if we knew them. And sometimes instead of writing essays we would do little cartoon strips of the different tales from history, and we loved it. And

she always encouraged you, even if your answer was dead wrong. She was a brilliant, brilliant teacher. It's interesting 'cause I think another teacher who was named Miss Potts would probably have been called "potty" or, um, given some nickname like that, but there was something about her that we respected so much that she just never had a nickname.

4. **Kate**
My favorite is named Mr. Brown. We call him Brownie but not to his face. We wouldn't dare. He's my homeroom teacher, and he's great. He'll joke and make fun of you but never in a horrible, nasty way. And we like to pull his leg, too. You know, he's bald, poor guy, totally bald, but when it's his birthday we'll ask him if he wants a comb or a brush or something like that. But there's a line we all know we can't cross. We have a lot of respect for him as a teacher, and he treats us totally fairly, but he also keeps his distance. He never tries to be one of us. If a teacher ever tries to be, you know, a teenager like us, same music, same clothes, same jokes, it just doesn't work. But there's another side to Brownie. He's also in charge of discipline at the school, so whenever a student, you know, misbehaves or mouths off to a teacher, they get sent to Mr. Brown, and he scares the pants off them. And when he shouts, boy, he is absolutely terrifying. No one, but no one, messes with Mr. Brown.

CD3 7

where   nose   mail   break   through   sent

CD3 8

Customer Waiter! I'm in a hurry. Will my pizza be long?
Waiter No, sir. It'll be round!

What's the difference between a sailor and someone who goes shopping?
One goes to sail the seas, the other goes to see the sales.

What's the difference between a jeweler and a jailer?
One sells watches, and the other watches cells.

CD3 9

A = Al   V = Vicky   B = Brian

A Welcome back, everybody. This is "News Fight," and I'm your host, Al Burns. Up next, fast food. We know it's delicious. We also know it isn't very good for us or for our kids. But wait till you hear what some people want to do about it! I'm here with Vicky Wilson. She's with a group called "Concerned Parents For Healthy Choices," and, believe it or not, these guys actually want to put a special tax on fast food. Welcome, Vicky.
V Thanks, Al. I'm glad to be here.
A So, Vicky, I mean, here's the thing. There are taxes on everything these days. Income tax, gas tax, property tax, everything. So why do you want to add a tax on my burger and fries?
V Well, Al, obviously no one likes paying taxes. But what really worries me is that the next generation is going to have so many problems with kids being overweight. There are far too many people who have a terrible diet, and they just go to the nearest hamburger joint and fill themselves up with junk.
A But that so-called "junk" tastes pretty good. Right, Vicky?
V A lot of people think so. But the main point is that fast food, junk food, is too cheap. If it was taxed, people would think twice before buying it.
A OK. Let's hear from another point of view. Joining the program is Brian Roberts. He's the president of a group called the National Fast Food Association, which represents fast food restaurants across the country. Brian, welcome to "News Fight."
B Thank you.
A So, what's your opinion on this crazy new tax?

B Al, if you ask me, this is a terrible idea. Firstly, it would be an infringement on individual freedom. Secondly, another way of saying fast food is convenience food, and that means it really suits the kind of lifestyle of people today. Another thing is that it would be a tax on people who are less well off.

A Vicky, how do you respond to that?

V If you want my opinion, I think almost everyone in this country can afford to eat healthy. Basically, the issue is laziness. As I understand it, these people just can't be bothered to buy fresh food and cook it.

A Whoa. "These people?!" I guess *you* don't eat fast food.

V To tell you the truth, I don't eat in these places personally, but that's not the point. The point I'm trying to make is that a tax will help people make better choices.

A What about you, Brian? Do you eat fast food?

B Actually, I'm seeing a friend for lunch, and we're going to have a burger. There's that new place that just opened, you know, down by the square. It's supposed to be pretty good. Anyway, as I was saying, this is about individual freedom. As far as I'm concerned, people should be allowed to eat what they want. I don't see what's wrong with that.

A Vicky? Any final thoughts?

V I suppose the problem is that we don't know what's in these burgers and pizzas. If people knew how bad they were, maybe they would change their habits.

A Fair enough. OK, everyone, we've got to take a commercial break now. When we come back, we'll have my exclusive, in-depth interview with the woman whose cat does that funny dance in that Internet video …

CD3 10

What really worries me is that …
But the main point is that …
If you ask me …
Another thing is that …
If you want my opinion …
As I understand it …
To tell you the truth …
That's not the point.
The point I'm trying to make is that …
Anyway, as I was saying …
As far as I'm concerned…
I suppose the problem is that …

CD3 33 See p. 116

UNIT 10

CD3 11

A You know that prehistoric man, the one they discovered in Italy years ago …

B You mean that guy in the Alps?

A Yeah, that's the one. He's supposed to be about 5,000 years old. They've done all sorts of tests on him, you know DNA tests and stuff, to find out about his life.

B What was he? Some sort of hunter?

A Well, they aren't sure. He could have been a hunter, or he could have been some kind of shepherd, you know, looking after his sheep up in the mountains. The mystery is, what was he doing up there? He might just have gotten lost for all we know.

B It must have been cold up there. How did he keep warm?

A I guess he lived in a cave and wore stuff like animal skins. They think he fell asleep while he was taking shelter from a snowstorm, so he may have died from cold and starvation. He shouldn't have gone up so high without the right, you know, protective clothing.

B I wonder what they did for food 5,000 years ago. They hunted wild animals, didn't they, with arrows and axes and things?

A Yeah, I guess they ate a lot of meat and berries and fruit. They might have even grown crops, you know, like grains to make bread.

B No, they can't have been that clever. I bet they didn't know how to do that. I'd have thought they just ate meat, you know, like carnivores.

A Who knows? Maybe these tests will tell us. I figure they didn't get around much. It would have been too difficult.

B Sure. I wouldn't have thought they traveled much at all. I bet they stayed in the same area. How old was he when he died?

A They think he was maybe 40 to 45, which must have been pretty old in those days.

B I bought that magazine, *New Scientist*, so we can read all about the results.

A You shouldn't have bothered. I downloaded them from the Internet. Let's take a look at them.

CD3 12

1. What was he?
   He could have been a hunter, or he could have been a shepherd.
2. What was he doing in the mountains?
   He might have been looking after his sheep, or he might have gotten lost.
3. Where did he live? What did he wear?
   He must have lived in a cave. He must have worn animal skins.
4. How did he die?
   He may have fallen asleep. He may have died of cold and starvation.
5. Was it a good idea to go so high?
   He shouldn't have gone so high on his own.
   He should have worn protective clothing.
6. What did he eat?
   He must have eaten a lot of meat and berries.
   They might have grown crops like grains to make bread.
   They can't have grown crops. I'd have thought they just ate meat.
7. Did they travel much?
   I wouldn't have thought they traveled much at all.
   They must have stayed in the same area.
8. How old was he when he died?
   He could have been between 40 and 45.
   That must have been pretty old in those days.

CD3 13

1. I *did* tell you about Joe's party. You must not have been listening.
2. Thanks so much for all your help. I couldn't have managed without you.
3. Flowers, for me! Oh, that's so nice, but you really shouldn't have.
4. Come on! We're only five minutes late. The movie may not have started yet.
5. I don't believe that Kathy's going out with Mark. She would have told me, I know she would.
6. We raced to get to the airport on time, but we shouldn't have worried. The flight was delayed.
7. We've got a letter here that isn't for us. The mailman must have delivered it by mistake.
8. You shouldn't have gone swimming in such rough seas. You could have drowned!

CD3 14

Hello?
Oh, it's you.
We're all right, no thanks to you. Why are you calling?
What do you mean, next Saturday? What about next Saturday?
Already! Is it the second Saturday of the month so soon? Yes, I suppose it is. All right, then.
Where are you thinking of taking them? The children always pester me if they don't know, especially Daniel.
The zoo! Again! Can't you think of anything else? They hated it last time. Nicky did, anyway.
That's not what she told me. Anyway, that's up to you. What time are you going to pick them up?
OK. I'll have them ready. By the way, when they come home after a day with you, they're always filthy. Can't Alison wash their clothes?
Well, she has enough time to go shopping and have lunch with her friends, from what the kids have told me.
All right! I don't want to argue about it.
I'll tell them you called. Bye.

CD3 15

1. **A** That exam was totally impossible!
   B You can say that again! I couldn't possibly have passed.
2. **A** You might as well apply for the job, even though you're too young.
   B Yes, why not! After all, I've got nothing to lose. You never know, I might be just the person they're looking for.
3. I know I shouldn't have eaten a whole tub of ice cream, but I just couldn't help it. I feel as fat as a pig now.
4. **A** I'm going to tell her exactly what I think of her.
   B I wouldn't do that if I were you. It could get really nasty.
5. **A** You should have told me that Jackie and Dave broke up!
   B Sorry! I thought you knew. Everybody else does.
6. **A** I think you should forget all about her and move on.
   B Believe me, I would if I could. But I just can't get her out of my mind. I think it must be love.
   A Oh no!
7. **A** You should have been here yesterday! You'd have died laughing!
   B Why? What was so funny?
   B Pedro was imitating the teacher, and he was so good, when the teacher walked in.
8. **A** Then I found out that Annie's been going out with … guess who? Dave!
   B Duh! I could have told you *that*. It's common knowledge. Where have you been?
9. I'd known this guy for five minutes when he asked me to marry him! I just couldn't believe it! Maybe he does that to every girl he meets.
10. **A** I could use a break.
    B Me, too. I'm dying for some coffee. This class has been going on forever.

CD3 16

Jim, who ran away from his nurse, and was eaten by a lion
There was a boy whose name was Jim;
His friends were very good to him.
They gave him tea, and cakes, and jam,
And slices of delicious ham,
And read him stories through and through,
And even took him to the zoo—

But there it was the dreadful fate
Befell him, I now relate.
You know—at least you ought to know,
For I have often told you so—
That children never are allowed
To leave their nurses in a crowd;
Now this was Jim's especial foible,
He ran away when he was able,
And on this inauspicious day
He slipped his hand and ran away!
He hadn't gone a yard when—bang!
With open jaws, a lion sprang,
And hungrily began to eat
The boy: beginning at his feet.
Now just imagine how it feels
When first your toes and then your heels,
And then by gradual degrees,
Your shins and ankles, calves and knees,
Are slowly eaten, bit by bit.
No wonder Jim detested it!
No wonder that he shouted "Hi!"
The honest keeper heard his cry,
Though very fat, he almost ran
To help the little gentleman.
"Ponto!" he cried, with angry frown
"Let go, sir! Down, sir! Put it down!"
The lion having reached his head,
The miserable boy was dead!
When nurse informed his parents they
Were more concerned than I can say.
His mother, as she dried her eyes,
Said, "Well—it gives me no surprise,
He would not do as he was told!"
His father, who was self-controlled
Bade all the children round attend
To James' miserable end,
And always keep a-hold of nurse
For fear of finding something worse.

UNIT 11

CD3 17

1. A No, I can't possibly go out tonight. I shouldn't have gone out last night.
   B Come on—we had a great time. It was a wild party!
   A I know it was.
   B So, when's your exam?
   A Tomorrow, 9 o'clock. If only I hadn't left *all* my studying till the last minute.
   B I wouldn't worry if I were you. You know you always do OK.
   A There's always a first time.
   B Good luck anyway.
2. A If only we could just fly off to that island.
   B That would be fantastic. I'd sit on a beach and read all day.
   A I'd just sleep forever. I can't remember the last time I got a full night's sleep.
   B Yeah. Sometimes I wish I'd never had kids. I mean, not *really*, but—
   A I know what you mean. No—you can't have an ice cream cone. I said no!
3. A Oh, man! What would you give to drive one of those?
   B Which one would you choose if you had the money?
   A That's a big "if!" But … mmm … if I won the lottery, I'd buy the Aston Martin.
   B I wouldn't—I'd go for the Ferrari.
   A In your dreams.
4. A Great shot, Charlie! Way to go!
   B Don't you wish you still played soccer?
   A Me? No. I was never any good. But *you* could have been a great player if you'd wanted.

B Nah! I wasn't as good as Charlie. Aaah—ooh, almost! Yes!
   A Yeah, he'll go far.
5. A Look, I know I shouldn't have been speeding, but it was only for two minutes.
   B I've already written the ticket.
   A Come on, couldn't you look the other way? It was literally one minute.
   B One minute, two minutes. You can't break the speed limit, it's as simple as that.
   A But I just wanted to get to the drugstore before it closed. I've got to pick up a prescription for my sick grandmother. Supposing you let it go just this once.
   B I don't care what you were doing. I'm just doing my job. You've got two weeks to pay.

CD3 18

1. A Would it be OK if I left a little early today? I have a dental appointment.
   B No problem. Just tell Janet to cover for you.
2. A Win? What do you mean? If you ask me, they don't stand a chance.
   B But they've been playing much better lately, don't you think?
   A Come on. They haven't won a game in months.
3. A If you knew what I know, you'd never go out with him again.
   B You're just jealous.
4. A Could I have a word with you if you've got a minute?
   B Yeah, of course, but I'm in a bit of a rush.
   A It's about that pay raise I was promised.
5. A Aren't you helping Jackie plan her wedding?
   B I am. It's a nightmare. If anything went wrong, I'd never forgive myself.
6. A How's it going?
   B OK. If all goes well, we should be finished by Friday. We've just got to put the finishing touches on the doors and windows.
7. A We arrived on a Tuesday and—
   B It was a Thursday, not a Tuesday, if I remember correctly.
   A Oh, Tuesday, Thursday—the day doesn't matter. I'll just never forget the blue of the water and the white of the sand.
8. A Well, if worse comes to worst, we can always postpone it.
   B I'd rather not. I've got a little headache. The sea air will do me good.
   A OK, if you're sure.
9. A You haven't made much progress, if any.
   B What do you mean? I've written 500 words.
   A Yeah, but you have to write 10,000.
10. A I don't think much of Nancy's new boyfriend. He's really cold and arrogant.
    B Actually, I don't think he's cold or arrogant. If anything, he's a little shy.
    A Shy! You wouldn't say that if you'd seen him at Ned's party!

CD3 19

1. In any relationship you have to be prepared to give and take. You can't have your own way all the time.
2. I didn't buy much at the mall. Just a few odds and ends for the kids. Socks for Ben and hairbands for Jane.
3. I'd been visiting Florida off and on for years before I finally moved there.
4. It's difficult to explain the ins and outs of the rules of baseball. It's so complicated.
5. A What did you get me for my birthday?
   B You'll have to wait and see.
6. A Oh, no! The Burtons are coming for lunch! I hate their kids!

B I'm sorry, but you'll just have to grin and bear it. It's only for an hour or so.
7. OK, you can have it for $90. That's my final offer, take it or leave it.
8. California has lots of faults, of course, but by and large, it's a nice place to live.

CD3 20 See p. 153

CD3 21

Well, my story, I guess it's in the supernatural category—which is—which is strange for me because I am a very down-to-earth person. I am basically pretty skeptical when people tell weird and wonderful stories. But there is just one time when something very weird and inexplicable happened to me.
Um, it was when I was in college, a long time ago, and I had a girlfriend, and the first time I stayed at her house I had this incredibly vivid dream. You know sometimes when you wake up and you're not sure what's more real, the dream or what's around you? It was like that. Nothing very momentous happened in the dream, but in the main part of it I was walking along a street in my hometown, and I bumped into my girlfriend unexpectedly, and we stood in the street and we kissed and everyone was looking, and it was just a really strange atmosphere. Right?
And I was just lying there, in bed, and I was just thinking how incredibly vivid this dream was. I could just remember every detail of the scene. And then my girlfriend came in with a cup of coffee for me. And she walked in the door and said, "Wow, I had this really strange dream last night." I just knew what she was going to say, it felt like that, and she went on to describe the dream she'd had and it was *exactly* the same as the dream I'd had. And then she looked at me and she said, "What's wrong?" Because I must have looked very, very shocked. And I asked her to describe the street where we were. And she described the shop that we were standing in front of, and she said it was a stationery store. She remembered that, selling pens and paper, and stuff like that, which is exactly right. And I was feeling pretty cold and shivery by this time.
Well, the really spooky part is that I knew it was the town that I had grown up in, but at this point she'd never been there, so she didn't know the town at all, and yet she was describing it very accurately. And I was… I was kind of obsessed by this point, and I wanted to make sure that it was not just a similar street and drew this little map of the street and asked her to describe things, and she put tons of details into it—like she could say exactly where the traffic lights and the crosswalk were. So, I don't know, it must have been my dream in a way because only I knew the town, but somehow I must have transmitted it to her. It's just inexplicable. Well, I saw a TV show last year where they said that it's called "dream telepathy," and they say that it's not that unusual in dreams. Well, it's never happened to me since, and to be honest, I can't say that I'd want it to because it was actually, strangely, very disturbing.

CD3 22

1. A I could kick myself. As soon as I'd handed it in, I remembered what the answer was.
   B Oh, I hate it when that happens! But do you think you still passed?
2. A I can't believe it! I've spent all morning trying to send this, and all I get is, "Ooops! Your message wasn't sent. Try again later."
   B What a pain! Have you tried calling the computer helpline?
3. A These instructions don't make any sense to me at all. If you can follow them, you're a genius.
   B Don't ask me! I had exactly the same trouble trying to put together a nightstand.

4. **A** It's not fair. I'd been looking forward to watching it all day and then the phone goes and rings!
   B Typical! And who was it? Anyone interesting?
5. **A** How many times do I have to tell you? Take them off *before* you come into the house!
   B Go easy on me! I was in a hurry. Anyway, they're not *that* muddy.
6. **A** You've got to be kidding. You promised you'd deliver it by Thursday at the latest. Now you're saying next week!
   B I'm very sorry, sir. I'm afraid there's nothing I can do about it. It's out of my hands.
7. **A** I went away to think about it, and of course, when I went back it was gone. I wish I'd just bought it then and there.
   B It's such a shame. It would have gone so well with your white jeans.
8. **A** What a waste of time! Ten minutes listening to music and, "All our lines are busy. Thank you for waiting."
   B I know, it drives me crazy. But worse still is that you never get to speak to a real person anyway!

CD3 23 See p. 97

UNIT 12

CD3 24

My grandfather, who's a widower, used to be a judge, and when he retired the year before last, he decided to go on an ocean cruise. He enjoyed the cruise very much. He sailed all around the world, and it sounded like a great experience. Anyway, the most interesting thing about this cruise was that he met an attractive widow. I think she's pretty rich, too. She's from California. Well, my grandfather invited her to have dinner with him, and they got along really well with one another. And, would you believe it, my grandfather fell in love? No kidding! He says that you can find love at any age. And the next thing we knew, he'd asked her to marry him. Apparently, they were married by the captain of the ship. It's so romantic. The whole family's amazed, but we're all very happy for him 'cause he's been pretty lonely since my grandmother died. I just hope I find love one day like Grandpa.

CD3 25

1. Do any of your friends like dancing?
2. What are the people in your class like?
3. I just sent my nephew $10 for his birthday.
4. Did you know Bob's training to be a vet, and he doesn't even like animals?
5. Isn't your mother Canadian?
6. What do you think the most important thing in life is?
7. I bet you've told lots of girls that you love them.
8. It's very kind of you to offer, but I can't take your car. You might have to use it this afternoon.
9. There was quite a crowd at your birthday party, wasn't there?

CD3 26

1. **A** Do any of your friends like dancing?
   B What do you mean, any? *All* my friends like dancing. We go every Saturday night.
2. **A** What are the people in your class like?
   B They're great. Every person in my class is really friendly. We all get along really well together.

3. **A** I just sent my nephew $10 for his birthday.
   B Well, I have five nieces. I gave $10 to each one for Christmas. And then I had nephews, cousins, in-laws, godchildren… It cost me a fortune.
   A I only have the one nephew for now. Thank goodness.
4. **A** Did you know Bob's training to be a vet, and he doesn't even like animals?
   B That's strange. Don't you think a love of animals is vital for a vet?
   A Of course. I guess Bob wanted to be a doctor, but he failed the exams.
5. **A** Isn't your mother Canadian?
   B Actually, *both* my parents are Canadian. My father was born in Montreal, but he moved to New York when he was eighteen.
6. **A** What do you think the most important thing in life is?
   B I think love is everything. If you can find true love, you'll be happy forever.
7. **A** I bet you've told lots of girls that you love them.
   B This time it's different. The love I have for you is forever. I've never felt like this before.
8. **A** It's very kind of you to offer, but I can't take your car. You might have to use it this afternoon.
   B Look, I have *two* cars. Borrow either one. I don't mind. I probably won't be using either anyway.
9. **A** There was quite a crowd at your birthday party, wasn't there?
   B Yeah, it was great to see everyone, and I think they all had a good time.

CD3 27

1. What's that song you're singing?
2. Look at this ladybug on my hand!
3. Did you hear that storm in the middle of the night?
4. Mmm! These strawberries are delicious!
5. Take those dirty shoes off! I've just cleaned in here.
6. I can't stand this weather. It's really getting me down.
7. Who was that man you were talking to this morning?
8. Do you remember when we were young? Those were the days!
9. Children have no respect for authority these days, do they?

CD3 28

1. **A** What was the meal like?
   B It was disgusting, every bit as bad as you said it would be.
2. **A** Did you apologize to all the guests?
   B Each and every one of them. I felt like I had to.
3. **A** They didn't all pass, did they?
   B All but three did. Three out of 20, that's not bad.
4. **A** Sorry, I only have 50 cents on me.
   B Don't worry. Every little bit helps, you know.
5. **A** When do you think you'll get there?
   B If all goes well, we should be there about six.
6. **A** Want to grab a bite to eat?
   B If it's all the same to you, I'd rather not.

CD3 29

1. Bernie
Personally, I'm just happy to be alive. I have this enormous appetite to get everything I can out of life. I know it sounds corny, but after all that I've been through I just appreciate each day. Uh—every single day I have with my wife and kids is much more than I thought I'd have a few years ago.

It all started in my 20s—I began to feel very run-down, and, being a pretty athletic person, it was clear something wasn't quite right. Anyway, I had some tests, and when the results came back, the doctor walked into the room and I just knew from his face that it was something awful. Uh, I'd been diagnosed with a rare liver disease, and he told me that if I didn't have a transplant, I'd be dead in 18 months. I went into denial. You see, I'd recently gotten married and our baby son had just been born, and I couldn't stand the thought of him not having a father. Anyway, I had the transplant and at first everyone was very optimistic, but in fact … my body rejected the transplant and … uh … from relief I fell back into despair. I had to wait for an exact match, a matching donor, to be found. It was torture not only for me but for my whole family. This time though, after the operation I knew right away it would be OK. It felt different. Eventually I started working again. These days the only thing that makes me unhappy is meeting people who don't realize what a gift life is—they just take all they have for granted. I could never do that. The birth of our daughter a year ago was just the icing on the cake for me.

2. Hayley
I = Interviewer   H = Hayley
I Teenagers get a bad rap, don't they?
H I know, and it's so unfair—you watch TV or read the papers and it's all kids getting high on drugs and booze and stuff.
I So, how do you and you friends get your kicks?
H Well, of course we like going out and having fun. We go to parties and dance and stuff…
I And drink?
H Well, actually, most of us just go for the dancing. I just love it when I'm dancing, I …
I Do you have a boyfriend?
H Not right now. Life's simpler that way. I'm really happier without one. You have a boyfriend and all they ever want to do is watch football, play football, talk about football. Boring! I have really good times with my girlfriends. We do things and have real conversations.
I So what do you talk about? Boys?
H OK, yeah sometimes. But lots of things. Honestly, the best times I've had are just nights talking with my friends.
I Do any of them have boyfriends?
H Oh yeah. Some girls have to have boyfriends. You know what I mean.
I What do you mean?
H Well, you know, they don't feel good about themselves unless some boy wants them. It's all they want to talk about, uh…
I And you don't like that?
H Of course not. It's pathetic. I want to do things for myself, by myself—not tie myself to one person. I had a boyfriend all last year—yeah, he was cute, but you can't have a relationship for life that begins when you're fifteen.
I Some people do.
H Not these days. I want to see the world, meet lots of people, get a good career before I settle down.
I Sounds exciting. Good luck with it all.

3. Tony
The kind of things that get me down are part political and part physical. I suppose like a lot of old, or older, people, I think the world has gone to pot. All these politicians come and go, but they don't make any difference, they all sound the same, they make promises and then break them. And then, on the physical side, I don't have the energy I used to have. I'm exhausted by lunchtime. I always seem to have aches and pains somewhere—knees, hip, shoulder, back.

The best thing I ever did was take early retirement. Honestly! It was like buying my life back. Suddenly I could do what I wanted. The first thing we did, Lizzie and me, was move to the country. We have a fantastic cottage by the sea, and we love taking our dog, Bonnie, for walks on the beach, or the cliffs, or the harbors. We have a big backyard, and there is no better feeling for me than spending the whole day outside. I like to walk around in the early morning, listening to the birds and smelling the fresh, early-morning air. I planted some fruit trees a year or so ago, and that's coming along well, and Lizzie and I are content just to putter in the vegetable garden, or cut the grass, or weed the flower beds. Having said that, we go out for lunch with friends pretty often or we have friends come and stay with us for the weekend. One of my favorite things to do is to sit out on the porch in the evening and watch the sunset with a good book.

4. **Tommy**
I = Interviewer   T = Tommy
I   So, what makes you happy, Tommy?
T   Mmmm ... my *best* thing is to go to Bigbury Beach.
I   Where's that?
T   It's where the ocean is.
I   Nice. What do you do there?
T   I play... I play with my brother in the tide pools and we have buckets and shovels and when the tide's in we go on the sea tractor and—
I   A sea tractor? What's that?
T   You know, it's when the tide comes in and you can't get to the island, so you go on the sea tractor. It's got big, big wheels, hugest wheels ever.
I   Bigger than you?
T   Yeah. This big. You have to climb up the steps at the back to get on it.
I   Wow! And it goes through the water to the island?
T   Yeah. I like it. It costs 60 cents.
I   Is that right? It sounds great, Tommy, and going on the sea tractor makes you happy. So, what makes you unhappy?
T   Uh ... uh, I think it's—it's—I think it's when birds die.
I   When *birds* die?
T   Yeah, I don't like it.
I   Have you *seen* birds die?
T   Yeah, our cat got one in the backyard, and it was dead and it made me sad.
I   Ah, I see. That *is* sad when a cat catches a bird.
T   Yeah, and I saw it lying on our porch. I didn't like it.

CD3 30
1. **A** I can't believe it. I failed again.
   B Don't worry. You'll have better luck next time.
   A But that was the second time.
   B Well, maybe you'll pass next time. You know what they say—third time's the charm!
2. **A** Come on. Get up! Get a life!
   B What do you mean?
   A Well, it's high time you did something other than watch soap operas all day.
   B Like what?
   A I dunno. Travel, see the world. Live life.
   B Boring.
   A I give up. Be a couch potato if that's what you want.
3. **A** Oh no! We missed it. It must have left right on time.
   B I thought we'd just make it.
   A What do we do now? There isn't another until 1 o'clock.
   B That's nearly two hours to kill!
   A More shopping?
   B Not on your life. I'm shopped-out! Let's just get a cup of coffee. There's a cafe on platform 1.

4. **A** How's it going?
   B Well, they've finished at last but not on time—almost four weeks late.
   A And how much is it all going to cost?
   B We haven't gotten the final bill yet—
   A Well, you can bet your life it'll be more than they estimated.
   B I know. We *were* going to have the kitchen decorated too, but enough's enough for the time being.
5. **A** How come Dave has such a cushy life? He never seems to do any work.
   B Didn't you know? He won the lottery.
   A You're kidding. I had no idea. I play the lottery every week and never win a thing.
   B Me neither. But that's life.

CD3 31 That's Life
That's life, that's what people say.
You're ridin' high in April,
Shot down in May.
But I know I'm gonna change that tune,
When I'm back on top in June.
That's life, funny as it seems.
Some folks get their kicks
Steppin' on dreams;
But I don't let it get me down,
'cause this ol' world keeps spinnin' around.
I've been a puppet, a pauper, a pirate,
A poet, a pawn, and a king.
I've been up and down and over and out
And I know one thing:
Each time I find myself flat on my face,
I pick myself up and get back in the race.
That's life, I can't deny it,
I thought of quitting,
But my heart just won't buy it.
If I didn't think it was worth a try,
I'd roll myself up in a big ball and die.

CD3 32
1. **A** Did you see the game last night?
   B No, but apparently it was a good one. We won, didn't we?
   A Actually, it was a tie, but it was really exciting.
2. **A** What do you think of Claire's new boyfriend?
   B Personally, I can't stand him. I think he'll dump her like all the rest. However, that's her problem, not mine.
   A Poor old Claire! She always picks the wrong ones, doesn't she? Anyway, we'll find out soon enough.
3. **A** I don't know how you can afford to buy all those fabulous clothes!
   B Hopefully, I'm going to get a bonus this month. My boss promised. After all, I did earn the company over $100,000 last year. Basically, I deserve it.
4. **A** She said some terrible things to me. I hate her!
   B All the same, I think you should apologize to her. If you ask me, you lose your temper too easily. You're being very childish. It's time you both grew up!
   A What? I never thought I'd hear you speak to me like that.
   B Honestly, I'm not taking sides. I just think you should make up.
5. **A** So, Billy. You say that this is the last record you're ever going to make?
   B Definitely.
   A But surely you realize how upset your fans are going to be?
   B Obviously, I don't want to hurt anyone, but basically, I'm fed up with pop music. I'd like to do something else. Ideally, I'd like to get into movies.

Grammar Reference

UNIT 1

1.1 The tense system

There are three classes of verbs in English: auxiliary verbs, modal verbs, and full verbs.

1 Auxiliary verbs

The auxiliary verbs are *be*, *do*, and *have*.

be

1. *Be* is used with verb + *-ing* to make continuous verb forms.
   You're lying. (present)
   They were reading. (past)
   I've been swimming. (present perfect)
   We'll be having dinner at 8 o'clock. (future)
   You must be joking! (infinitive)

2. *Be* is used with the past participle to make the passive.
   These books are printed in Hong Kong. (present)
   Where were you born? (past)
   The car's been serviced. (present perfect)
   The city had been destroyed. (past perfect)
   This work should be done soon. (infinitive)

do

1. *Do/does/did* are used in the Present Simple and the Past Simple.
   Do you live near here? (question)
   She doesn't understand. (negative)
   When did they arrive? (question)

2. *Do/does/did* are used to express emphasis when there is no other auxiliary.
   I'm not interested in sports, but I do like tennis.
   "If only she had a car!" "She does have a car!"
   "Why didn't you tell me?" "I did tell you!"

have

Have is used with the past participle to make perfect verb forms.
Have you ever tried sushi? (present)
My car had broken down before. (past)
I'll have finished soon. (future)
I'd like to have met Napoleon. (infinitive)
Having had lunch, we cleaned up. (participle)

Other uses of auxiliary verbs

1. In question tags.
   It's cold today, isn't it?
   You don't understand, do you?
   You haven't been to China, have you?

2. In short answers. *Yes* or *No* alone can sound abrupt.
   "Are you hungry?" "No, I'm not."
   "Do you like jazz?" "Yes, I do."
   "Did you have a nice meal?" "Yes, we did."
   "Has she seen the mess?" "No, she hasn't."

3. In reply questions. These are not real questions. They are used to show that the listener is paying attention and is interested. They are practiced on p. 29 of the Student Book.
   "The party was awful." "Was it? What a pity."
   "I love hamburgers." "Do you? I hate them."
   "I've bought you a present." "Have you? How kind!"

2 Modal auxiliary verbs

These are the modal auxiliary verbs.

can	could	may	might	will	would
should	must	ought to	need		

They are auxiliary verbs because they "help" other verbs. They are different from *be*, *do*, and *have* because they have their own meanings.
He must be at least 70. (= probability)
You must try harder. (= obligation)
Can you help me? (= request)
She can't have gotten my letter. (= probability)
I'll help you. (= willingness)
Modal auxiliary verbs are dealt with in Units 5, 7, 9, 10, and 11.

3 Full verbs

Full verbs are all the other verbs in the language. For example:

run	walk	eat	love	go	talk	write

The verbs *be*, *do*, and *have* can also be used as full verbs with their own meanings.
Have you been to school today?
I want to be an engineer.
I do a lot of business in Russia.
The vacation did us a lot of good.
They're having a fight.
Have you had enough to eat?

1.2 English tense usage

English tenses have two elements of meaning: time and aspect.

Time

1. The time referred to is usually obvious.
   English people drink tea. (all time)
   Shh! I'm watching this program! (now)
   I'll see you later. (future)
   I went out with Jenny last night. (past)

2. Sometimes a present tense form can refer to the future.
   I'm going out tonight. (Present Continuous for near future)
   The train leaves at 10:00 tomorrow. (Present Simple for a timetable)
   If you see Peter, say hello from me. (Present Simple in a subordinate clause)

3. Sometimes a past tense form can refer to the present.
   I wish I could help you, but I can't.
   This use of unreal tense usage is dealt with in Unit 11.

The simple aspect

1. The simple aspect describes an action that is seen to be complete. The action is viewed as a whole unit.
   The sun rises in the east. (= all time)
   When I've read the book, I'll lend it to you. (= complete)
   She has red hair. (= permanent)
   He always wore a suit. (= a habit)
   It rained every day of our vacation. (= the whole two weeks)
   This store will close at 7:00 this evening. (= a fact)

2. Remember the verbs that rarely take the continuous. This is because they express states that are seen to be permanent and not subject to frequent change.

Verbs of the mind	know understand believe think mean
Verbs of emotions	love hate like prefer care
Verbs of possession	have own belong
Certain other verbs	cost need contain depend

3. The simple aspect expresses a completed action. For this reason we must use the simple, not the continuous, if the sentence contains a number that refers to "things done."

*She's **written three** letters this morning.*
*I **drink ten** cups of tea a day.*
*He **read five** books while he was on vacation.*

Simple tenses are dealt with further in Units 2, 3, and 5.

The continuous aspect

1. The continuous aspect focuses on the duration of an activity. We are aware of the passing of time between the beginning and the end of the activity. The activity is not permanent.

*I**'m staying** with friends until I find a house. (= temporary)*
*What **are** you **doing** on your hands and knees? (= in progress)*
*I**'ve been studying** English for years. (And I still am.)*
*Don't call at 8:00. We**'ll be eating**. (= in progress)*

2. Because the activity is seen in progress, it can be interrupted.

*We **were walking** across a field when we were attacked by a bull.*
*"**Am I disturbing** you?" "No. I**'m** just **doing** the ironing."*

3. The activity may not be complete.

*I **was writing** a report on the flight home. (I didn't finish it.)*
*He **was drowning**, but we saved him. (He didn't die.)*
*Who's **been drinking** my coffee? (There's some left.)*

4. The action of some verbs, by definition, lasts a long time, for example, *live, work, play*. The continuous gives these actions limited duration and makes them temporary.

*Hans **is living** in London while he**'s learning** English.*
*I**'m working** as a waiter until I go to college.*
*Murray **has been playing** well recently. Maybe he'll win Wimbledon.*

5. The action of some other verbs lasts a short time, for example, *lose, break, cut, hit, crash*. They are often found in the simple.

*I **lost** all my money.   I**'ve crashed** your car. Sorry.*
*She's **cut** her finger.   He **hit** me.*

In the continuous, the action of these verbs seems longer or habitual.

*I**'ve been cutting** the grass. (= for hours)*
*He **was hitting** me. (= again and again)*

Note

We cannot say a sentence such as *~~I've been crashing your car~~* because it suggests an activity that was done deliberately and often.
Continuous tenses are dealt with further in Units 2, 3, and 5.

The perfect aspect

The perfect aspect expresses two ideas.

1. The action is completed before another time.

*Have you ever **been** to the U.S.? (= some time before now)*
*When I arrived, Peter **had left**. (= some time before I arrived)*
*I'll **have finished** the report by 10:00. (= some time before then)*

2. The exact time of the verb action is not important. The perfect aspect refers to indefinite time.

*Have you **seen** my wallet anywhere? I've lost it. (= before now)*
*We'll **have arrived** by this evening. (= before this evening)*

The exception to this is the Past Perfect, which *can* refer to definite time.

*I recognized him immediately. I **had met** him **in 1992** at college.*
Perfect tenses are dealt with further in Units 2, 3, and 5.

Active and passive

1. Passive sentences move the focus of attention from the subject of an active sentence to the object.

*Shakespeare **wrote** Hamlet in 1599.*
***Hamlet**, one of the great tragedies, **was written** in 1599.*

2. In most cases, *by* and the agent are omitted in passive sentences. This is because the agent is not important, isn't known, or is understood.

My car was stolen yesterday.
This house was built in the 17th century.
She was arrested for shoplifting.

3. Sometimes we prefer to begin a sentence with what is known and end a sentence with what is "new." In the passive, the "new" can be the agent of the active sentence.

*"What a lovely painting!" "Yes. It was painted **by Canaletto**."*

4. In informal language, we often use *you* or *they* to refer to people in general or to no person in particular. In this way we can avoid using the passive.

***You** can buy anything in Macy's.*
***They're** building a new airport soon.*

5. There are many past participles that are used more like adjectives.

*I'm very **impressed** by your work.*
*You must be **disappointed** with your exam results.*
*I'm **exhausted**! I've been on my feet all day.*

Passive sentences are dealt with further in Unit 3.

UNIT 2

Introduction to the Present Perfect

1. Many languages have a past tense to refer to past time, and a present tense to refer to present time. English has these, too, but it also has the Present Perfect, which relates past actions to the present.

2. The use of the Past Simple roots an action in the past, with no explicit connection to the present. When we come across a verb in the Past Simple, we want to know *When?*

3. The use of the Present Perfect always has a link with the present. When we come across a verb in the Present Perfect, we want to know how this affects the situation now.

4. Compare these sentences.

*I **lived** in Rome. (But not anymore.)*
*I**'ve lived** in Rome, Paris, and New York. (I know all these cities now.)*
*I**'ve been living** in New York for ten years. (And I'm living there now.)*
*She**'s been married** three times. (She's still alive.)*
*She **was married** three times. (She's dead.)*
***Did** you **see** the Renoir exhibition? (It's finished now.)*
***Have** you **seen** the Renoir exhibition? (It's still on.)*
***Did** you **see** that program on TV? (I'm thinking of the one that was on last night.)*
***Did** you **enjoy** the movie? (Said as we're leaving the theater.)*
***Have** you **enjoyed** the vacation? (Said near the end of the vacation.)*
*Where **have** I **put** my glasses? (I want them now.)*
*Where **did** I **put** my glasses? (I had them a minute ago.)*
*It **rained** yesterday. (= past time)*
*It**'s been snowing**. (There's snow still on the ground.)*

2.1 Present Perfect Simple and Continuous

See the introduction to the perfect aspect and the continuous aspect in Unit 1. These tenses have three main uses.

Unfinished past

The verb action began in the past and continues to the present. It possibly goes on into the future, as well.

We've lived in this house for 20 years.
Sorry I'm late. Have you been waiting long?
I've been a teacher for five years.
I've been working at the same school all that time.

Notes

- There is sometimes little or no difference between the simple and the continuous.

  I've played
  I've been playing | *tennis since I was a kid.*

- The continuous can sometimes suggest a more temporary situation. The simple can sound more permanent.

  I've been living with a host family for six weeks.
  The castle has stood on the hill overlooking the sea for centuries.

- Certain verbs, by definition, suggest duration, for example, *wait, rain, snow, learn, sit, lie, play, stay.* They are often found in the continuous.

  It's been raining all day.
  She's been sitting reading for hours.

- Remember that state verbs rarely take the continuous.

  I've known Joan for years. *I've been knowing
  How long have you had that car?* *have you been having
  I've never understood why she likes him.* *I've never been understanding

Present result

The verb action happened in the past, usually the recent past, and the results of the action are felt now.

You've changed. What have you done to yourself?
I've lost some weight.
I've been doing some exercise.
I'm covered in mud because I've been gardening.

In this use, the simple emphasizes the completed action. The continuous emphasizes the repeated activities over a period of time.

Notes

- Certain verbs, by definition, suggest a short action, for example, *start, find, lose, begin, stop, break, die, decide, cut.* They are more often found in the simple.

  We've decided to get married.
  I've broken a tooth.
  I've cut my finger.

  In the continuous, these verbs suggest a repeated activity.

  I've been stopping eating junk food for years.
  You've been losing everything lately. What's the matter with you?
  I've been cutting wood.

- The use of the simple suggests a completed action.

  I've painted the bathroom.

  The use of the continuous suggests a possibly incomplete action.

  I'm tired because I've been working. (Finished? Not finished?)
  Someone's been drinking my tea. (There's some left.)

- The continuous can be found unqualified by any further information.

  My hair's wet because I've been swimming.
  We're tired because we've been working.
  "Why is your face red?" "I've been running."
  The simple sounds wrong in this use.
  I've swum. *We've worked.* *I've run.*

- Sometimes there is little difference between the Past Simple and the Present Perfect.

  Where | *did you put*
  have you put | *my keys?*

Indefinite past

The verb action happened at an unspecified time in the past. The actual time isn't important. We are focusing on the experience at some time in our life.

Have you ever had a serious illness?
She's never been abroad.
Have you ever been flying in a plane when it's hit an air pocket?

Note

- Notice these two sentences.

  She's been to Mexico. (At some time in her life.)
  She's gone to Mexico. (And she's there now.)
  The first is an example of indefinite past.
  The second is an example of present result.

UNIT 3

Narrative tenses

Past Simple and Present Perfect

See the introduction to the perfect aspect and the simple aspect on pp. 136–137. The Past Simple differs from all three uses of the Present Perfect.

1. The Past Simple refers to **finished past**.
   Shakespeare wrote plays. (He's dead.)
   I've written short stories. (I'm alive.)

2. There is **no present result**.
   I hurt my back. (But it's better now.)
   I've hurt my back. (And it hurts now.)

3. It refers to **definite past**.

   I saw him | *last night.*
   | *two weeks ago.*
   | *on Monday.*
   | *at 8:00.*

   Compare this with the indefinite adverbials found with the Present Perfect.

   I've seen him | *recently.*
   | *before.*

   I haven't seen him | *since January.*
   | *yet.*
   | *for months.*

   I've | *never*
   | *just* | *seen him.*

Note

Even when there is no past time adverbial, we can "build" a past time in our head.

Did you have a good trip? (The trip's over. You're here now.)
Thank you for dinner. It was lovely. (The meal is finished.)
Where did you buy that shirt? (When you were out shopping the other day.)

3.1 Past Simple

The Past Simple is used:

1. to express a finished action in the past.
   Columbus discovered America in 1492.

2. to express actions that follow each other in a story.
   I heard voices coming from downstairs, so I put on my nightgown and went to investigate.

3. to express a past state or habit.

*When I **was** a child, we **lived** in a small house by the sea. Every day I **walked** for miles on the beach.*

This use is often expressed with *used to*.

*We **used to** live …*
*I **used to** walk …*

See Unit 9 for more information on *used to*.
See Unit 11 for information on the Past Simple used for hypothesis.

3.2 Past Continuous

See the introduction to the continuous aspect on p. 137.
The Past Continuous is used:

1. to express an activity in progress before and probably after a time in the past.
   *I called at 4:00, but there was no reply. What **were** you **doing**?*

2. to describe a past situation or activity.
   *The cottage **was looking** so cozy. A fire **was burning** in the fireplace, music **was playing**, and the most delicious smells **were coming** from the kitchen.*

3. to express an interrupted past activity.
   *I **was taking** a bath when the phone rang.*

4. to express an incomplete activity in the past.
   *I **was reading** a book during the flight. (But I didn't finish it.)*
   *I **watched** a movie during the flight. (the whole film)*

5. to express an activity that was in progress at every moment during a period of time.
   *I **was working** all day yesterday.*
   *They **were fighting** for the whole vacation.*

Notes

- The Past Simple expresses past actions as simple, complete facts. The Past Continuous gives past activities time and duration.
  "What did you do last night?"
  *"I **stayed** at home and **watched** football."*
  *"I **called** you last night, but there was no answer."*
  *"Oh, I **was watching** football and I didn't hear the phone. Sorry."*

- Notice how the questions in the Past Continuous and Past Simple refer to different times.
  When we arrived, Jan was ironing. She stopped ironing and made some coffee.
  *What **was** she **doing** when we arrived? She was ironing.*
  *What **did** she **do** when we arrived? She made some coffee.*

3.3 Past Perfect

See the introduction to the perfect aspect and the continuous aspect on p. 137.
The Past Perfect is used to look back to a time in the past and refer to an action that happened before then.

*She was crying because her cat **had died**.*
*I arrived to pick up Dave, but he **had** already **left**.*
*Keith was fed up. He'**d been looking** for a job for months, but he'**d found** nothing.*

Notes

- The continuous refers to longer actions or repeated activities. The simple refers to shorter, complete facts.
  *He'**d lost** his job and his wife **had left** him. Since then he'**d been sleeping** badly, and he **hadn't been eating** properly.*

- The Past Perfect can refer to definite as well as indefinite time.
  *I knew his face immediately. I'**d** first **met** him **in October 1993**.* (= definite)
  *I recognized her face. I'**d seen** her somewhere **before**.* (= indefinite)

3.4 Past Perfect and Past Simple

1. Verbs in the Past Simple tell a story in chronological order.
   *John **worked** hard all day to prepare for the party. Everyone **had** a good time. Even the food **was** all right. Unfortunately, Andy **upset** Peter, so Peter **left** early. Pat **came** looking for Peter, but he **wasn't** there.*
   *It **was** a great party. John **sat** and **looked** at all the mess. He **felt** tired. It **was** time for bed.*

2. By using the Past Perfect, the speaker or writer can tell a story in a different order.
   *John sat and looked at all the mess. It **had been** a great party, and everyone **had had** a good time. Even the food **had been** all right. Unfortunately, Andy upset Peter, so Peter left early. Pat came looking for Peter, but he'**d** already **gone**.*
   *John felt tired. He'**d been working** all day to prepare for the party. It was time for bed.*

Note

For reasons of style, it is not necessary to have every verb in the Past Perfect.

… Andy upset Peter … Peter left …

Once the time of "past in the past" has been established, the Past Simple can be used as long as there is no ambiguity.

3.5 Time clauses

1. We can use time conjunctions to talk about two actions that happen one after the other. Usually the Past Perfect is not necessary in these cases, although it can be used.
   *After I'**d taken/took** a bath, I **went** to bed.*
   *As soon as the guests **left/had left**, I **started** cleaning up.*
   *I **sat** outside until the sun **had gone/went** down.*

2. The Past Perfect can help to make the first action seem separate, independent of the second, or completed before the second action started.
   *When I **had read** the paper, I threw it away.*
   *We stayed up until all the guests **had gone**.*

3. Two verbs in the Past Simple can suggest that the first action led into the other, or that one caused the other to happen.
   *When I **heard** the news, I **burst** out crying.*
   *As soon as the alarm **went off**, I **got up**.*

4. The Past Perfect is more common with *when* because it is ambiguous. The other conjunctions are more specific, so the Past Perfect is not so essential.
   *As soon as all the guests **left**, I cleaned the house.*
   *Before I **met** you, I didn't know the meaning of happiness.*
   *When I **opened** the door, the cat jumped out.*
   *When I'**d opened** the mail, I made another cup of tea.*
   See Unit 11 for information on the Past Perfect used for hypothesis.

UNIT 4

4.1 Questions

Question forms

Notice these question forms.

- Subject questions with no auxiliary verb
  *Who **broke** the window?*
  *What **happens** at the end of the book?*

- Questions with prepositions at the end
  *Who is your letter **from**?*
  *What are you talking **about**?*

- Question words + noun/adjective/adverb
  *What **sort** of music do you like?*

How big is their new house?
How fast does your car go?

- Other ways of asking *Why?*
  What did you do that for?
  How come you got here before us?
  How come …? expresses surprise. Notice that there is no inversion in this question form.

what and *which*

1. *What* and *which* are used with nouns to make questions.
   What size shoes do you wear?
   Which of these curries is the hottest?

2. Sometimes there is no difference between questions with *what* and *which*.
   What/which is the biggest city in your country?
   What/which channel is the game on?

3. We use *which* when the speaker has a limited number of choices in mind.
   There's a blue one and a red one. Which do you want?
   We use *what* when the speaker is not thinking of a limited number of choices.
   What car do you drive?

Asking for descriptions

1. *What is X like?* means Give me some information about X because I don't know anything about it.
   What's your capital city like?
   What are your parents like?

2. *How is X?* asks about a person's health and happiness.
   How's your mother these days?
   Sometimes both questions are possible. *What … like?* asks for objective information. *How … ?* asks for a more personal reaction.
   "What was the party like?" "Noisy. Lots of people. It went on till 3."
   "How was the party?" "Great. I danced all night. Met lots of great people."
   How was your trip?
   How's your new job going?
   How's your meal?

Indirect questions

There is no inversion and no *do/does/did* in indirect questions.
I wonder what she's doing. *I wonder ~~what is she doing~~.*
I don't know where he lives. *I don't know ~~where does he live~~.*
Tell me when the train leaves.
Do you remember how she made the salad?
I didn't understand what she was saying.
I have no idea why he went to India.
I'm not sure where they live.
He doesn't know whether he's coming or going.

4.2 Negatives

Forming negatives

1. We make negatives by adding *not* after the auxiliary verb. If there is no auxiliary verb, we add *do/does/did*.
   I haven't seen her for ages.
   It wasn't raining.
   You shouldn't have gone to so much trouble.
   We don't like big dogs.
   They didn't want to go out.

2. The verb *have* has two forms in the present.
   I don't have ⎫
   I haven't got ⎬ *any money.*
   But … *I didn't have any money.*

---

3. Infinitives and *-ing* forms can be negative.
   We decided not to do anything.
   I like not working. It suits me.

4. *Not* can go with other parts of a sentence.
   Ask him, not me.
   Buy me anything, but not perfume.

5. When we introduce negative ideas with verbs such as *think, believe, suppose,* and *imagine,* we make the first verb negative, not the second.
   I don't think you're right. *~~I think you aren't~~ …*
   I don't suppose you want a game of tennis?

6. In short answers, the following forms are possible.

   Are you coming? ⎧ *"I think so."*
   ⎪ *"I believe so."*
   ⎨ *"I hope so."*
   ⎪ *"I don't think so."*
   ⎩ *"I hope not."*

   I think not is possible. *~~I don't hope so~~ is not possible.

Negative questions

1. Negative questions can express various ideas.
   Haven't you finished school yet? (surprise)
   Don't you think we should wait for them? (suggestion)
   Wouldn't it be better to go tomorrow? (persuasion)
   Can't you see I'm busy? Go away! (criticism)
   Isn't it a lovely day! (exclamation)

2. In the main use of negative questions, the speaker would normally expect a positive situation, but now expresses a negative situation. The speaker therefore is surprised.
   Don't you like ice cream? Everyone likes ice cream!
   Haven't you done your homework yet? What have you been doing?

3. Negative questions can also be used to mean *Confirm what I think is true.* In this use it refers to a positive situation.
   Haven't I met you somewhere before? (I'm sure I have.)
   Didn't we speak about this yesterday? (I'm sure we did.)

4. The difference between the two uses can be seen clearly if we change them into sentences with question tags.
   You haven't done your homework yet, have you? (negative sentence, positive tag)
   We've met before, haven't we? (positive sentence, negative tag)

UNIT 5

Introduction to future forms

There is no one future tense in English. Instead, there are several verb forms that can refer to future time. Sometimes, several forms are possible to express a similar meaning, but not always.

5.1 *will* for prediction

1. The most common use of *will* is as an auxiliary verb to show future time. It expresses a future fact or prediction – *at some time in the future this event will happen.* This use is uncolored by ideas such as intention, decision, arrangement, willingness, etc.
   I'll be 30 in a few days.
   It will be cold and wet tomorrow, I'm afraid.
   Who do you think will win the game?
   You'll feel better if you take this medicine.
   I'll see you later.
   This is the nearest English has to a neutral, pure future tense.

2. *Will* for a prediction can be based more on an opinion than a fact or evidence. It is often found with expressions such as *I think …, I hope …, I'm sure … .*
   I think the Democrats will win the next election.
   I hope you'll come and visit me.
   I'm sure you'll pass your exams.

3. *Will* is common in the main clause when there is a subordinate clause with *if, when, before,* etc. Note that we don't use *will* in the subordinate clause.
   You'll break the glass *if* you aren't careful.
   When you're ready, *we'll start* the meeting.
   I won't go until you arrive.
   As soon as Peter comes, *we'll have* lunch.

5.2 *going to* for prediction

Going to can express a prediction based on a present fact. There is evidence now that something is sure to happen. We can see the future from the present.
Careful! That glass is going to fall over. Too late!
Look at that blue sky! It's going to be a lovely day.

Notes

- Sometimes there is little or no difference between *will* and *going to.*
  We'll ⎱
  We're going to ⎰ *run* out of money if we aren't careful.

- We use *going to* when we have physical evidence to support our prediction.
  She's going to have a baby. (Look at her stomach.)
  Chicago is going to win. (It's 14–0, and there are only five minutes left.)
  That glass is going to fall. (It's rolling to the edge of the table.)

- We can use *will* when there is no such outside evidence. Our prediction is based on our own personal opinion. It can be more theoretical and abstract.
  I'm sure you'll have a good time at the party. (This is my opinion.)
  I think Chicago will win. (Said the day before the game.)
  The glass will break if it falls. (This is what happens to glasses that fall.)

- Compare the sentences.
  I bet John will be home late. The traffic is always bad at this time. (= my opinion)
  John's going to be home late. He left a message on the answering machine. (= a fact)
  Don't lend Keith your car. He'll crash it. (= a theoretical prediction)
  Look out! We're going to crash! (= a prediction based on evidence)

5.3 Decisions and intentions – *will* and *going to*

1. *Will* is used to express a decision or intention made at the moment of speaking.
   I'll call you back in a minute.
   Give me a call some time. We'll go out together.
   "The phone's ringing." "I'll get it."

2. *Going to* is used to express a future plan, decision, or intention made before the moment of speaking.
   When she grows up, she's going to be a ballet dancer.
   We're going to get married in the spring.

5.4 Other uses of *will*

1. *Will* as a prediction is an auxiliary verb that simply shows future time. It has no real meaning.
   Tomorrow will be cold and windy.

2. *Will* is also a modal auxiliary verb, and so it can express a variety of meanings. The meaning often depends on the meaning of the main verb.
   I'll help you carry those bags. (= offer)
   Will you marry me? (= willingness)
   Will you open the window? (= request)
   My car won't start. (= refusal)
   I'll love you forever. (= promise)

5.5 Present Continuous for arrangements

1. The Present Continuous is used to express personal arrangements and fixed plans, especially when the time and place have been decided. A present tense is used because there is some reality in the present. The event is planned or decided, and we can see it coming. The event is usually in the near future.
   I'm having lunch with Brian tomorrow.
   What time are you meeting him?
   Where are you having lunch?
   What are you doing tonight?

2. The Present Continuous for future is often used with verbs of movement and activity.
   Are you coming to the dance tonight?
   I'm meeting the director tomorrow.
   We're playing tennis this afternoon.

3. The Present Continuous is used to refer to arrangements between people. It is not used to refer to events that people can't control.
   It's going to rain this afternoon. *~~It's raining this afternoon.~~*
   The sun rises at 5:30 tomorrow. *~~The sun is rising~~ ...*

Notes

- Sometimes there is little or no difference between the Present Continuous and *going to* to refer to the future.
  We're seeing ⎱
  We're going to see ⎰ Hamlet *at the theater tonight.*

- When there is a difference, the Present Continuous emphasizes an arrangement with some reality in the present; *going to* expresses a person's intentions.
  I'm seeing my girlfriend tonight.
  I'm going to ask her to marry me. *~~I'm asking~~ ...*
  What are you doing this weekend?
  What are you going to do about the broken toilet? (= What have you decided to do?)

5.6 Present Simple for timetables

1. The Present Simple refers to a future event that is seen as unalterable because it is based on a timetable or calendar.
   My flight leaves at 10:00.
   Classes start on April 4.
   What time does the movie *start?*
   It's my birthday tomorrow.

2. It is used in subordinate clauses introduced by conjunctions such as *if, when, before, as soon as, unless,* etc.
   We'll have a picnic if the weather stays fine.
   When I get home, I'll cook dinner.
   I'll leave as soon as it stops raining.

5.7 Future Continuous

1. The Future Continuous expresses an activity that will be in progress before and after a time in the future.
   Don't call at 8:00. We'll be having dinner.
   This time tomorrow I'll be flying to New York.

2. The Future Continuous is used to refer to a future event that will happen in the natural course of events. This use is uncolored by ideas such as intention, decision, arrangement, or willingness. As time goes by, this event will occur.
   Don't worry about our guests. They'll be arriving any minute now.
   We'll be going right back to the game after the break. (said on television)

5.8 Future Perfect

The Future Perfect refers to an action that will be completed before a definite time in the future. It is not a very common verb form.

I'll have done all my work by this evening.

UNIT 6

Expressing quantity

6.1 Quantifiers

1. The following can be used before a noun.

some/any	much/many	each/every	more/most
a little/little	a few/few	both	fewer/less	several
all/no	enough

With countable nouns only	With uncountable nouns only	With both
(not) many cigarettes a few cars very few trees fewer books several answers	(not) much luck a little cheese very little experience less time	some money some eggs (not) any water (not) any friends more/most wine more/most people all/no work all/no children enough food enough apples

With singular count nouns only	With plural count nouns only
each boy every time	both parents

2. Most of the quantifiers can be used without a noun. *No, all, every,* and *each* cannot.

Do you have any money?	***Not much/a little/enough.***
Are there any eggs?	***A few/not many.***
Have some wine.	*I don't want **any**.*
How many people came?	*Very **few**.*
Have some more tea.	*I've got **some**.*
Did Ann or Sam go?	***Both**.*

3. Most of the quantifiers can be used with *of* + *the/my/those,* etc. + noun. *No* and *every* cannot.

*They took **all of my money**.*
*Take **a few of these tablets**.*
***Some of the people** at the party started dancing.*
*Were **any of my friends** at the party?*
*Very **few of my friends** live at home.*
***Not much of the food** was left.*
*I've missed **too many of my French classes**.*
*I couldn't answer **several of the questions**.*
*I'll have **a little of the strawberry cake**, please.*
***Both of my children** are smart.*
*I feel tired **most of the time**.*
*I've had **enough of your jokes**.*

4. For *no* and *every,* we use *none* and *every one* or *all.*

***None of the audience** was listening.*
***All of the hotels** were booked.*

In formal, written English, *none* is followed by a singular form of the verb.

***None** of the guests **has** arrived yet.*

But in informal English, a plural verb is possible.

***None** of my friends **exercise**.*
***None** of the lights **are** working.*

Note

When we use *none* with a plural noun or pronoun, the verb can be singular or plural. Grammatically, it should be singular, but people often use the plural when they speak.

*None of my friends **is** coming.*
*None of my friends **are** coming.*

some, any, somebody, anything

1. The basic rule is that *some* and its compounds are used in affirmative sentences, and *any* and its compounds in negatives and questions.

*I need **some** help.*
*I need **somebody** to help me.*
*Give me **something** for my headache.*
*I don't need **any** shopping.*
*We can't go **anywhere** without being recognized.*
*Is there **any** sugar left?*
*Did **anyone** call me last night?*

2. *Some* and its compounds are used in requests or invitations, or when we expect the answer "yes."

*Do you have **some** money you could lend me?*
*Would you like **something** to eat?*
*Did **someone** call me last night?*
*Can we go **somewhere** quiet to talk?*

3. *Any* and its compounds are used in affirmative sentences that have a negative meaning.

*He **never** has **any** money.*
*You made **hardly any** mistakes.*
*I made the cake myself **without any** help.*

4. *Any* and its compounds are used to express *It doesn't matter which/who/where.*

*Take **any book** you like. I don't mind.*
***Anyone** will tell you 2 plus 2 is 4.*
*Sit **anywhere** you like.*
*I eat **anything**. I'm not fussy.*

nobody, no one, nowhere, nothing

1. These are more emphatic forms.

*I saw **nobody** all weekend.*
*I've eaten **nothing** all day.*

2. They can be used at the beginning of sentences.

***No one** was saved.*
***Nobody** understands me.*
***Nowhere** is safe any more.*

much, many, a lot of, lots of, a great deal of, a large number of, plenty of

1. *Much* and *many* are usually used in questions and negatives.

*How **much** does it cost?*
*How **many** people came to the party?*
*Is there **much** unemployment in your country?*
*I don't have **much** money.*
*Will there be **many** people there?*
*You don't see **many** snakes in England.*

2. We find *much* and *many* in affirmative sentences after *so, as,* and *too.*

*He has **so much** money that he doesn't know what to do with it.*
*She doesn't have **as many** friends as I have.*
*You make **too many** mistakes. Be careful.*

3. In affirmative sentences, the following forms are found.

Spoken/informal
*There'll be **plenty of food/people**. (uncount and count)*
*We've got **lots of time/friends**. (uncount and count)*
*I lost **a lot of my furniture/things**. (uncount and count)*

Written/more formal
A great deal of money was lost during the strike. (uncount)
A large number of strikes are caused by bad management. (count)

Many world leaders are quite young. (count)
Much time is wasted in trivial pursuits. (uncount)

4. These forms are found without nouns.
"Do you have any socks?" "Yeah. **Lots**."
"How many people were there?" "**A lot**."
Don't worry about food. We've got **plenty**.

little/few/less/fewer

1. *A little* and *a few* express a small amount or number in a positive way. Although there is only a little, it is probably enough.
Can you lend me **a little sugar**?
A few friends are coming around tonight.

2. *Little* and *few* express a small amount in a negative way. There is not enough.
Very few people passed the exam.
There's **very little milk** left.

3. *Fewer* is the comparative of *few*; *less* is the comparative of *little*.
Fewer people use suface mail these days. (= count noun)
I spend **less and less time** doing what I want to. (= uncount noun)
It is becoming more common to find *less* with a count noun. Many people think that this is incorrect and sounds terrible.
*~~Less people use surface mail.~~
*~~You should invite less people next time.~~

all

1. We do not usually use *all* to mean *everybody/everyone/everything*.
Everybody had a good time.
Everything was ruined in the fire.
I said hello to **everyone**.
But if *all* is followed by a relative clause, it can mean *everything*.
All (that) I own is yours.
I spend **all** I earn.
This structure can have a negative meaning, expressing ideas such as *nothing more* or *only this*.
All I want is a place to sleep.
All I had was a cup of coffee and some toast.
All that happened was that he pushed her a bit, and she fell over.

2. Before a noun with a determiner (for example *the, my, this*) both *all* and *all of* are possible.
You eat **all (of) the time**.
All (of) my friends are coming tonight.
Before a noun with no determiner, we use *all*.
All people are born equal.

3. With personal pronouns, we use *all of*.
All of you passed. Well done!
I don't need these books. You can have **all of them**.

UNIT 7

7.1 Introduction to modal auxiliary verbs

1. These are the modal auxiliary verbs.

can	could	may	might	should
will	would	must	ought to	shall

They are used with great frequency and with a wide range of meanings. They express ideas such as willingness and ability, permission and refusal, obligation and prohibition, suggestion, necessity, promise and intention. All modal auxiliary verbs can express degrees of certainty, probability, or possibility.

2. They have several characteristics.

- There is no *-s* in the third person.
He can swim.
She must go.

- There is no *do/does* in the question.
May I ask a question?
Shall we go?

- There is no *don't/doesn't* in the negative.
You shouldn't tell lies.
You won't believe this.

- They are followed by an infinitive without *to*. The exception is *ought*.
*It might **rain**.*
*Could you **help**?*
*We ought **to be** on our way.*

- They don't really have past forms or infinitives or *-ing* forms. Other verbs are used instead.
*I **had** to work hard when I was young.*
*I'd love **to be able to** ski.*
*I hate **having** to get up in the morning.*

- They can be used with perfect infinitives to refer to the past. For more information, see Grammar Reference Unit 10 on p. 146.
*You should **have told** me that you can't swim.*
*You might **have drowned**!*
*She must **have been** crazy to marry him.*

7.2 Modal auxiliary verbs of probability, present and future

The main modal auxiliary verbs that express probability are described here in order of certainty. *Will* is the most certain, and *might/could* are the least certain.

will

Will and *won't* are used to predict a future action. The truth or certainty of what is asserted is more or less taken for granted.
*I'**ll see** you later.*
*His latest book **will be** out next month.*

must and can't

1. *Must* is used to assert what we infer or conclude to be the most logical or rational interpretation of a situation. We do not have all the facts, so it is less certain than *will*.
*You say he walked across the Sahara Desert! He **must be** crazy!*
*You **must be** joking! I simply don't believe you.*

2. The negative of this use is *can't*.
*She **can't have** a ten-year-old daughter! She's only 21 herself.*
*"Whose coat is this?" "It **can't be** Mary's. It's too small."*

should

1. *Should* expresses what may reasonably be expected to happen. Expectation means believing that things are or will be as we want them to be. This use of *should* has the idea of *if everything has gone according to plan*.
*Our guests **should be** here soon (if they haven't gotten lost).*
*This homework **shouldn't take** you too long (if you've understood what you have to do).*
*We **should be moving** into our new house soon (as long as nothing goes wrong).*

2. *Should* in this use has the idea that we want the action to happen. It is not used to express negative or unpleasant ideas.
*You **should pass** the exam. You've worked hard.*

You should fail the exam. You haven't done any work at all.
We would say … *I don't think you'll pass the exam.*

may and *might*

1. *May* expresses the possibility that an event will happen or is happening.
   *We **may go** to Greece this year. We haven't decided yet.*
   *"Where's Ann?" "She **may be taking** a bath, I don't know."*

2. *Might* is more tentative and slightly less certain than *may*.
   *It **might rain**. Take your umbrella.*
   *"Where's Peter?" "He **might be** upstairs. There's a light on."*

3. Learners of English often express these concepts of future possibility with *perhaps* or *maybe … will* and so avoid using *may* and *might*. However, these are widely used by native speakers, and you should try to use them.

could

1. *Could* has a similar meaning to *might*.
   *You **could be** right. I'm not sure.*
   *That movie **could be** worth seeing. It got good reviews.*

2. *Couldn't* is not used to express a future possibility. The negative of *could* in this use is *might not*.
   *You **might not be** right.*
   *That movie **might not be** any good.*

3. *Couldn't* has a similar meaning to *can't* above, only slightly weaker.
   *She **couldn't have** a ten-year-old daughter! She's only 21 herself.*

Related verbs

Here are some related verb forms that express probability.
*William's so brainy. He**'s sure to pass** the exam.*
*We're having a picnic tomorrow, so it**'s sure to rain**.*
*You**'re likely to find** life very different when you live in China.*
*Are you **likely to come across** Judith while you're in Oxford?*

7.3 Other uses of modal auxiliary verbs and related verbs

Here is some further information about modal auxiliary verbs, but it is by no means complete. See a grammar book for more details.

Ability

1. *Can* expresses ability. The past is expressed by *could*.
   *I **can** speak three languages.*
   *I **could** swim when I was three.*

2. Other forms are provided by *be able to*.
   *I've never **been able to** understand her. (Present Perfect)*
   *I'd love **to be able to** drive. (infinitive)*
   ***Being able to drive** has transformed my life. (-ing form)*
   *You**'ll be able to** walk again soon. (future)*

3. To express a fulfilled ability on one particular occasion in the past, *could* is not used. Instead, we use *was able to* or *managed to*.
   *She **was able to** survive by clinging onto the wrecked boat.*
   *The prisoner **managed to** escape by climbing onto the roof.*

Advice

1. *Should* and *ought* express mild obligation or advice. *Should* is much more common.
   *You **should go** to bed. You look very tired.*
   *You **ought to** take things easier.*

2. We use *had better* to give strong advice, or to tell people what to do. There can be an element of threat – "If you don't do this, something bad will happen."
   *You**'d better** get a haircut before the interview. (If you don't, you won't get the job.)*
   *I'm late. I**'d better** get a move on. (If I don't, I'll be in trouble.)*

Note

The form is always past (*had*), but it refers to the immediate future.
*She**'d better** start revising. The exams are next week.*

Obligation

1. *Must* expresses strong obligation. Other verb forms are provided by *have to*.
   *You **must** try harder!*
   *What time **do** you **have to** start work?*
   *I **had to** work hard to pass my exams. (Past Simple)*
   *You**'ll have to** do this exercise again. (future)*
   *We might **have to** spend less money. (infinitive)*
   *She**'s never had to** do a single day's work in her life. (Present Perfect)*
   *I hate **having to** get up early. (-ing form)*

2. *Must* expresses the opinion of the speaker.
   *I **must** get my hair cut. (I am telling myself.)*
   *You **must** do this again. (Teacher to student)*
   Must is associated with a more formal, written style.
   *Candidates **must** answer three questions. (On an exam)*
   *Books **must** be returned by the end of the week. (Instructions in a library)*

3. *Have to* expresses a general obligation based on a law or rule, or based on the authority of another person.
   *Children **have to** go to school until they're 16. (It's the law.)*
   *Mom says you **have to** clean your room.*

4. *Can't* expresses negative obligation. *Don't have to* expresses the absence of obligation.
   *You **can't** steal. It isn't right.*
   *You **don't have to** go to England if you want to learn English.*

5. *Have got to* is more informal than *have to*.
   *I've **got to** go now. See you!*
   *Don't stay out late. We've **got to** get up early tomorrow.*

6. Here are some related verb forms that express obligation.
   *Visitors **are required to** have a visa.*
   *When you're 18, you**'re supposed to** take responsibility for yourself.*
   *You **aren't supposed to** park on double yellow lines.*
   *You **need to** think carefully before you make a decision.*
   *He **doesn't need to** work. He's a millionaire.*

Permission

1. *May*, *can*, and *could* are used to ask for permission.
   ***May** I ask you a question?*
   ***May** I use your phone?*
   ***Can/Could** I go home? I don't feel well.*
   ***Can/Could** I borrow your car tonight?*

2. *May* is used to give permission, but it sounds very formal. *Can* and *can't* are more common.
   *You **can** use a dictionary in this exam.*
   *You **can't** stay up till midnight. You're only five.*
   *You **can't** use cell phones during the flight. It's forbidden.*

3. To talk about permission generally, or permission in the past, we use *can*, *could*, or *be allowed to*.
   *Children **can/are allowed to** do what they want these days.*

   I | *couldn't* / *wasn't allowed to* | *go out on my own until I was 16.*

4. Here are some related verb forms that express permission.
   *Passengers **are not permitted to** use cell phones.*
   *My parents **don't allow** me to*
   *I'm **not allowed to** stay out late.*
   *My parents **don't let** me*
   Note that this sentence with *let* is not possible in the passive.
   I'm not let …

Willingness and refusal

1. *Will* expresses willingness. *Won't* expresses a refusal by either people or things. *Shall* is used in questions.
   I'll help you.
   *She says she **won't** get up until she's had breakfast in bed.*
   *The car **won't** start.*
   ***Shall** I give you a hand?*
2. The past is expressed by *wouldn't*.
   *My mom said she **wouldn't** give me any more money. Isn't she mean?*

Requests

Several modal verbs express a request.
***Can/could/will/would** you do me a favor?*
***Can/could** I open the window?*
Modal verbs are also dealt with in Units 9, 10, and 11.

UNIT 8

8.1 Introduction to relative clauses

It is important to understand the difference between two kinds of relative clauses.

1. Defining relative (DR) clauses qualify a noun, and tell us exactly which person or thing is being referred to.
   *She likes people **who are fun to be with**.*
   *Politicians **who tell lies** are odious.*
   *A corkscrew is a thing **you use to open a bottle of wine**.*
   She likes people on its own doesn't mean very much; we need to know which people she likes.
   who tell lies tells us exactly which politicians are odious. Without it, the speaker is saying that all politicians are odious.
   A corkscrew is a thing doesn't make sense on its own.
2. Non-defining relative (NDR) clauses add secondary information to a sentence, almost as an afterthought.
   *My friend Andrew, **who is Scottish**, plays the bagpipes.*
   *Politicians, **who tell lies**, are odious.*
   *My favorite building is Durham Cathedral, **which took over 200 years to build**.*
   My friend Andrew is clearly defined. We don't need to know which Andrew is being discussed. The clause *who is Scottish* gives us extra information about him.
   The clause *who tell lies* suggests that all politicians tell lies. It isn't necessary to identify only those that deceive – they all do!
   My favorite building is clearly defined. The following clause simply tells us something extra.
3. DR clauses are much more common in the spoken language, and NDR clauses are more common in the written language. In the spoken language, we can avoid a NDR clause.
   My friend Andrew plays the bagpipes. He's Scottish, by the way.
4. When we speak, there is no pause before or after a DR clause, and no commas when we write. With NDR clauses, there are commas before and after, and pauses when we speak.
   I like the things you say to me. (No commas, no pauses)
   My aunt (pause), *who has been a widow for twenty years* (pause), *loves traveling.*

Defining relative clauses

1. Notice how we can leave out the relative pronoun if it is the object of the relative clause. This is very common.

   Pronoun left out
   Did you like the present ( ) I gave you?
   Who was that man ( ) you were talking to?
   The thing ( ) I like about Dave is his sense of humor.

2. We cannot leave out the pronoun if it is the subject of the clause.

   Pronoun not left out
   *I met a man **who** works in advertising.*
   *I'll lend you the book **that** changed my life.*
   *The thing **that** helped me most was knowing I wasn't alone.*

3. Here are the possible pronouns. The words in brackets are possible, but not as common. ____ means "nothing."

	Person	Thing
Subject	who (that)	that (which)
Object	____ (that)	____ (that)

Notes

- *That* is preferred to *which* after superlatives, and words such as *all*, *every(thing)*, *some(thing)*, *any(thing)*, and *only*.
  *That's the **funniest** movie **that** was ever made.*
  ***All that**'s left is a few slices of cheese.*
  *Give me **something that**'ll take away the pain.*
  *He's good at **any** sport **that** is played with a ball.*
  *The **only** thing **that**'ll help you is rest.*
- *That* is also preferred after *it is …*
  ***It is** a movie **that** will be very popular.*
- Prepositions usually come at the end of the relative clause.
  *Come and meet the people I work **with**.*
  *This is the book I was telling you **about**.*
  *She's a friend I can always rely **on**.*

Non-defining relative clauses

1. Relative pronouns *cannot* be left out of NDR clauses.

   Relative pronoun as subject
   *Paul Jennings, **who has written several books**, addressed the meeting.*
   *His last book, **which received a lot of praise**, has been a great success.*

   Relative pronoun as object
   *Paul Jennings, **who I knew in college**, addressed the meeting.*
   *His last book, **which I couldn't understand at all**, has been a great success.*

2. Look at the possible pronouns. *Whom* is possible, but not as common.

	Person	Thing
Subject	… , who … ,	… , which … ,
Object	… , who (whom) … ,	… , which … ,

Note
Prepositions can come at the end of the clause.
*He talked about theories of market forces, which I'd never even heard **of**.*
In a more formal written style, prepositions come before the pronoun.
*The privatization of railways, **to which** the present government is committed, is not universally popular.*

which

Which can be used in NDR clauses to refer to the whole of the sentence before.
*She arrived on time, **which** amazed everybody.*
*He gambled away all his money, **which** I thought was ridiculous.*
*The coffee machine isn't working, **which** means we can't have any coffee.*

whose

Whose can be used in both DR clauses and NDR clauses.
*That's the woman **whose son was killed recently**.*
*My parents, **whose only interest is gardening**, never go away on vacation.*

what

What is used in DR clauses to mean *the thing that*.
*Has she told you **what**'s worrying her?*
***What** I need to know is where we're meeting.*

why, when, where

1. *Why* can be used in DR clauses to mean *the reason why*.
   *I don't know **why** we're arguing.*

2. *When* and *where* can be used in DR clauses and NDR clauses.
   *Tell me **when** you expect to arrive.*
   *The hotel **where** we stayed was excellent.*
   *We go walking on Mondays, **when** the rest of the world is working.*
   *He works in Baltimore, **where** my sister lives.*

8.2 Participles

1. When present participles (*-ing*) are used like adjectives or adverbs, they are active in meaning.
   *Modern art is **interesting**.*
   *Pour **boiling** water onto the pasta.*
   *She sat in the corner **crying**.*

2. When past participles (*-ed*) are used like adjectives or adverbs, they are passive in meaning.
   *I'm **interested** in modern art.*
   *Look at that **broken** doll.*
   *He sat in his chair, **filled** with horror at what he had just seen.*

3. Participles after a noun define and identify in the same way as relative clauses.
   *I met a woman **riding** a donkey. (= who was riding …)*
   *The car **stolen** in the night was later found abandoned. (= that was stolen …)*

4. Participles can be used as adverbs. They can describe:

- two actions happening at the same time.
   *She sat by the fire **reading** a book.*

- two actions that happen one after another.
   ***Opening** his case, he took out a gun.*
   If it is important to show that the first action is completed before the second action begins, we use the perfect participle.
   ***Having finished** lunch, we set off on our journey.*
   ***Having had** a shower, she got dressed.*

- two actions that happen one because of another.
   ***Being** stingy, he never bought anyone a Christmas present.*
   ***Not knowing** what to do, I waited patiently.*

5. Many verbs are followed by *-ing* forms.
   *I **spent** the vacation **reading**.*
   *Don't **waste** time **thinking** about the past.*
   *Let's **go swimming**.*
   *He **keeps on asking** me to go out with him.*

UNIT 9

9.1 Expressing habit

Present Simple

1. Adverbs of frequency come before the main verb, but after the verb *to be*.
   *We **hardly ever** go out.*
   *She **frequently** forgets what she's doing.*
   *We don't **usually** eat fish.*
   *I **rarely** see Peter these days.*
   *We are **seldom** at home in the evening.*
   *Is he **normally** so bad-tempered?*

2. *Sometimes, usually,* and *occasionally* can come at the beginning or the end of a sentence.
   ***Sometimes** we play cards.*
   *We go to the movies **occasionally**.*
   The other adverbs of frequency don't usually move in this way.
   *Always I have tea in the morning.

Present Continuous

1. The Present Continuous can be used with *always* to express a habit which happens often and perhaps unexpectedly. It happens more than is usual.
   *I like Peter. He's **always smiling**.*
   *She's **always giving** people presents.*

2. However, there is often an element of criticism with this structure. Compare these sentences said by a teacher.
   *Pedro always **asks** questions in class. (This is a fact.)*
   *Pedro is **always asking** questions in class. (This annoys the teacher.)*

3. There is usually an adverb of frequency with this use.
   *I'm **always losing** my keys.*
   *She's **forever leaving** the water running.*

will and would

1. *Will* and *would* express typical behavior. They describe both pleasant and unpleasant habits.
   *He'**ll** sit in his chair for hours on end.*
   *She'**d** spend all day long gossiping with the neighbors.*
   Would cannot be used to express a state.
   *He'd live in a large house.

2. *Will* and *would*, when decontracted and stressed, express an annoying habit.
   *She **WOULD** make us wash in ice-cold water.*

used to + infinitive

1. This structure expresses a past action and/or a state. It has no present equivalent.
   *When I was a child, we **used to go** on vacation to Florida. (action)*
   *He **used to live** in a large house. (state)*

2. Notice the negative and the question.
   *Where **did** you **use to** go?*
   *We **didn't use to** do anything interesting.*

3. We cannot use *used to* with a time reference + a number.
   *We used to go there for vacation 10 years/three times.
   But …
   *We **used to** go there every year.*

be/get used to + noun + -ing form

1. This is totally different from *used to* + infinitive. It expresses an action that was difficult, strange, or unusual before, but is no longer so. Here, *used* is an adjective, and it means *familiar with*.
   *I found it difficult to get around New York when I first came, but I'm **used to it** now.*
   *I'm **used to getting** around New York by subway.*

2. Notice the use of *get* to express the process of change.
   *I'm **getting used to** the climate.*
   *Don't worry. You'**ll get used to** eating with chopsticks.*

UNIT 10

10.1 Modal auxiliary verbs 2

Modal auxiliary verbs of probability in the past

1. All modal auxiliary verbs can be used with the perfect infinitive. They express the same varying degrees of certainty as explained on p. 143. Again, *must have* is the most certain, and *might/may/could have* is the least certain.
   *It **must have been** a good party. Everyone stayed till dawn.*
   *The music **can't have been** any good. Nobody danced.*
   *Where's Pete? He **should have been** here ages ago!*
   *He **may have gotten** lost.*
   *He **might have decided** not to come.*
   *He **could have been** in an accident.*

2. *Would have thought* is common to express an assumption or supposition.

I'd have thought they'd be here by now. Where are they?
You'd have thought she'd remember my birthday, wouldn't you?
Wouldn't you have thought they'd call if there was a problem?

Other uses of modal verbs in the past

should have

1. *Should have* can express advice or criticism about a past event. The sentence expresses what is contrary to the facts.
   You should have listened to my advice. (You didn't listen.)
   I shouldn't have lied to you. I'm sorry. (I did lie.)
   You shouldn't have told her you hated her. (You did tell her.)

2. Look at these sentences.
   You should have been here yesterday!
   You should have seen his face!
   Should have is used here for comic effect. The suggestion is *because it was so funny!*

3. *Shouldn't have* also expresses an action that was done, but it wasn't necessary. It was a waste of time.
   I shouldn't have gotten up so early. The train was delayed.
   "I've bought you a new pen, because I lost yours." "You shouldn't have bothered. I've got hundreds."

could have

1. *Could have* is used to express an unrealized past ability. Someone was able to do something in the past but didn't do it.
   I could have gone to college, but I didn't want to.
   We could have won the game. We didn't try hard enough.
   I could have told you that Chris wouldn't come. He hates parties.
   I was so angry with her, I could have killed her!

2. It is used to express a past possibility that didn't happen.
   You fool! You could have killed yourself!
   We were lucky. We could have been caught in that traffic jam.
   When I took the burned meal out of the oven, I could have cried!

3. It is used to criticize people for not doing things.
   You could have told me that Sue and Jim had split up!
   I've been cleaning the house for hours. You could at least have cleaned your bedroom!

might have

1. The above use of *should have* can also be expressed with *might have*.
   You might have helped instead of just sitting on your backside!

2. *I might have known/guessed that …* is used to introduce a typical action of someone or something.
   I might have known that Peter would be late. He's always late.
   The car won't start. I might have guessed that would happen.

UNIT 11

11.1 Hypothesizing

First and second conditionals

1. First conditional sentences are based on fact in real time. They express a possible condition and its probable result in the present or future.
   If you pass your exams, I'll buy you a car.

2. Second conditional sentences are not based on fact. They express a situation which is contrary to reality in the present and future. This unreality is shown by a tense shift from present to past. They express a hypothetical condition and its probable result.
   If I were taller, I'd join the police force.
   What would you do if you won the lottery?

Notes

- The difference between first and second conditional sentences is not about time. Both can refer to the present and future. By using past tense forms in the second conditional, the speaker suggests the situation is less probable, or impossible, or imaginary. Compare the pairs of sentences.
  If it rains this weekend, we'll … (said in England where it often rains)
  If it rained in the Sahara, it would … (this would be most unusual)
  If global warming continues, we'll … (I'm a pessimist.)
  If global warming continued, we'd … (I'm an optimist.)
  If you come to my country, you'll have a good time. (possible)
  If you came from my country, you'd understand us better. (impossible)
  If I am elected as a member of Congress, I'll … (said by a candidate)
  If I ruled the world, I'd … (imaginary)

- We can use *were* instead of *was*, especially in a formal style.
  If the situation were the opposite, would you feel obliged to help?
  I'd willingly help if it were possible.

Third conditional

1. Third conditional sentences are not based on fact. They express a situation which is contrary to reality in the past. This unreality is shown by a tense shift from past to Past Perfect.
   If you'd come to the party, you'd have had a great time.
   I wouldn't have met my wife if I hadn't gone to France.

2. It is possible for each of the clauses in a conditional sentence to have a different time reference, and the result is a mixed conditional.
   If we had brought a map (we didn't), we would know where we are (we don't).
   I wouldn't have married her (I did) if I didn't love her (I do).

Other structures that express hypothesis

1. The tense usage with *wish*, *if only*, and *I'd rather* is similar to the second and third conditionals. Unreality is expressed by a tense shift.
   I wish I were taller. (But I'm not.)
   If only you hadn't said that! (But you did.)
   I'd rather you didn't wear lots of make-up. (But you do.)
   I'd rather you … is often used as a polite way to tell someone to do something differently. The negative form *I'd rather you didn't …* is especially useful as a polite way to say "no."
   "I'll come in with you." "I'd rather you waited outside."
   "Can open the window?" "I'd rather you didn't."

Notes

- *wish … would* can express regret, dissatisfaction, impatience, or irritation because someone WILL keep doing something.
  I wish you'd stop criticizing me.
  I wish you'd do more to help in the house.
  I wish it would stop raining.

- If we are not talking about willingness, *wish … would* is not used.
  I wish my birthday wasn't in December. (*~~I wish it would be~~ …*)
  I wish I could stop eating junk food. (*~~I wish I would~~ is strange because you should have control over what you are willing to do.)*
  I wish he would stop eating junk food.
  This is correct because it means *I wish he were willing to …*

UNIT 12

12.1 Determiners

There are two kinds of determiners.

1. The first kind identifies things.
   articles – *a/an, the*
   possessives – *my, your, our …*
   demonstratives – *this, that, these, those*

2. The second kind are quantifiers, expressing *how much* or *how many*.
   some, any, no
   each, every, either, neither
   much, many, more, most
   (a) little, less, least
   (a) few, fewer, fewest
   enough, several
   all, both, half
   another, other
   Determiners that express quantity are dealt with in Unit 6.

each and *every*

1. *Each* and *every* are used with singular nouns. *Each* can be used to talk about two or more people or things. *Every* is used to talk about three or more.
   ***Every/each** time I come to your house it looks different.*
   ***Each/every** bedroom in our hotel is decorated differently.*

2. In many cases, *each* and *every* can both be used with little difference in meaning.
   We prefer *each* if we are thinking of people or things separately, one at a time. We use *every* if we are thinking of the things or people all together as a group.
   ***Each** student gave the teacher a present.*
   ***Every** policeman in the state is looking for the killer.*

enough

1. When *enough* is used as a determiner, it comes before the noun.
   *We don't have **enough food**.*

2. When it is used as an adverb, it comes after the adjective, adverb, or verb.
   *Your homework isn't **good enough**.*
   *I couldn't run **fast enough**.*
   *You don't **exercise enough**.*

Articles

The use of articles is complex as there are a lot of "small" rules and exceptions. Here are the basic rules.

a/an

1. We use *a/an* to refer to a singular countable noun which is indefinite. Either we don't know which one, or it doesn't matter which one.
   *They live in **a** lovely house.*
   *I'm reading **a** good book.*
   *She's expecting **a** baby.*

2. We use *a/an* with professions.
   *She's **a** lawyer.*

the

1. We use *the* before a singular or plural noun, when both the speaker and the listener know which noun is being referred to.
   *They live in **the** green house across from **the** library.*
   ***The** book was recommended by a friend.*
   *Watch **the** baby! She's near **the** fireplace.*
   *I'm going to **the** mall. Do you want anything?*
   *I'll see you at **the** gym later.*
   *"Where's Dad?" "In **the** yard."*

2. We use *the* when there is only one.
   ***the** world   **the** Mississippi River   **the** Atlantic Ocean*

3. We use *the* for certain places which are institutions. Which particular place isn't important.
   *We went to **the** movies/theater last night.*
   *We're going to **the** beach.*

a followed by *the*

We use *a* to introduce something for the first time. When we refer to it again, we use *the*.
*I saw **a** man walking **a** dog in the park today. **The** man was tiny and **the** dog was huge!*

Zero article

1. We use no article with plural and uncountable nouns when talking about things in general.
   ***Computers** have changed our lives.*
   ***Love** is eternal.*
   ***Dogs** need a lot of exercise.*
   *I hate **hamburgers**.*

2. We use no article with meals.
   *Have you had **lunch** yet?*
   *Come around for **dinner** tonight.*
   *But … We had **a** lovely lunch in an Italian restaurant.*

Extra Materials

EVERYDAY ENGLISH
Social expressions and the music of English

CD1 13

A Excuse me, is this yours?

B Let me see. Yes, it is. Thank you. I must
   have dropped it.

A Is Chicago your final destination?

B Yeah, I'll be home soon. What about you?

A I have a connecting flight to L.A.

B Oh, do you live there?

A Actually, no. I'm going there for work. I live in
   New York, in Soho.

B Lucky you! I just love shopping there!

A Yeah, you and thousands of others!

B What do you mean?

A Well, you know, the tourists. There are just
   so many, all year round.

B Right, that's too bad. You don't like tourists,
   huh?

A Well, I shouldn't really complain.

B Why not? You can complain if you want.

A Not really—you see, I work in the travel
   industry, so I make a living from tourists.

PRACTICE
Exchanging information

Student A
Ask and answer questions to complete the information about Tony
and Maureen Wheeler.

> How many people does it employ?

> Five hundred. Where does it have offices?

> In the U.S., France, England, and Australia.

Lonely Planet is one of the outstanding publishing successes of
the past three decades. It employs more than . . . people *(How
many?)* and has offices in the U.S., England, and Australia. Its
headquarters are in Melbourne.

Tony and Maureen Wheeler have been writing *Lonely Planet*
guidebooks for . . . *(How long?)*. They have written more than 650
guides. They sell . . . copies a year *(How many?)* in 118 countries.
The books have been translated into 17 languages.

Tony lived . . . *(Where?)* when he was young. He lived all over the world
because of his father's job. He studied . . . at Warwick University
(What?), then he studied business at the London Business School.

Maureen was born in . . . *(Where?)*. She went to London at the
age of 20 because she wanted to see the world. Three days later
she met Tony . . . *(Where?)*. In 1972 they traveled overland across
Europe, through Asia, and on to Australia. The trip took six months.
They wrote their first book, called . . . *(What?)*, on their kitchen table in
Melbourne. They have lived in Melbourne
off and on for over 30 years.

Together they have been to . . . countries
(How many?). Tony says that the most
amazing place he has ever visited is a
remote hilltop city called Tsaparang in
the Himalayan mountains.

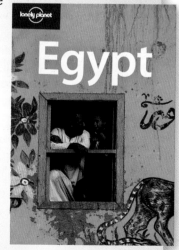

They are currently in . . . *(Where?)*. On
this trip, they are researching a new
edition of their guide to the country.

In 2007, he sold his shares in the
company to . . . *(Who . . . to?)*. He says,
"I've had a wonderful time, it's been
terrific, but it has now gotten too much
like a business."

SPEAKING AND LISTENING
Dreams come true

These are the top 15 things that people most wanted to do before they die.

1 swim with dolphins
2 go scuba diving on the Great Barrier Reef
3 go whale-watching
4 dive with sharks
5 go skydiving
6 fly in a hot-air balloon
7 fly in a fighter plane
8 go on safari
9 see the Northern Lights
10 visit Machu Picchu
11 climb Sydney Harbor Bridge
12 get away to a paradise island
13 drive a Formula 1 car
14 go white-water rafting
15 walk the Great Wall of China

PRACTICE
News and responses

Student A
Read the newspaper story. Then tell the story to your partner.

WOMAN BARRED FROM TOP STORE

As fashion-conscious GILLY WOODWARD left Harrods, the famous London department store, last Friday, she felt proud of the $200 designer jeans that she had just bought. But when Gilly, 31, came back the next day for more shopping, she was barred from entry for wearing the same jeans.

Gilly, now back home in Toronto, had been staying with friends in London for a few days. She explained what had happened.

"I was walking through the doors when I was stopped by a security guard. He pointed at my knees and said that my jeans were torn, and I couldn't enter. I tried to tell him that I had bought them in Harrods the day before and that the torn parts were fashionable. But he didn't listen. He told me to get out. By this time, a crowd of people had gathered. I left immediately. I had never felt so embarrassed."

A spokesperson from Harrods said that the dress code had been introduced in 1989, and it states: no beachwear, no backpacks, no torn jeans.

SPEAKING
Career Quiz: How ambitious are you?

Mainly a answers
You are ambitious and competitive. You may be talented and hardworking, but your success is often due to your own self-promotion. This approach will probably earn you success and riches, but be careful never to turn your back on anyone.

Mainly b answers
You are ambitious but too sensitive to others' feelings to be hugely successful. You are always looking for approval. You will have to put yourself first sometimes. Take a few tips from your ambitious colleagues, and you'll have more success.

Mainly c answers
You have very little ambition. Clearly work is not the most important thing in life for you. This is by no means a bad decision, but try to act as if you have a bit of ambition before your colleagues tell the boss about you.

PRACTICE
Quiz time!

Group A

Music
1. Louis Armstrong played jazz music. *(What kind?)*
2. A violin has four strings. *(How many?)*

Sports
3. A bronze medal is given to the person who comes in third in the Olympic Games. *(What?)*
4. Golf was first played in Scotland. *(Where?)*

Science
5. The Sun is the nearest star to the earth. *(Which?)*
6. Albert Einstein developed the theory of relativity. *(Who?)*

Geography
7. The capital of New Zealand is Wellington. *(Which country?)*
8. The Richter scale measures earthquakes. *(What?)*

History
9. President John F. Kennedy was assassinated in 1963. *(Which year?)*
10. Nelson Mandela was in prison for twenty-eight years. *(How long ... for?)*

PRACTICE
Exchanging information

Student B
Ask and answer questions to complete the information about Tony and Maureen Wheeler.

> How many people does it employ?

> Five hundred. Where does it have offices?

> In the U.S., France, England, and Australia.

Lonely Planet is one of the outstanding publishing successes of the past three decades. It employs more than 500 people and has offices in . . . *(Where?)*, Its headquarters are in Melbourne.

Tony and Maureen Wheeler have been writing *Lonely Planet* guidebooks for over 30 years. They have written . . . guides *(How many?)*. They sell around 5.5 million copies a year in 118 countries. The books have been translated into . . . languages *(How many?)*.

Tony lived in many different countries when he was young. He lived all over the world because . . . *(Why?)*. He studied engineering at Warwick University, then he studied business at . . . *(Where?)*.

Maureen was born in Belfast. She went to London at the age of 20 because . . . *(Why?)*. Three days later she met Tony on a bench in Regent's Park. In 1972 they traveled overland across Europe, through Asia, and on to Australia. The trip took . . . *(How long?)*. They wrote their first book, called *Across Asia on the Cheap*, on their kitchen table in Melbourne. They have lived in Melbourne off and on for over . . . *(How long?)*.

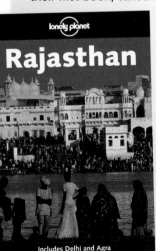

Together they have been to more than 100 countries. Tony says that the most amazing place he has ever visited is . . . *(What?)*.

They are currently in India. On this trip, they are . . . *(What . . . doing . . . ?)*.

In 2007, he sold his shares in the company to BBC Worldwide. He says, ". . . ." *(What?)*.

PRACTICE
Exchanging information

Information for Tony Wheeler

BACKGROUND
- Father worked for British Airways
- Lived in Pakistan, the Bahamas, the U.S.
- Lived overseas for most of my school days

EDUCATION
- Educated mainly in Britain and the U.S. Most of my secondary education was in the U.S.
- Came back to England to do my college entrance exams when I was 16
- Went to Warwick University to study engineering

WORK
- Started a career in engineering, did this for a couple of years in Coventry, England
- Went to do an MBA in business studies in London

LONELY PLANET GUIDES
- First one came out in 1973
- Idea came because a lot of people were asking us questions about our trip across Asia
- Worst moment was when we first started the business. We didn't have enough money.
- Best moment was doing something that no one had done before. Our guides were the first of their kind.
- The secret of our success is that people can rely on us, so they keep coming back to us.
- If you want to get into travel writing, you have to have traveled a lot. You have to be able to write well. You have to believe in what you're doing. Wanting to do it is far more important than wanting to make money.

FAMILY
- Two children, a girl and a boy

VACATIONS
- Like walking and diving

FUTURE
- Would like to go back to Nepal
- Am looking forward to spending a long time in Australia. In my opinion, there's no better place in the world to be alone.

PRACTICE
News and responses

Student B
Read the newspaper story. Then tell the story to your partner. Show him/her the photo.

Man fined for keeping tiger in apartment

A MAN WHO kept a 400-pound tiger in his apartment in Harlem, New York has been fined $2,500 and forbidden from owning animals for ten years.

Brian Jackson, 31, had bought the Bengal tiger, named Ming, when it was just a three-month-old cub. It had been living in his fourth-floor apartment for three years, eating raw meat provided by Jackson, who worked as a butcher. Neighbors had often complained of strange smells and loud noises.

Jackson's unusual pet came to light because he had had to go to the hospital with cuts and bites to his arm. The tiger had attacked him in an apparent attempt to capture and kill a cat that he also kept in the apartment.

Police officers scaled down the outside of the building and fired tranquilizer darts through an open fourth-floor window. They removed the tiger, and also an alligator, to a New York animal shelter.

A neighbor said, "We liked having Ming here. He was cool. My worry is that he won't like the country. He's a city cat, and he likes jazz and hip-hop."

PRACTICE

Quiz time!

Group B

Music
1. 50 Cent performs rap music. *(What kind?)*
2. Michael Jackson's brothers formed a pop group called The Jackson Five. *(Whose?)*

Sports
3. The Marathon is the longest running race in the Olympic Games. *(What ... called?)*
4. Baseball was first played in the United States in the 19th century. *(Where and when?)*

Science
5. A butterfly has six legs. *(How many?)*
6. Charles Darwin developed the theory of evolution. *(Which theory?)*

Geography
7. Alaska is the biggest state in the U.S. *(Which state?)*
8. The Atlantic and Pacific Oceans are linked by the Panama Canal. *(Which oceans?)*

History
9. President John F. Kennedy was assassinated in Dallas, Texas. *(Which city and state?)*
10. The Concorde flew for the last time in 2003. *(In which year?)*

EVERYDAY ENGLISH
Role play

A = Anna   **B** = Ben   **H** = Henry   **K** = Kim

B Kim! Hello! Great to see you. Come on in. Let me take your coat.

K Thanks so much. Oh, these are for you.

A What lovely flowers! How nice of you! Thank you so much. Now, I don't think you know Henry. Let me introduce you. Henry, this is Kim.

H Hello, Kim. Nice to meet you. I've heard a lot about you.

K …

H Where exactly are you from, Kim?

K …

H That's interesting. And what are you doing in Seattle?

K …

H And how do you find Seattle, Kim? Is it like home, or is it very different?

K …

B Now, Kim. What would you like to drink?

K …

B Sure. I'll just get that for you.

K …

A OK, everybody. Dinner's ready. Come and sit down. Kim, can you sit next to Henry?

K …

B Does everybody have a glass? Cheers, everybody!

K …

A Kim, help yourself. Would you like some Parmesan parsnips?

K …

A Well, they're parsnips coated in Parmesan cheese and roasted. Would you like to try some?

K …

A Hey, no problem. Well, *bon appétit* everyone!

UNIT 9 p. 78

The Man Who Planted Trees

"Only when the last tree has died and the last river has been poisoned and the last fish has been caught will we realize that we can't eat money."

The answer is 5, a Native American. The saying is a proverb from the Cree, a Native American group found across Canada.

UNIT 3 p. 26

The Clinging Woman

A man (whose name we never learn) wakes up early one morning to see a woman hanging from her balcony. He calls the police, who come to rescue her. His neighbors treat him as a hero. He thinks he did nothing that was brave and wants to forget the whole episode. Two weeks later the woman comes to his door to thank him. She introduces herself as Lydia Simpson.

They get to know each other and have meals together. One evening he asks her why she tried to kill herself. She replies that she had been engaged to be married, but the man had left her for someone else.

He is attracted to her because she is neat, feminine, and self-reliant. In time they get married. She is the perfect wife and homemaker. They have a close, intense relationship, with very few outside people coming into their lives.

The man is promoted at work. He needs to find a secretary. Lydia proposes herself. He tries to explain that it wouldn't be a good idea for his wife to be his secretary as well, but she takes this as a rebuff of his love. The next day she tries to commit suicide again by gassing herself in the oven. She is rushed to the hospital, where she confesses to him that she had also tried to kill herself when she was 17 because a boy had let her down.

The man is determined to devote the rest of his life to looking after his wife. He refuses to go on a business trip to Canada in order to stay with her. They decide not to have children. Their own company is enough for them. He gets sick and does some work from home with Lydia acting as his secretary. He becomes depressed and even contemplates suicide himself. As he approaches forty he sees himself trapped.

His company is opening an office in Australia, and he is offered the opportunity of going there for three months. But he is worried because this will take him away from home. He tries to put off telling Lydia, but she eventually finds out. She reacts very badly but helps him to prepare for the trip. He knows that she will probably try to kill herself again. He also thinks about suicide as a way out of this suffocating relationship.

He discovers Lydia has taken an overdose of sleeping pills. She is still alive. He is about to call for an ambulance when he makes a big decision. He goes out of the house and doesn't come back until several hours later when he knows his wife will have died.

UNIT 11 p. 93

VOCABULARY AND PRONUNCIATION
Word pairs

CD3 20

A Are you going to take a vacation this year?

B I'd love to—but we'll have to wait and see. We're kind of broke at the moment.

A We're hoping to rent that farmhouse in Vermont, but it's touch and go whether we will.

B Why's that?

A Well, I don't know if I can get the time off work.

B But I thought they were good about giving you time off.

A Yeah, they are, by and large, but we're a small company and we have to cover for each other, so there's a lot of give and take.

B Yeah, I can see that. At least *you* got away last year. I'm sick and tired of not being able to go anywhere.

A You get away now and then, don't you?

B More "then" than "now." We used to spend the occasional weekend in the country, but since the kids came along it's more difficult. Oh, for the peace and quiet of the countryside—uh, but I don't suppose we'd get much peace or quiet, even if we *could* afford to go, what with three kids and two dogs.

A Is Chris fed up too?

B You know Chris. Never complains, just grins and bears it.

A I tell you what. If we do manage to get that farmhouse, why don't you all join us? It's huge.

B Oh, that's so nice! Uh, but I don't know. Wouldn't we be spoiling your vacation? What would Pat think? What if ...

A Oh, just come along! The offer's there—you can take it or leave it!

B I can't tell you how much I appreciate it. It would be great, but can I talk to Chris about it first?

A Of course. I'm sure you'll want to go through all the pros and cons together.

B I can't think of many cons. It's just too good to be true. Thank you so much.

A Well, as I said, the offer's there. Let's hope I get the time off work—we'll have a great time together.

LISTENING AND SPEAKING
The interpretation of dreams

a. Buildings and houses are symbols of yourself. The upstairs represents your conscious mind and the lower floors and cellar your hidden self. The cramped feeling of the cellar indicates frustration and a need to expand your activities or thinking. Decayed or crumbling buildings indicate that your self-image has suffered. Treat yourself to a few activities that make you feel good about yourself.

b. This dream symbolizes rediscovering a part of yourself. There may be something that you have neglected or repressed. It could be that you had an ambition in life and only now have found the opportunity to try again.

There may also have a literal interpretation. If you're worried about finances, now may be the time to start a new venture.

c. This dream highlights a loss of self-control. It may represent your insecurity, a lack of self-confidence, a fear of failure, or an inability to cope with a situation. There could also be a literal interpretation. You may have noticed something unsafe—a loose stair rail, wobbly ladder, or insecure window. Check it out. The dream may be a warning.

ÖTZI THE ICEMAN

He died 5,300 years ago. He was 46 years old and 5 feet 2 inches tall. He had a beard.

His last meal was goat steak and bread baked in charcoal.

He wore goatskin leggings, a deerskin jacket, a thick grass cape, and a bearskin hat.

He stuffed his leather shoes with grass to keep out the cold.

He lived his entire life in a world just 50 kilometers across.

He knew how to look after himself. He had over 70 items in his possession, including flints for skinning animals and sharpening tools. In his backpack he carried herbs with pharmaceutical properties, dried fruit, and flint and tinder for starting fires.

He was probably a herdsman or hunter, but on this day he was a warrior. He had an axe and a longbow and arrows tipped with a flint.

No one knows how the battle started. Perhaps Ötzi and his companions deliberately entered enemy territory, or perhaps they were ambushed or attacked one another.

From the DNA on his clothing and weapons and the injuries to his body, Ötzi's last and fatal fight can be reconstructed with some precision.

Ötzi stabbed one of his enemies with his flint dagger. He shot an arrow into another and managed to retrieve the valuable weapon before shooting it again. He killed or wounded at least three men, but the hand-to-hand fighting was ferocious. Ötzi tried to hold off one assailant and suffered a deep wound in one hand that left three fingers useless.

Ötzi put up a fierce fight until an arrow, fired from behind, entered his shoulder and penetrated close to his lung. Ötzi retreated into the mountains but not before lifting a wounded companion onto his back. The blood of the injured man mixed with Ötzi's, soaking into his jacket.

Finally, high in the Ötzal Alps, Ötzi staggered into a small ravine and collapsed. It took two more days before he died, and the ice closed over him.

THE PACE OF LIFE
How well do you use your time?

Answers to quiz

Mostly a answers
You're a daydreamer. Did you actually manage to finish the quiz? You have little control over your life. Chaos surrounds you. Perhaps you tell yourself that you are being creative, but the truth is that you are frightened of failure, so you don't try. Your abilities remain untested and your dreams unfulfilled.

Mostly b answers
You represent balance and common sense. Your ability to manage your life is impressive, and you know when to relax. You understand that the best decisions are never made in an atmosphere of pressure. You are able to meet deadlines and look ahead to make sure crises don't happen.

Mostly c answers
You live in hope that something or somebody will make everything in life work out for you. "I'll get around to it," you tell yourself. What you don't tell yourself is that you alone can manage your life. You are expert at putting things off until later and finding excuses when you do so. Forget these excuses. The right time is now.

Mostly d answers
You are certainly an achiever. Superman or superwoman. You know how to get a job done, and you are proud of the way you manage your life. You are obsessive about putting every second of the day to the best use and get irritated by people who are not like you and prefer to take life at a slower pace. Learn to relax a little. Remember, stress kills.

Irregular Verbs

Base form	Past Simple	Past participle
be	was/were	been
become	became	become
begin	began	begun
break	broke	broken
bring	brought	brought
build	built	built
buy	bought	bought
can	could	been able
catch	caught	caught
choose	chose	chosen
come	came	come
cost	cost	cost
cut	cut	cut
do	did	done
drink	drank	drunk
drive	drove	driven
eat	ate	eaten
fall	fell	fallen
feel	felt	felt
fight	fought	fought
find	found	found
fly	flew	flown
forget	forgot	forgotten
get	got	gotten
give	gave	given
go	went	gone/been
grow	grew	grown
have	had	had
hear	heard	heard
hit	hit	hit
keep	kept	kept
know	knew	known
leave	left	left
lose	lost	lost
make	made	made
meet	met	met
pay	paid	paid
put	put	put
read /riːd/	read /rɛd/	read /rɛd/
ride	rode	ridden
run	ran	run
say	said	said
see	saw	seen
sell	sold	sold
send	sent	sent
shut	shut	shut
sing	sang	sung
sit	sat	sat
sleep	slept	slept
speak	spoke	spoken
spend	spent	spent
stand	stood	stood
steal	stole	stolen
swim	swam	swum
take	took	taken
tell	told	told
think	thought	thought
understand	understood	understood
wake	woke	woken
wear	wore	worn
win	won	won
write	wrote	written

Verb Patterns

Verb + -ing

like love enjoy hate finish stop	swimming cooking

Verb + to + infinitive

choose decide forget manage promise need help hope try want would like would love	to go to work

Verb + -ing or to + infinitive

begin start	raining/to rain

Modal auxiliary verbs

can could will would	go arrive

OXFORD
UNIVERSITY PRESS

198 Madison Avenue, New York, NY 10016 USA

Great Clarendon Street, Oxford OX2 6DP UK

Oxford University Press is a department of the University of Oxford. It furthers the University's objective of excellence in research, scholarship, and education by publishing worldwide in

Oxford New York

Auckland Cape Town Dar es Salaam Hong Kong Karachi
Kuala Lumpur Madrid Melbourne Mexico City Nairobi
New Delhi Shanghai Taipei Toronto

With offices in

Argentina Austria Brazil Chile Czech Republic France Guatemala
Hungary Italy Japan Poland Portugal Singapore South Korea Switzerland
Thailand Turkey Ukraine Vietnam

OXFORD and OXFORD ENGLISH are registered trademarks of Oxford University Press in certain countries.

© Oxford University Press 2010

Database right Oxford University Press (maker)

Editorial Director: Laura Pearson
Publishing Manager: Erik Gundersen
Managing Editor: Louisa van Houten
Development Editor: Tracey Gibbins
Design Director: Susan Sanguily
Design Manager: Maj-Britt Hagsted
Associate Design Manager: Michael Steinhofer
Image Editor: Trisha Masterson
Design Production Manager: Stephen White
Senior Manufacturing Coordinator: Eve Wong
Production Coordinator: Elizabeth Matsumoto

ISBN: 978-0-19-472902-4 Student Book with Multi-ROM (Pack)
ISBN: 978-0-19-472904-8 Student Book (Pack Component)
ISBN: 978-0-19-472916-1 Multi-ROM (Pack Component)

Printed in China

This book is printed on paper from certified and well-managed sources.

10 9 8 7 6 5 4 3 2 1

Acknowledgements

The authors and publisher are grateful to those who have given permission to reproduce the following extracts and adaptations of copyright material:

p6 "Expat e-mail: Chile" by Ian Walker-Smith, BBC news, 11 February 2003. Reproduced by permission of BBC. p8 "Expat Tales: Daniel Allum" BBC, Source: http://news.bbc.co.uk/2/hi/uk_news/2573893.stm p27 "The Clinging Woman" from *Collected Short Stories* by Ruth Rendell.1988 copyright Ruth Rendell, reproduced by permission of PFD on behalf of Ruth Rendell. pp44–45 "Today's Teenagers are Just Fine" *Mail on Sunday*, December 2008. pp62–63 "Meet the Kippers" by Ray Connolly, *Daily Mail*, 18 November 2003. Reproduced by permission of Atlantic Syndication. pp78–79 "The Man Who Planted Trees" by Jean Giono. Adapted from "The Man Who Planted Trees" by Jean Giono with kind permission of Peter Owen Publishers, Ltd. London. pp86–87 "The Tarzan of Central Park" by Alexander Chancellor, *The Independent*, 8 October 1986. p88 "Jim and the Lion" from *Cautionary Verses* by Hilaire Belloc. Reprinted by permission of PFD on behalf of The Estate of Hilaire Belloc © The Estate of Hilaire Belloc, 1930. pp102–103 "A Life in the Day of Mary Hobson" by Caroline Scott, *The Sunday Times Magazine*, 30 November 2003. Reproduced by permission of NI Syndication. p104 "That's Life" Words and Music by Dean Kay & Kelly Gordon © 1964 Bibo Music Publishers, USA. Universal Music Publishing Limited. All rights reserved. International Copyright Secured. p118 "A Darwin Award, Larry was a Truck Driver" from www.tech-sol.net as shown on 14 June 2004. Reproduced by permission of Mike Guenther, Techsol.

Sources: pp98–99 Based on copyright material "How's Your Timing" by Celia Brayfield.

Although every effort has been made to trace and contact copyright holders before publication, this has not been possible in some cases. We apologize for any apparent infringement of copyright and if notified, the publisher will be pleased to rectify any errors or omissions at the earliest opportunity.

Illustrations by: p2 Barb Bastian; p3 Map Resources (map); p4 Andy Hammond; p6 Stefan Chabluk (map); p8 Map Resources (map); p9 Chris Patterson/www.CartoonStock.com (home made); p9 Vahan Shirvanian/www.CartoonStock.com (homework); p12 Stefan Chabluk (map); p13 Stefan Chabluk (map); p19 Carroll Zahn/www.CartoonStock.com; p25 Barb Bastian (cover); p27 Matt Vincent/Anna Goodson Illustration Agency; p30 Paul Gilligan/Stock Illustration Source/Getty Images (Woman/boy); p31 Paul Gilligan/Stock Illustration Source/Getty Images (Woman/couple/man/office); p38 Mike Balswin/ www. CartoonStock.com; p47 Roy Nixon/www.CartoonStock.com; p52 Barb Bastian; p57 © The New Yorker Collection 1993 Robert Mankoff/The Cartoon Bank (cartoon); p68 Gavin Reece; p78 Adapted from "The Man Who Planted Trees" by Jean Giono, with kind permission of Peter Owen Publishers (acorns/planting); p79 Adapted from "The Man Who Planted Trees" by Jean Giono, with kind permission of Peter Owen Publishers (village/forest); p80 Andy Hammond/Illustration Web (fan/sunglasses); p82 Stefan Chabluk (map); p88 Illustrations by Edward Gorey, from "Jim" in Cautionary Tales for Children by Hilaire Belloc by kind permission of the Edward Gorey Charitable Trust (zoo/lion); p89 Illustrations by Edward Gorey, from "Jim" in Cautionary Tales for Children by Hilaire Belloc by kind permission of the Edward Gorey Charitable Trust (lion/policeman/lost/father); p89 Gill Button (hand); p96 Tim Maars (man/wall/spade); p97 John Morris/ www.CartoonStock.com; p118 Mark Duffin.

The publishers would like to thank the following for permission to reproduce photographs:

Commissioned Photography:
p10 MM Studios (objects); p28 MM Studios (banknote); p39 Gareth Boden; p41 Gareth Boden (packing); p63 Gareth Boden (Family); p73 Gareth Boden (Health/Vacancies/Worton/Chestnut); p90 Gareth Boden (car/mothers); p91 Gareth Boden (soccer); p91 Gareth Boden/Oxford University Press (woman); p109 MM Studios; p113 MM Studios (products).

Cover Photography:
Pixtal/AGE Fotostock: (top left); Photo Alto/Jupiter Images: James Hardy (top center); dbimages/Alamy: Roy Johnson (top right); PhotoAlto/AGE Fotostock/: Vincent Hazat (left center); Masterfile: (right center); Masterfile: (bottom right); ASP/Getty Images: Kirstin Scholtz (bottom left).

Stock Photography:
p1 Michael Blann/Digital Vision/Getty Images; p3 Jon Arnold Images Ltd/Alamy (motorbike); p3 Imagestate Media Partners Limited - Impact Photos/Alamy (class); p5 DMAc/Alamy (woman); p5 dbimages/Alamy (street); p6 Ian Walker-Smith (Walker-Smith); p6 D. Nunuk/Science Photo Library (Observatory); p7 Roger Ressmeyer/Corbis UK Ltd.; p8 redbrickstock.com/Alamy (boy); p8 Jim Reed/Getty Images (field); p10 Dmytro Korolov/Shutterstock (fruit); p10 Corbis UK Ltd. (kitten); p10 Jeff Greenberg/Alamy (newspaper); p10 E.Fitkau/Getty Images (motorcycle); p11 Comstock Select/Corbis UK Ltd.; p12 Peter Newark's Pictures (Polo); p12 akg-images (Manuscript); p12 K. Su/Corbis UK Ltd. (camels); p13 Digital Vision/Punchstock (backpackers); p14 Courtesy of Maureen, Tony & Tashi Wheeler/Lonely Planet (Peru); p14 Courtesy of Maureen, Tony & Tashi Wheeler/Lonely Planet (Rajastan); p14 Lonely Planet (Egypt); p15 Courtesy of Maureen, Tony & Tashi Wheeler/Lonely Planet (Wheelers); p15 D. & J.Heaton/SC Photos/Alamy (Uluru); p15 Tim Davis/Corbis UK Ltd. (eleephants); p15 Sergio Pitamitz/Corbis UK Ltd. (Venice); p15 Gavin Hellier/Photographer's Choice /Getty Images (Greece); p15 David Davis Photoproductions/Alamy (Thailand); p16 Ashley Cooper/Corbis UK Ltd.; p18 Gary Peral/Stockshot/Alamy (rafting); p18 R. Cook/Alamy (plane); p18 Jeff Rotman/Alamy (Shark); p18 Pascal Rondeau/Stone/Getty Images (racecar); p18 View Stock China/Alamy (China); p18 D. Tipling/Image State/Alamy (aurora); p18 Bob Krist/Corbis UK Ltd. (dolphins); p20 Courtesy of Maureen, Tony & Tashi Wheeler/Lonely Planet (Tashi, 6 photos); p22 T. McMullen/AP Photo (Man); p22 Ruslan Nassyrov/iStockphoto (phone); p22 J.Agarwal/SCPhotos/Alamy (falls); p22 John Cleare Mountain Camera (mountain); p23 Marnie Burkhart/Masterfile UK Ltd.(nerd); p23 National Pictures (climber); p24 BBC Photograph Library; p25 David Levenson/Getty Images (Rendell); p28 S Dennett/John Connor Press associates (girls); p29 ACE STOCK LIMITED/Alamy; p32 D. Durfee/Getty Images; p33 N. Schaefer/Corbis UK Ltd. (looking); p33 J-L. Pelaez Inc/Corbis UK Ltd. (report); p33 R.Faris/Corbis UK Ltd. (cookies); p33 Tobi Corney/Photographer's Choice/Getty Images (smile); p34 Bettmann/Corbis UK Ltd.; p35 Tim Graham/Getty Images (Diana/Newspapers); p36 NASA/Science Photo Library (Earthrise); p36 NASA (astronauts); p36 Robin Scagell/Johnson Space Centre/Galaxy Picture Library (rock); p37 Mike Segar/Reuters/Corbis UK Ltd. (Carolyn); p37 Popperfoto/ Getty Images (funeral); p40 thinkstock/Punchstock (couple); p40 Tom McCarthy/Transparencies, Inc. (baseball); p40 Alvis Upitis/Riser /Getty Images (cooking); p41 Juice Images/Alamy (studying); p41 Image Source Pink/Alamy (guitar); p42 Wagner/The Flight Collection/Alamy; p43 Onslow Auctions Limited/Mary Evans Picture Library (pagoda); p43 Lordprice Collection/Alamy (India); p43 Onslow Auctions Limited/Mary Evans Picture Library (Canadian); p44 Joe Plimmer/Mail On Sunday (Darius/Fraser); p45 Joe Plimmer/Mail On Sunday (Harry/Sarah); p46 Bill Cannon/Digital Vision/Oxford University Press; p48 Jon Arnold Images Ltd/Alamy (Boston); p48 Adam Kazmierski/iStockphoto (Friends); p49 MBI/Alamy (headset); p49 S.E.A. Photo/Alamy (cellphone); p49 Chris King/Oxford University Press (kitchen); p50 John Angerson/Alamy; p51 Tony Buckingham/Rex Features; p53 David H. Wells/Corbis UK Ltd.; p54 Stephen Chernin/Getty Images; p55 Apple Computer Inc. (iphone); p55 Tony Avelar/AFP/Getty Images (Jobs); p56 Ariel Skelley/ Corbis UK Ltd.; p57 David Lees/The Image Bank/Getty Images (businessmen); p58 Comstock/Punchstock; p59 David Schmidt/Masterfile UK Ltd. (men); p59 Comstock/Corbis UK Ltd. (sofa); p59 Glow Asia RF/ Alamy (smiling); p60 Jeff Morgan education/Alamy (woman); p60 Fredrik Skold/Alamy (Park); p61 Bob Thomas/Stone /Getty Images (family); p61 Janet Wishnetsky/Corbis UK Ltd. (Indian); p61 Brand X Pictures/Punchstock (chapel); p61 Comstock/Punchstock (woman); p62 Wolfgang Amri/iStockphoto; p63 Getty Images (smiling); p63 thinkstock/Punchstock (woman); p64 Edgar Argo/CartoonStock; p65 Photolibrary Group; p66 Bruce Ackerman/Rex Features; p67 Stewart Cook/Rex Features; p69 Shepard Sherbell/SABA/Corbis UK Ltd. (Siberia); p69 Hartmut Schwarzbach/argus/Still Pictures (Pyramid); p70 Eye Ubiquitous/Alamy (Station); p70 Sandra Baker/Alamy (crowd); p71 Gavin Gough/Alamy (restaurant); p71 Russell Kord/Alamy (square); p72 Mike Powell/Stone/Getty Images (audience); p72 Dave Lewis/Rex Features (Oscar); p73 RC Hall Photography (AAA); p73 David McNew/Getty Images (DMV); p73 Geri Engberg Photography (Storage); p73 Karlene and Lowell Schwartz (Mortgage/Hardward); p73 Light Photographic (repair); p75 Chris Moorhouse/Evening Standard/Hulton Archive/Getty Images; p76 H. Armstrong Roberts/Corbis UK Ltd.; p77 Purestock/Kwame Zikomo/Superstock Ltd. (woman); p77 Inti St Clair/Digital Vision/Getty Images (man); p77 William Vanderson/Fox Photos/Hulton Archive/ Getty Images (1930); p81 Alex Wong/Meet the Press/Getty Images; p82 www.iceman.it/South Tyrol Museum of Archaeology (Iceman); p82 Vienna Report Agency/Sygma/Corbis UK Ltd. (mummy); p83 www.iceman.it/ South Tyrol Museum of Archaeology (quiver/body/shoes/axe/cap/dagger/wood/bow); p84 Ghislain & Marie David de Lossy/The Image Bank /Getty Images; p85 Atlantide Phototravel/Corbis UK Ltd. (New York); p85 Andy Roberts/Stone/Getty Images (painting); p85 Bob Redman (Redman); p86 Digital Vision/Oxford University Press; p87 Bob Redman (sitting/standing/climbing); p90 Bill Fritsch/Brand X Pictures/Alamy (trooper); p92 Stephen Rose - Rainbow/Science Faction/Corbis UK Ltd. (House); p92 Chris Rout/Alamy (Couple); p93 Grant Faint/Photodisc/Oxford University Press; p94 Grant Faint/Photodisc/Oxford University Press; p99 Robert Daly/Stone/Getty Images; p101 Maximilian Stock Ltd/Science Photo Library (Grandad); p101 Donata Pizzi/The Image Bank /Getty Images (couple); p101 Katja Zimmermann/Taxi/Getty Images (family); p101 Liz & John Soars (tractor); p101 Nick Daly/Stone/Getty Images (guitar); p103 Pal Hansen/ News International Syndication; p105 Redferns/Getty Images; p106 Biddiboo/Photographer's Choice/Getty Images; p107 van hilversum/Alamy; p108 Stephanie Maze/Corbis UK Ltd.; p110 Bettmann/Corbis UK Ltd.; p111 Dynamic Graphics Group/Creatas/Punchstock; p112 Jeff Greenberg/Alamy; p113 Widmann/F1online/Alamy (burger); p115 Bill Ross/Corbis UK Ltd. (Brownstones); p115 Frank Tozier/Alamy (Musicians); p116 Sean Justice/Stone/Getty Images; p117 iwish/Alamy; p119 World Films Enterprises/Corbis UK Ltd. (Talking); p149 Corbis UK Ltd. (Talking); p149 Lonely Planet (Egypt); p151 Courtesy of Maureen, Tony & Tashi Wheeler/Lonely Planet; p152 AP Photo/NYPD/Press Association Images; p153 www.iceman.it/South Tyrol Museum of Archaeology.